FEDERAL LAW OF EMPLOYMENT DISCRIMINATION

IN A NUTSHELL

SEVENTH EDITION

By

MACK A. PLAYER

Dean and Professor of Law, Emeritus
Santa Clara University
School of Law

WEST®

Mat #41334261

Nutshell Series, In a Nutshell and the Nutshell Logo are trademarks registered in the U.S. Patent and Trademark Office.

© 1976, 1981, 1992 WEST PUBLISHING CO.
© West, a Thomson business, 1999, 2004
© 2009 Thomson Reuters
© 2013 LEG, Inc. d/b/a West Academic Publishing

  610 Opperman Drive
  St. Paul, MN 55123
  1-800-313-9378

West, West Academic Publishing, and West Academic are trademarks of West Publishing Corporation, used under license.

Printed in the United States of America

ISBN: 978–0–314–28535–5

To

*Jeanne, Allen, Evan, Hugo, and Audrey
Player*

PREFACE AND ACKNOWLEDGEMENTS

In the generation since publication of the first edition of this work, employment discrimination law has evolved to where few observations made in 1976 remain enact. And just when one thinks the pace of change begins to slow, there are seismic shifts. Such change has happened in the relatively short time since the 6th Edition.

This Nutshell is designed assist four groups: (1) students enrolled in employment discrimination or employment law courses, either in law schools or in similar courses in business or management schools, (2) attorneys not regularly working in this area who need a refresher or "big picture" overview, (3) non-attorney professionals, such as human resource managers, EEO officers, and union officials, who seek relatively plain English overviews of the area, and finally (4) lay persons, such as employees, who seek a relatively easy-to-read condensation and explanation of the federal law in this area.

As should be obvious, a "Nutshell" is not a scholarly work or a reference source. It is an introduction, a doubly condensed summary, not unlike the lecture a professor might give to summarize a topic that had been explored in depth. Accordingly, **THIS SUMMARY SHOULD NOT BE RELIED UPON FOR LEGAL ADVICE. READERS SHOULD SECURE COMPETENT LEGAL COUNSEL OR**

**CONSULT   MORE   ENCYCLOPEDIC
REFERENCES.**

Organization: After the introductory overview and coverage in chapters 1–4, Chapter 5 defines the basic elements of liability: "employment," "terms and conditions of employment," "discrimination," and "because of." Part II defines the classes protected, and not protected, by the core employment discrimination statutes. Part III begins the focus on these basic principles as applied to employee *selection and retention.* Part IV focuses on discrimination *among workers* in their compensation, insurance plans, pensions and retirement, leaves and job reassignment. Finally, chapter 25 examines the miscellaneous distinctions that constitute "terms or conditions of employment," in particular the creation of a "hostile work environment"—aka "harassment"—and the important protection against retaliation. Part V concludes the work with an overview of remedies and enforcement.

Federal Law: Federal law is the focus. Significant discrimination law often is found at the state and local level, producing differences that make generalization or summarization of local law in the space of a nutshell impossible. For a full picture, readers should also consult state and local sources.

A Citation **Caution:** This work does not pretend to be "scholarly" in that references are sporadic and incomplete. It provides only a sampling of the hundreds of cases that are published each year. Moreover, citations may refer to the general topic area, and do not necessarily provide direct support for the point in the text. They often are inserted for their dicta or because the case gives an overview or summary of the area. In short, cases are used to give the reader a source to begin a more in-depth search. Page and parallel citations are omitted in deference to readability and length. Statements are often paraphrased, omitting awkward internal quotation marks. Largely irrelevant subsequent histories such as certiorari denied are omitted. Accordingly cited authority should not be relied upon without confirming its applicability and continuing viability.

Statements often reflect the author's view of likely outcomes in unsettled areas, or the "better" approach, without a note of qualification or direct reference to conflicting views. The reader may be in a jurisdiction that has not confronted the issue or has adopted a contrary position.

Apology: I apologize for use of language that suggests a lack of sensitivity, and for any offense it may cause. It is often difficult to consistently identify groups as they themselves prefer, particularly when the statutes or the courts use dated or different terms. I have done my best to be reasonably descriptive while avoiding unnecessary offense. I have refrained from using the popular "African-American" in that the term, while inoffensive, is both under and over inclusive. The persons suffering race or color discrimination because they have dark skin may or may not be of African origins, or may have African roots but not be an American. Thus, I used "black" as a race, in contrast to "white," when I refer to white skinned persons of Western-European origins. "Indians," meaning peoples whose roots are in pre-Columbian America, is used in the statutes to refer to American Indians, a reference many find offensive. However, to totally abandon that word would, at best, be awkward. Latino or Hispanic? Latino may more accurately describe peoples of Central and South American origins who speak Latin based languages, which suggests inclusion of French and Italian. "Hispanic" is more narrow, focusing on Spanish American culture, but suggests exclusion of Portuguese (thus Brazilian). Even "Hispanic" has become increasingly confusing, witness a debate over whether the current Pope, who was born and reared in Argentina, but whose parents were Italian, is "Hispanic." I have elected to use the more historic reference to peoples of Latin/American origins as being "Hispanic."

Occasionally, I have reproduced terns or curses that most would find offensive, perhaps hurtful, but to do otherwise, particularly when the words are in the reported decision, would be misleading and would fail to give the full and accurate impact on the victims of the curse. For example, it is doubtful that a racist supervisor would be calling a black employee "The N . . . word," and if he did, I suspect the impact on his audience would be far different. Other offensive terms have no well-used, polite substitutes. Accordingly, I have refrained from resorting to euphemisms. With the recognition that such words themselves are offensive curses, I apologize for any discomfort caused in seeing them in print.

Acknowledgments: My full, often unnamed, partner in this and other works is my spouse Jeanne M.L. Player, now retired from years as an employment law litigator, and more recently as an EEOC administrative judge. Here, as elsewhere, Jeanne has contributed ideas and text, provided corrective direction, served as a sounding board, and has been my editor for words, style, and content. I must acknowledge, too, the indirect contribution of Professor Martin H. Malin, of Chicago Kent College of Law, my co-author of the West Casebook, **Employment Discrimination Law** (2012). Ideas in the casebook and accompanying teacher's manual naturally found their way here, and thus were based on contributions from Professor Malin. Nonetheless, all errors, misstatements, etc. herein are mine.

MACK A. PLAYER

July 2013

OUTLINE

PART 2. PROTECTED CLASSES

PART 3. SELECTING THE WORKFORCE: ESTABLISHING DISCRIMINATORY HIRING, PROMOTIONS, AND DISMISSALS

PART 4. DISCRIMINATION IN THE WORK PLACE: COMPENSATION AND OTHER "TERMS AND CONDITIONS OF EMPLOYMENT"

PART 5. COMPLIANCE AND ENFORCEMENT

TABLE OF CASES

References are to Pages

FEDERAL LAW OF EMPLOYMENT DISCRIMINATION

SEVENTH EDITION

PART 1

INTRODUCTION

CHAPTER 1

"EMPLOYMENT DISCRIMINATION" DEFINITION

1.01: "EMPLOYMENT DISCRIMINATION:" BOUNDARIES

"Employment discrimination" occupies the wide, ill defined region between "civil rights" and "labor law." The subject has historical and ideological civil rights roots in that it promises individuals a right to be free from invidious, class-based discrimination in the work place. Nonetheless, discrimination in the work place deals with the employment relationship, or "labor law," which has been regulated for generations by evolving common law principles, and since the early 20th Century by federal labor relations statutes.

There are three general categories of "employment law"—labor relations, employee rights, and work place discrimination—which overlap and contribute to each other. While the complete practitioner of employment law needs to be knowledgeable in all three areas, the practicalities of teaching and learning require that each must be considered and studied separately. This work focuses on invidious work place discrimination.

The Constitution protects public employees against infringement of fundamental liberties, such as speech, association, and privacy, and provides minimal levels of "due process" protection when "tenured" public employees are severely disciplined. While within the realm of "employment discrimination" this complex area of equal protection and due process of law must be left to the study of constitutional law.

1.02: THE BIG THREE "CORE"

It is generally accepted that the three statutes administered by the federal Equal Employment Opportunity Commission (EEOC) form the core of employment discrimination law: (1) *Title VII of the Civil Rights Act of 1964 ("Title VII")* prohibits work place discrimination because of race, color, national origin, sex, and religion. 42 U.S.C. 2000–e. (2) *The Age Discrimination in Employment Act (ADEA)* prohibits work place discrimination because of one's "age." 29 U.S.C. 623 and,(3) *The Americans With Disabilities Act (ADA)* proscribes discrimination against "qualified individuals" on the basis of mental or physical disability. 42 U.S.C. 1201 (various).

1.03: SIX "SUPPLEMENTS"

Six statutes supplement the "core three" and must be touched upon in a study of work place discrimination: (1) *The Civil Rights Act of 1866,* 42 U.S.C.A. 1981, *(or "1981")*, which proscribes race discrimination in the making and enforcing of contracts. (2) *The Equal Pay Act of 1963 (EPA),* 29 U.S.C. 206(d), requires employers to provide male and female workers with equal rates of pay for work that is "equal." (3) *The Family and Medical Leave Act,* 29 U.S.C. 2601(FMLA), imposes on large employers an obligation to provide unpaid leave for "eligible" employees for the pregnancy, child bearing and serious medical needs of the employee and the employee's children, spouse, and parents. (4) *The Immigration Reform and Control Act of 198 4, 8* U.S.C. 102 (IRCA), sets national immigration policy, but in doing so duplicates Title VII in its prohibition of "national origin" discrimination, and proscribes some discrimination on the basis of citizenship. (5) *The Genetic Information and Non–Discrimination Act of 2008, (GINA),* 42 U.S.C. 2000ff, prohibits inquiries into, and employer reliance upon, medical information and physical conditions that might disclose genetic information. (6) *The Uniformed Services Employment and Reemployment Act of 1994 (USERA),* 38 U.S.C. 4311, prohibits discrimination against persons because of their uniformed military service.

1.04: FEDERAL VS. STATE LAW

The focus of this work is upon *federal law.* However, unlike many aspects of federal law (in particular federal labor relations statutes), federal employment discriminations statutes *do not* pre-empt state law when state law provides protection *parallel to or greater than* protection provided by federal law. Federal law provides the floor, minimal protection. State law can, and occasionally does, provide more or additional protections. *California Fed. Sav. & Loan Ass'n v. Guerra,* 479 U.S. 272 (1987).

State employment discrimination statutes tend to mirror federal statutory language, and where the language is similar, state courts usually are guided by federal precedents. However, many states add classes of protection not found in the federal statutes, such as prohibiting discrimination because of marital status and sexual orientation. State statutes may prohibit forms of age or disability discrimination not proscribed by federal law, and often provide more expansive coverage, reaching smaller employers, than does federal law. States may have more efficient administrative mechanisms and allow different remedies, such as no-cap damages, for successful plaintiffs.

CHAPTER 2
COMMON LAW CONTEXT

2.01: DEFAULT AND SUPPLEMENT

Common law is important because it provides: (1) *the default position;* where the statutes have no application, state common law defines the rights of the parties, and can serve as a (2) *supplement* to both state and federal statutory law by creating additional rights and remedies.

2.02: AT–WILL DOCTRINE

A. PRIVATE EMPLOYERS

In the United States, unless restricted by statute or regulated by contract, the employment relationship is "at will." As an "at-will" relationship, employment may be entered or *terminated* by either party for any or no reason. *Payne v. Western & Atlantic R.R.,* 81 Tenn. 507 (1884). This "American Rule" was contrary to the English common law. See, Blackstone's *"Commentaries on the Law of England, Book I,"* Chapter 14 (1765).

The "at will" doctrine, founded on "liberty of contract," was so embedded that until the late 1930s legislative attempts to limit the ability of employers to hire and dismiss employees was deemed to be a violation of the 5th and 14th Amendments to the Constitution. Ultimately, the power to limit private employers' common law "right" to discharge employees was sustained in *NLRB v. Jones &*

Laughlin Steel Corp., 301 U.S. 1 (1937). Congress is now deemed to have the power to regulate discrimination in the work place under the Constitution's Article I "commerce power." To the extent the statutes regulate invidious discrimination, such as race or sex, Congress is granted plenary power under section 5 of Amendment 14. *Fitzpatrick v. Bitzer,* 427 U.S. 445 (1976).

B. PUBLIC EMPLOYERS

Until the 1960s the "at will" doctrine was applied to public employees. Employment with the government was deemed to be a "privilege" rather than a "right," and thus could be terminated for any reason even if the discharge undermined a fundamental freedom such as speech. *McAuliffe v. Mayor of New Bedford,* 155 Mass. 216, 29 N.E. 517 (1892) (Holmes). The "right-privilege" concept was overruled in *Pickering v. Board of Education,* 391 U.S. 563 (1968). Public employees may no longer be dismissed for exercising rights enjoyed by the citizenry at large, such as free speech, religion, etc. Nevertheless, public employees not otherwise protected by contractual or statutory "tenure" statutes, or civil service regulations, may be dismissed for "no cause" without violating the Constitution. *Kelley v. Johnson,* 425 U.S. 238 (1976).

2.03: WRONGFUL DISCHARGE

A. GENERAL PRINCIPLE

Most states currently recognize some limits on an employer's right to dismiss its employees. Discharges that undermine well defined public policy will be considered "wrongful," thus providing the discharged employee with a remedy under state tort law. *Cf. Weider v. Skala,* 80 N.Y.2d 628 (1992) (rejecting common law limits on "at will" employment). A discharge is not "wrongful" simply because it was arbitrary, unreasonable, "unfair," or lacked "good cause." *Wilburn v. Mid–South Health Dev. Inc.,* 343 F.3d 1274 (10th Cir. 2003).

Foley v. Interactive Data Corp., 765 P.2d 373 (Cal. 1988), states the basic principle of when public policy limits an employer's right to discharge "at will" workers:

> "The policy in question [being undermined by the discharge] must involve a matter that affects society at large rather than a purely personal or proprietary interest of the plaintiff or employer; in addition, the policy must be 'fundamental,' 'substantial' and 'well established' at the time of the discharge."

B. PRINCIPLE APPLIED

The division among the states, which is considerable, is in the application of the basic principle to the varying and often unique state policies. The public policies that are violated by the discharge of an employee can be categorized: *(1)*

Violations of the law: Dismissing employees for refusing to engage in actions that would subject them to possible criminal prosecution is almost universally recognized as being "wrongful." *Wegenseller v. Scottsdale Mem. Hosp.,* 710 P.2d 1015 (Ariz. 1985) (indecent exposure). *(2) Exercising legal obligations,* such as service on a jury or obeying a subpoena, is recognized by most courts. *Nees v. Hocks,* 536 P.2d 512 (Ore. 1975). *Cf., Demarco v. Publix Supermarkets,* 360 So.2d 134 (Fla. App. 1978) (firing employee because he filed a lawsuit on behalf of minor daughter injured by alleged negligence of his employer did not undermine the state constitutional right of the individual to free access to the courts). *(3) "Retaliation"* for invoking statutory protections designed to protect the employee, such as filing a workers' compensation claim or an occupational safety complaint also is widely accepted as a fundamental public policy. *Frampton v. Central Indiana Gas Co.,* 297 N.E.2d 425 (Ind. 1973). *(4) "Whistleblowing"*—dismissing an employee for reporting the employer's violations of laws designed to protect the public at large, such as reporting the employer's violation of consumer safety, banking, or environmental codes, is widely, but not universally considered "wrongful." *Compare, Frennd v. Nycomed Amersham,* 326 F.3d 1070 (9th Cir. 2003), with *Bergin v. Liquidebt Systems,* 548 F.3d 533 (7th Cir. 2008). *(5) Miscellaneous policies:* States may view various of their policies sufficiently strong to protect employees against retaliation. For example, Missouri encourages its citizens to become organ donors. Discharging an employee electing to become a donor was a wrongful discharge. *Delaney v. Signature Health Care Foundation,* 376 S.W.3d 55 (Mo.App. 2012).

Regardless of the impact upon public policies, liability will not attach to an employer's refusal to *hire* applicants; (*Sanchez v. Philip Morris, Inc.,* 992 F.2d 244 (10th Cir. 1993)); refusal to transfer or offer promotions to workers; (*White v. State of Washington,* 929 P.2d 396 (Wash. 1997)); harassment, or threats of discharge. *Below v. Skarr,* 569 N.W.2d 510 (Iowa 1997).

2.04: CONTRACTS

A. HISTORICALLY

At one time courts found that the employment "at will" rule was such a fundamental right that the parties could not contractually limit the mutual and reciprocal rights of the parties to quit or be dismissed "at will." *Morris v. Park Newspapers of Georgia, Inc.,* 255 S.E.2d 131 (Ga.1979). Even where contractual modifications in the "at will" doctrine were accepted, there was a presumption that an at-will relationship could be overcome only by clear, explicit, unambiguous contractual language. *Savage v. Spur Distributing Co.,* 228 S.W.2d 122 (Tenn. 1949). Representations of "permanent employment" or dismissal only for "good cause" were deemed too vague to be promises that could be enforced. *Muller v. Stronberg Carlson Corp.,* 427 So.2d 266 (Fla. App. 1983). Setting an annual salary did not imply a promise that employment would be from year to year. *Buian v. J.L. Jacobs & Co.* 428 F.2d 531 (7th Cir. 1970).

Even clear, unambiguous promises of tenure for a fixed period were denied enforcement if they lacked "mutuality." The employee providing services was not seen as adequately "mutual" consideration for the employer's promises of a fixed tenure. *Chastain v. Kelly–Springfield Tire Co.*, 733 F.2d 1479 (11th Cir. 1984). To make promises of tenure binding, the employee had to provide some *additional* consideration, such as a payment of money or a return promise not to quit during the term.

B. CURRENTLY

Representations in the employment context now are analyzed in light of general objective principles of contract law, judged for their enforceability as any other alleged "promise" (that is, would a reasonable person believe that a binding legal obligation was being offered). *Weiner v. McGraw Hill, Inc.*, 457 N.Y.Supp.2d 193, 433 N.2d 441 (1982). The notion that distinct, additional consideration must be provided by the employee other than undertaking and remaining in that employment is being abandoned. *Worley v. Wyoming Bottling Co.*, 1 P.3d 615 (Wyo. 2000). Courts today also are willing to apply traditional concepts of promissory estoppel to find that when the offeree/employee reasonably relies to her detriment on a promise of permanent employment by leaving her current employment or by moving long distances, the promisor/employer is estopped to deny the promise. *Thompson v. St. Regis Paper Co.*, 685 P.2d 1081 (Wash. 1984). Finally, implied-in-fact promises to discharge a worker only for good cause can be drawn from a pattern of past performance and relationships. *Pugh v. See's Candies, Inc.,* 171 Cal.Rptr. 917 (1981).

"Employee handbooks" that contain promises that dismissal is warranted only for specified reasons and that internal grievance processes will be followed when discipline is proposed are judged for their enforceability as any other alleged "promise," and thus are regularly enforced as binding contractual obligations. *Toussaint v. Blue Cross & Blue Shield of Mich.,* 292 N.W.2d 880 (Mich.1980).

C. LIMITATIONS AND DISCLAIMERS

Hortatory statements of future intent, such as the use of "may," will not limit the employer's right to dismiss employees, particularly when coupled with clear reference to employment being "at will". *See, Reid v. Sears, Roebuck & Co.,* 790 F.2d 453 (6th Cir. 1986). When the document's language makes unambiguous commitments limiting the employer's right to discharge workers, followed by a disclaimer that the commitments are not binding, the disclaimers, to be effective, should be prominently featured and utilize unambiguous disclaiming language. *Jones v. Central Peninsula General Hosp.,* 779 P.2d 783 (Alaska, 1989) (one sentence in an 85 page document was ineffective disclaimer of otherwise binding promises).

2.05: "GOOD FAITH AND FAIR DEALING"

Traditional contract law provides that, "Every contract imposes on each party a duty of good faith and fair dealing in its performance and enforcement." Rest. Contracts 2nd, sec. 205. This implied-in-law duty is breached by failing to act with honesty in fact, unreasonably, or outside the reasonable expectations of the parties. Most courts have rejected the application of this doctrine to employment contracts. "Were we to adopt such a rule, we fear that we would tread perilously close to abolishing completely the at-will doctrine which employees can and should get *only* through collective bargaining agreements or tenure provisions." *Wagenseller v. Scottsdale Mem. Hosp.,* 710 P.2d 1025 (Ariz. 1985). Courts will apply the "good faith and fair dealing" doctrine to situations where an employer dismisses the employee to *avoid* payment of obligations such as profit sharing or pension benefits. *Mitford v. de Lasal,* 666 P.2d 1000 (Alaska 1983).

2.06: TRADITIONAL TORTS

In dealing with employees, employers may commit traditional torts such as intentional infliction of emotional harm, invasion of privacy, or defamation. Harassment of a worker may involve assault and battery or intentional infliction of emotional harm. If an employer attempts to unjustifiably interfere with the former employee's employment elsewhere, the employer may commit the tort of unjustified interference with contract. These are in addition to rights created by the statutes, and can be joined with any statutory claim.

CHAPTER 3
OVERVIEW AND HISTORY

3.01 THE THREE CORE STATUTES

Employment discrimination law is a patchwork of prohibitions and protections found in three core and at least six supplemental and occasionally overlapping statutory schemes. The statutes do not create a code requiring general fairness. They prohibit discrimination because of particular classes identified for protection (*e.g.,* race, color, national origin, sex (including pregnancy and childbirth), religion, age, disability, etc.), and retaliation for asserting rights created by the statutes.

A. TITLE VII OF THE CIVIL RIGHTS ACT OF 1964 (TITLE VII)

The Civil Rights Act of 1964 was a key aspect of the massive civil rights initiative of President Lyndon B. Johnson. Title VII is but one title of that Act. The premise of the legislation was supported by a vast majority of moderate and progressive legislators of both parties. It was vigorously opposed by most legislators from the southeastern states. The bill having passed the House of Representatives faced potentially blocking opposition in the Senate. To avoid the bill being held in Senate committees dominated by southern "conservatives," Senate leadership placed the bill directly on the floor for debate. During this debate numerous changes and "clarifications" from the House-passed bill were adopted. This floor debate with accompanying memoranda is the primary legislative history of the statute. In order to override a Senate filibuster a number of additional compromises were accepted. The Senate-passed bill, which differed significantly from the House-passed bill, was not submitted to a conference committee, as is traditional, but went directly to the House of Representatives where the Senate bill was debated and approved without amendment and became effective July 1965. Thus, aside from the Senate debates, Title VII produced relatively little useful legislative history.

Title VII was amended in 1972, primarily strengthening enforcement procedures, and in 1978, by the Pregnancy Discrimination Act (PDA). It was substantially overhauled by the Civil Rights Act of 1991, and in 2009 a "technical" amendment clarified the time limitations in which to file pay discrimination claims.

B. THE AGE DISCRIMINATION IN EMPLOYMENT ACT OF 1967 (ADEA)

The ADEA is not an amendment to Title VII but a distinct statutory scheme limited to age discrimination. However, key substantive provisions of the ADEA are identical to the language of Title VII. Where language of the ADEA and Title VII is similar the courts give similar interpretations. Nevertheless, the ADEA contains numerous provisos and defenses not found in Title VII, and provides distinct enforcement procedures and remedies.

During the Congressional debate of Title VII an amendment that would have added "age" as a class protected by Title VII was rejected, but the legislation directed the Secretary of Labor to undertake a study of age discrimination and report back to Congress with recommended legislation. The Secretary's report (the "Wirtz Report") completed in 1965, served as the basis for the ADEA. The ADEA received broad bipartisan support.

The ADEA prohibition of discrimination because of "age" initially applied only to persons between the ages of 40 and 65. The ADEA was expanded in 1974 to cover state and local governments and prohibit age discrimination by federal employers. In 1978 the protected age class was extended from 65 to 70, and specified that retirement plans could not force retirement prior to age 70. There were important but rather technical amendments in 1982 and 1984. In 1986 the upper age limit of 70 was eliminated. The "Older Worker Benefits Protection Act" amendments in 1990 addressed two problems: calculation of fringe benefit reductions for workers as they age and the waiver of rights under the ADEA.

The original Act assigned enforcement responsibilities to the Secretary of Labor (rather than the EEOC). However, in a 1978 reorganization President Carter transferred enforcement responsibilities to the EEOC. The Civil Rights Act of 1991 focused on amending Title VII, but did attempt to bring ADEA *procedures* more into conformity with Title VII procedures.

C. THE AMERICANS WITH DISABILITIES ACT
OF 1990 (ADA)

The roots of the ADA lie in the Rehabilitation Act of 1973 which was a sweeping statute designed to provide "handicapped" persons with rehabilitation services, full access to federally sponsored programs, such as education and research, and architectural access to public buildings. It also proscribed discrimination in employment (Sections 501, 503 and 504), but with operative language much different from Title VII and the ADEA. Section 503 of the Act (29 U.S.C. 793) requires that most contracts with the federal government contain a provision that "in employing persons to carry out such contract * * * [the contracting entity] shall take affirmative action to employ and advance in employment qualified handicapped individuals." Section 504 (29 U.S.C. 794) provides that "no otherwise qualified handicapped individual * * * shall solely by reason of his handicap * * * be subjected to discrimination under any program receiving federal financial assistance or under any program or activity conducted by any [federal] Executive agency." Section 501 prohibits "handicap" discrimination against federal employees. In 1978 amendments defined with more precision the meaning of "handicap" as applied to the employment provisions of the Act, expanded the provisions applicable to federal agencies, and provided for private remedies to enforce section 504 (incorporating the remedies of Title VI of the 1964 Civil Rights Act). In 1987 the Act was expanded to cover all programs or activities of the *entity* receiving federal financial support, not just the particularly activity or program directly supported by the federal aid.

The ADA is a comprehensive statute that provides a wide range of protections for persons with disabilities, including, but not limited to, employment. *The ADA did not repeal the Rehabilitation Act.* Indeed, it amended the Rehabilitation Act to insure conformity, and directed that judicial decisions and administrative interpretations of the Rehabilitation Act would continue to be applicable to the ADA. The Rehabilitation Act, not the ADA, provides the protection for federal employees.

The employment sections of the ADA replicate in large measure the operative substantive provisions of Title VII, but amplify the prohibitions with more precision and detail than does Title VII. The ADA incorporates by reference coverage, procedures, and remedies of Title VII.

The ADA was extensively amended in 2008 by the Americans With Disabilities Act Amendments Act (ADAAA). The amending legislation itself provides extensive analysis of the Supreme Court decisions that the legislation was "correcting." The EEOC issued extensive regulatory interpretations with a detailed "appendix" that discusses the statute, its legislative history, and the EEOC's interpretation of the amended Act. 29 C.F.R. Part 1630.

3.02 ENFORCEMENT INTRODUCTION

A. PRIVATE INITIATIVE

Enforcement of the substantive rights created by the core statutes usually depends on individual victims initiating the process by filing charges of discrimination and "exhausting" administrative processes of the Equal Employment Opportunity Commission (EEOC) and any state enforcement agency. Upon exhaustion of the state and federal administrative process, enforcement requires a law suit filed either by the EEOC or the charging party. *Infra,* Chapter 29.

B. THE EQUAL EMPLOYMENT OPPORTUNITY COMMISSION (EEOC)

The EEOC is the federal agency created by Title VII of the Civil Rights Act of 1964 to interpret and enforce that statute. That authority has been expanded to include the Age Discrimination in Employment Act (ADEA), the Americans With Disabilities Act (ADA), and the Equal Pay Act (EPA). Regional offices of the EEOC are located in major cities. The EEOC has six functions:

(1) Intake and Investigation

Individuals seeking legal redress *must* first file a written charge with the EEOC that indicates the nature of the alleged discrimination. The EEOC notifies the party charged with discrimination, and is directed to investigate the charge. The agency is granted broad pre-litigation subpoena power to secure disclosure of relevant information. *University of Penn. v. EEOC,* 493 U.S. 182 (1990).

(2) Conciliation

If the investigation of the charge discloses reasonable cause to believe a violation has occurred, the EEOC is directed to attempt an informal resolution through conciliation. If informal resolution fails, the EEOC is directed to notify the charging party of the failure and give him notice of a right to sue. The charging party then is free to file a law suit against the charged entity in a state or a federal district court.

(3) Resolution

The EEOC does have some adjudicatory responsibilities for charges filed by high level state employees and federal employees. *Infra,* Chapter 30. The EEOC *does not* conduct formal administrative or adversarial hearings to resolve private and most state government employee charges. It's efforts are limited to conciliation. The judicial action that typically follows the exhaustion of EEOC conciliation requirements is a trial *de novo*, independent from any fact finding the EEOC may have undertaken as part of its investigation and conciliation efforts.

(4) Litigation

While most enforcement suits are brought by private parties, the EEOC, Office of General Counsel, is authorized to file suit in the name of the Commission but only after conciliation efforts by the

Commission have been undertaken and have failed to produce a satisfactory resolution of the charge. The EEOC is empowered to intervene in suits previously filed by private parties, and may file friend of court briefs on points of law.

(5) Interpretation and Guidance

The EEOC has some authority, particularly under the ADA, to promulgate formal interpretive regulations. It also has the authority, frequently exercised, to issue less formal interpretive guidelines and policy statements. These guidelines assist employers in compliance and advise employees of their rights and procedural responsibilities. The courts give these guidelines varying degrees of deference.

(6) Record Gathering and Keeping

Through regulations the EEOC requires covered employers to maintain employment records and file statistical reports with the Commission.

CHAPTER 4

COVERAGE OF THE CORE STATUTES

4.01: GENERALLY

Coverage of Title VII, the ADEA, and the ADA is broad but not universal. Coverage applies to defined "employers," "labor organizations," and "employment agencies." "Employer" coverage is central in defining the coverage of "labor organizations" and "employment agencies." There are a number of expressed and implied exclusions from coverage. Coverage is not jurisdictional, meaning that the lack of coverage will be waived by the failure of the defendant to raise the issue in a timely fashion. *Arbaugh v. Y & H Corp.*, 546 U.S. 500 (2006).

4.02: "EMPLOYER" COVERAGE

A. "PERSON AFFECTING COMMERCE"

For coverage a "person" first must "affect commerce." "Person" includes individuals or legal entities such as partnerships and corporations. "Affecting commerce" is an expression that Congress exercised the full extent of its authority granted under Article I of the Constitution. Use of the term was not intended to limit coverage to "commercial" or profit seeking enterprises. State and local governments and charitable organizations can be covered employers. *Martin v. United Way,* 829 F.2d 445 (3d Cir. 1987).

B. NUMBER OF "EMPLOYEES"

Coverage is determined by the number of employees employed by the "person" or entity. The minimum number of employees for coverage of both Title VII and the ADA is 15 employees. The ADEA coverage requires employers to have 20 employees.

C. PERIOD OF TIME

To be a covered "employer" the person must employ the requisite number of either 15 or 20 employees *"each working day* for *twenty* or more calendar *weeks* in the *current or previous calendar year."* The requisite 20 weeks need not be consecutive weeks. Thus, coverage may extend to employers with a work force that fluctuates or is seasonal.

As coverage can be established by the number of employees in either the current or the previous year, an employer with fewer than the required number of employees when it took an employment action or when the charge was filed will be covered if during 20 weeks the *previous year,* the employer had the requisite number of employees.

"Each working day" during the calendar week is determined by the employer's *payroll* for that week, not whether the employees were actually on the job each working day of the week. Accordingly, part-time employees who work only a few days during a

week will be counted to determine coverage. *Walters v. Metro. Educ. Enter.,* 519 U.S. 202 (1997).

D. "EMPLOYEE"

As "employer" coverage depends upon the number of "employees," it is necessary to determine whether the individuals performing services for the employer are doing so as "employees." Individuals performing non-employment services, such as "independent contractors," are not "employees" of the employer. *Clackamas v. Gastroenterology Assoc. v. Wells,* 538 U.S. 440 (2003), directed that in making the determination of whether a worker was an "employee" courts must apply the common law standard which depends heavily on the "right of control" as to the manner and means of the worker's performance. *Clackamas, supra,* involved physicians who were shareholders working in a professional corporation that provided medical services for patient/customers. The trial court had applied a version of an "economic realities" standard that focused on the economic dependence of the worker on the corporation. The court of appeals affirmed on the grounds that as the defendant had adopted a business model that treated its shareholder/physicians as "employees" of the defendant corporation, it could not deny that these workers were its "employees." The Supreme Court reversed and remanded for an evaluation of the relationship applying a common law "right of control" standard.

(1) Independent Contractor

Distinguishing between "employees" and "independent contractors" can be difficult and requires weighing many factors. The independent contractor typically has a distinct place of business, provides his own tools, may have the right to "subcontract" some tasks, has flexibility as to when and how to perform the assigned tasks, provides similar services to more than one entity, and has the entrepreneurial opportunity for profit or risk of loss. By contrast, the time, place, and manner of performance of "employees" are set and controlled by the employer. See Restatement of Agency, section 2(2).

(2) "Employer"

The common law distinguishes "masters" (or employers) from "servants" (or employees). "An employer is the person or group of persons who owns and manages the enterprise" and will not be counted to determine coverage. *Clackamas Gastroenterology Assoc. v. Wells, supra.* Thus, even if the owners, partners, or proprietors of an enterprise work beside their "employees" and receive compensation, they are not considered "employees." Managing partners, high level controlling executives, and corporate board members are not "employees" even if they provide management advice for which they are compensated. *Zimmerman v. North Am. Signal Co.,* 704 F.2d 347 (7th Cir. 1983).

(3) Volunteers

"Employees" receive economic compensation and form an economic relationship with an entity. Persons who volunteer their services for charitable institutions are not its "employees." *Havistola v. Community Fire Co. of Sun, Inc.*, 6 F.3d 211 (4th Cir. 1998).

(4) Students

Students enrolled in an educational institution are not "employees" of the institution. The relationship is one of education, even if the student performs incidental services as a condition to receiving grants or a reduction in tuition. If the student performs independent services, such as working in the library or student cafeteria, that have no relationship to the academic program they will be considered an "employee" of the institution. *Pollack v. Rice University*, 28 FEP 1273 (S.D. Tex. 1982), *aff'd* 690 F.2d 902 (5th Cir. 1982).

(5) Interns and Trainees

Individuals performing services for *non-academic institutions* as part of their academic program at a bona fide academic institution, that are monitored by the academic institution, and for which the students receive academic credit from the institution rather than compensation from the employer, will not be considered "employees" of either institution. However, individuals performing services for employers in on-the-job training programs *administered by the employer* will be considered "employees" even if they receive no immediate compensation and are labeled as "interns" or "trainees." *See,* Department of Labor regulations regarding "employees" subject to the Fair Labor Standards Act. http://www.dol.gov/compliance/laws/comp-flsa.htm.

E. JOINT EMPLOYERS

Employees of two or more distinctly owned entities may be combined when operations, management, and employee relations decisions of the two entities are centrally coordinated or controlled. Common ownership or the fact that one is a wholly owned subsidiary of the other is not alone sufficient "integration" of actual operations for the two to be considered joint employers. *Papa v. Katy Indus. Inc.,* 166 F.3d 937 (7th Cir. 1999).

4.03: STATE AND LOCAL GOVERNMENTS: STATUTES AND THE CONSTITUTION

State and local governmental employers with the requisite number of employees are covered by the statutes. In addition, employees of public employers, state, local, and federal are protected by the Constitution. Violations are remedied via suits under 42 U.S.C. 1983. Race, sex, religious, and national origin discrimination are subject to "heightened judicial scrutiny," and broadly parallel protection accorded these classes by the Fifth and Fourteenth Amendments. In addition, the Constitution provides substantive protections not provided private sector employees, such as limits on discrimination by public employers on the basis of the employee's First Amendment right of free public speech (*Connick v. Myers,* 461 U.S. 138 (1983)), the right to join and participate in political or social associations (*Rutan v. Republican Party of Ill.,* 497 U.S. 62 (1990)), and the broad constitutional right of privacy. *Skinner v. R.R. Executives Ass'n.,* 489 U.S. 602 (1989).

Public employees who have a legitimate claim of entitlement to continued employment have constitutionally protected rights to procedural due process before they are severely disciplined or dismissed that include notice of reasons for discipline or dismissal and an opportunity to challenge the evidence before an impartial decision-maker. *Cleveland Bd. of Educ. v. Loudermill,* 470 U.S. 532 (1985).

Finally, civil services statutes and regulations usually provide detailed processes and standards for the selection, promotion, discipline, and dismissal of public employees that generally prohibit all forms of discrimination and require some form of cause before the tenured public employee may be discharged.

4.04: FEDERAL GOVERNMENT

Federal executive agencies are specifically *excluded* from the statutory definition of "employer." However, separate provisions of Title VII and the ADEA prohibit discrimination by federal executive department employers, and are interpreted to provide the same protections provided employees of private entities. The consequence of this awkward structure is that dramatically different procedures and remedies are applicable to federal government employees. *Infra,* Chapter 30.

Disability discrimination claims by federal employees are regulated not by the ADA but by the Rehabilitation Act of 1973. However, those two statutory schemes provide similar, if not identical, substantive protections.

4.05: FOREIGN GOVERNMENTS

Foreign governments operating in the United States in their sovereign capacity, such as embassies and consulates, are implicitly immune from general employment laws of the United States. *McCulloch v. Sociedad Nacional de Marineos de Honduras,* 372 U.S. 10 (1963). However, this implicit exemption for sovereign activity does not extend to commercial activity of the foreign state such as operating airlines or commercial banks. *Wickes v. Olympic Airways,* 745 F.2d 363 (6th Cir. 1984).

4.06: FOREIGN OWNED EMPLOYERS

Commercial employers doing business in the United States will be subject to American employment law. However, treaties between the United States and the "guest nation" frequently permit companies of the "guest nation" to prefer nationals of the "guest nation" for certain positions, such as executives, specialists, and technical experts. Such treaties, however, usually apply only to companies *incorporated* in the "guest nation." Unless clearly stated otherwise in the treaty, companies incorporated in the United States will not be covered by such treaties even when they are wholly owned subsidiaries of a foreign entity. *Sumitomo Shoji America, Inc. v. Avagliano,* 457 U.S. 176 (1982).

If the treaty is applicable, but by its terms is not "self-executing," it will have no impact on U.S. domestic law until U.S. legislation implements the treaty. Many commercial treaties either are self-executing or have been implemented by legislation. When there is a conflict between terms in the treaty and domestic legislation, the latest in time will prevail. *Medellin v. Texas,* 522 U.S. 491 (2008). In situations governed by a treaty, the treaty will be strictly and narrowly construed to avoid any conflict with domestic U.S. law. *MacNamara v. Korean Airlines,* 863 F.2d 1135 (3d Cir. 1988).

4.07: INNOCENCE ABROAD?

The statutes cover American incorporated companies and their subsidiaries operating abroad as to their treatment of U.S. citizens working at a foreign site. The core statutes do not apply to non-citizens (aliens) employed and working outside of the United States. Moreover, U.S. law is not applied to an employer's extra-territorial employment actions if compliance with U.S. employment law would violate the law of the host nation.

4.08: EMPLOYERS EXPRESSLY EXCLUDED

A. INDIAN TRIBES

Recognized tribes of Native Americans are specifically excluded by Title VII from being "employers." The exclusion applies not just to the tribe's governmental entities but also to the tribe's commercial activity (such as operating retail outlets and casinos). While the other two core statutes have no similar exclusion, exclusion is implied at least as to a tribe's semi-sovereign governmental entities. *EEOC v. Fond du Lac Heavy Equipment Co.*, 986 F.2d 246 (8th Cir. 1993) (ADEA).

B. PRIVATE MEMBERSHIP CLUBS

Title VII and the ADA, but not the ADEA, exclude from the definition of "employer" non-profit membership clubs (other than labor organizations) which are exempt from taxation under the Internal Revenue Code. Although the statutes provide no further definition, the courts have concluded that to meet the definition of a "club" the organization must: (1) impose meaningful conditions of membership, and (2) have a defined social or recreational purpose that promotes a common literary, scientific, or political objective. Athletic and country clubs generally meet this definition. Credit unions, nursing homes, and hospitals open to large segments of the public do not. *Quijano v. University Fed. Credit Union*, 617 F.2d 129 (5th Cir. 1980).

4.09: RELIGIOUS ORGANIZATIONS

A. "RELIGIOUS" DISCRIMINATION

Title VII does not exempt religious organizations from coverage but specifically permits them to discriminate on the basis of religion. 42 U.S.C. 2000e–1. This allowance extends not only to religious discrimination against individuals involved in the religious activities of the religious organization, but also to individuals engaged in *secular activities* of the religion so long as the secular activity has some relationship to the church and its religious mission. *Corp. of Presiding Bishop v. Amos,* 483 U.S. 327 (1987) (exemption applicable to a church operated, but secular, gymnasium, and this exemption does not violate 1st Amendment prohibition of "establishment" of religion).

B. "RELIGIOUS ORGANIZATION"

A purely secular, for-profit business is not a "religious organization" entitled to discriminate on the basis of religion, simply because its proprietors hold sincere religious beliefs and use their secular business to promote those beliefs, such as by requiring its employees to attend employer organized religious services. *EEOC v. Townley Eng. & Mfg. Co.,* 859 F.2d 610 (9th Cir. 1988). Some authority holds that to qualify as a "religious organization" permitted to engage in religious discrimination the organization must be owned or significantly controlled by an established religious order. *LeBoon v. Lancaster Jewish Community Cntr. Ass'n.,* 503 F.3d 217 (3d Cir. 2007). *Spencer v. World*

Vision, Inc. 633 F.3d 723 (9th Cir. 2011), held, however, that a humanitarian relief organization may be deemed "religious" even though it is not directly affiliated with a religious organization if it: (1) was organized for a religious/ethical purpose, (2) was primarily engaged in pursuing that purpose, (3) held itself out to the public as engaging in that defined purpose, and (4) refrained from significant commercial enterprises. Concurring judges added a fifth element: that the organization have tax exempt status as a charitable, non-profit organization.

Educational institutions with a connection to an organized religion that claim the exemption allowing the institution to engage in religious discrimination will be analyzed in terms of the extent of the relationship of the school to an organized religious group, the history and stated mission of the school, the funding and administrative influence on the institution by a religious order, the religious orientation of its curriculum, and the religious affiliation of its students and faculty. *Killinger v. Samford Univ.*, 113 F.3d 196 (11th Cir. 1997) (7% of the school's funding from the church was sufficient to make the educational institution "religious"). However, merely because an educational institution was founded by a religious organization and maintains a formal, albeit distant, identification to that religion is not sufficient to make it "religious" when the school's modern mission, goals, activities, finance, direction, and curriculum have evolved into the institution being predominately secular. *EEOC v. Kamehameha Schools,* 990 F.2d 458 (9th Cir. 1993). Nevertheless, requiring that an *individual* be of a particular religion to teach specific courses in religion may be justified as a bona fide occupational qualification necessary to teach courses in religion even at a secular institution. *Pime v. Loyola Univ. of Chicago,* 803 F.2d 351 (7th Cir. 1986) (being Catholic is BFOQ for teaching religion classes at a Jesuit founded but secular university). *Infra*, Chapter 12.

C. "MINISTERIAL EXEMPTION"

The statutes do not expressly exempt religious organizations from charges of discrimination on the basis of race, color, national origin, sex, age, or disability. However, the "establishment" and "free exercise" of religion clauses of the First Amendment limit governmental intrusion into management and affairs of religious organizations that would include the selection, pay, assignment, or dismissal of "ministers" or teachers of the religion, and of those involved in the central pastoral mission of the religious organization. This constitutional imperative requires an exemption from statutory demands as applied to such positions. *Hosanna–Tabor Evangelical Lutheran Church v. EEOC,* ___ U.S. ___, 131 S.Ct. 1783 (2011). *Hosanna–Tabor* applied this implicit "ministerial" exemption to a "called teacher" of secular subjects (*i.e.*, math, science, language, music, and gym) in a primary school operated by the defendant religious organization even though the employee was not a fully ordained member of the clergy or authorized to perform the church's holy rites. The Court held that a detailed comparison of secular vs. religious job duties was not warranted when both the church and the employee deemed the employee to be a "minister" of the religion.

In addition to recognized "ministers" in the religious organization, the implicit exemption extends to persons who hold positions important to the church's spiritual mission. Lay teachers of theology at religiously affiliated educational institutions (such as nuns at a Catholic affiliated secular university) and teachers in seminaries or yeshivas are not subject to the statutes because they perform the core religious functions of preserving and conveying the organization's religious doctrine. *EEOC v. Southwestern Baptist Theological Seminary,* 651 F.2d 277 (5th Cir. 1981).

Hosanna–Tabor noted that applying the "ministerial exemption" for non-ministers is not subject to formulaic generalizations. In making the necessary case-by-case evaluation courts have balanced two factors: (1) duties of the employee, and (2) doctrine of the religion. The religion cannot claim First Amendment protection against race, sex, national origin, age, or disability discrimination in the purely secular *operations* of the religion, such as operating hospitals or retirement centers. *Employment Div., Dep't of Hum. Res. of Oregon v. Smith,* 494 U.S. 872 (1990). There is no exemption for a church's secular *activities* on church premises (*e.g.,* janitorial or clerical) even if compliance with statutory requirements violate principles of the religion. *See, Catholic Charities of Sacramento v. Superior Court,* 109 Cal.Rptr.2d 176 (2001), *aff'd* 85 P.3d 67 (2004) (availability of contraceptives for lay employees required by state law does not conflict with the constitutional rights of the Church).

A thin line often separates activities of a religion that are secular and subject to the law and sectarian activities protected by the First Amendment. For example, an "editorial secretary" at a publishing house operated by the religion to publish its religious materials was not subject to the religious ministerial exemption because her tasks were clerical and editorial, rather than religious. *EEOC v. Pacific Press Pub. Ass'n,* 676 F.2d 1272 (9th Cir. 1982). The lay "director of religious formation" for the Roman Catholic diocese was not subject to the ministerial exemption because his duties, in their totality, were viewed as primarily administrative. *Skrzypezak v. Roman Catholic Diocese of Tulsa,* 611 F.3d 1228 (10th Cir. 2010). However, as music was an integral part of the religious services, the post of the church's "music director" was subject to the implied exemption. *Tomic v. Catholic Dioceses of Peoria,* 442 F.2d 1036 (7th Cir. 2006).

Hosanna–Tabor, supra, emphasized that courts must refrain from ordering religious organizations to violate church doctrine in their sectarian activities. *Hankins v. Lyght,* 441 F.3d 96 (2d Cir.2006) (mandatory retirement imposed on the Church's ministers, prohibited by the ADEA, is not subject to challenge). However, the church may not be immunized from discrimination practiced by *its ministers* when the discrimination is prohibited by church doctrine and the discrimination does not affect tangible job benefits. In such cases, the conflict between secular law and church doctrine are minimized. *Elvig v. Calvin Presbyterian Church,* 375 F.3d 951 (9th Cir. 2004) (sexual harassment claims *not* subject to the exemption). *Contra: Kennedy v. St. Joseph's Ministries,* 657 F.3d 189 (4th Cir. 2011) (exemption *applies* to ministers charged with harassment).

4.10: "LABOR ORGANIZATION" COVERAGE

A "labor organization" is defined by the statutes as one which exists in whole or in part to deal with covered "employers." This "dealing" must concern "employee" grievances, labor disputes or terms and conditions of employment. A "labor organization" is covered, however, only if it maintains a union hiring hall, or has a minimum number of *members* (15 under Title VII and ADA; 25 under the ADEA). In addition, the labor organization with the requisite number of *members* (or operates a hiring hall) must be: (1) certified as the exclusive bargaining representative by the National Labor Relations Board, (2) be actively seeking such exclusive representation, *or* (3) is chartered as an organization which represents employees of a defined "employer." Most organizations that appear to laypersons as a labor union will be covered "labor organizations."

In dealing with its *own employees*, a labor organization is covered only if it has the requisite number of *employees*. Accordingly, even if the union is covered as a "labor organization," if not covered as an "employer" it will not have its relationship with its *employees* covered.

4.11: "EMPLOYMENT AGENCY" COVERAGE

The statutes define "employment agencies" as "any person regularly undertaking, with or without compensation, to procure employees for an employer." Coverage of employment agencies is not dependent upon the number of employees of the agency, but upon the agency's relationship to covered "employers." Thus, even a large agency that is covered in its employment relations as an "employer" but limits its placement activity to referrals to individuals not covered as "employers" (such as baby sitters or home health care workers) will not be covered in its referral activity. Moreover, referring independent contractors (such as "handyman" or security services) to "employers" is not covered as the agency is not referring "employees" for "employment."

To be covered the agency must also satisfy a non-statutory, common sense conception of the term in that its primary purpose is that of procuring employees for an employer or employers. Thus, a newspaper which prints "help wanted" advertisements is not considered an employment agency. *Greenfield v. Field Enterprises, Inc.*, 4 FEP Cases 548 (N.D.Ill. 1972). Professional certification agencies, such as bar associations or medical boards, are not considered employment agencies. While an academic institution incidentally may aid its students or graduates in finding employment, the institution will not, *per se*, be an employment agency. However, the placement or career service office dedicated to procuring employment prospects will be an "employment agency" even though it receives no compensation for the service. *Kaplowitz v. University of Chicago,* 387 F.Supp. 42 (N.D.Ill. 1974). State and local government employment services divisions are covered "employment agencies." *Pegues v. Miss. State Emp. Serv.,* 699 F.2d 760 (5th Cir. 1983).

CHAPTER 5

PRINCIPLES OF ACTIONABLE "DISCRIMINATION"

5.01: "EMPLOYMENT"

A. "RIGHT OF CONTROL?"

A covered "employer's" action must adversely affect a "term or condition of *employment.*" Thus, a director of a corporation removed from that position, allegedly because of his religious beliefs, has not been denied "employment," and thus has no Title VII claim. *Mariotti v. Mariotti Bld Products, Inc.* 714 F.3d 76 (3d Cir. 2013). A hospital that is a covered "employer" will not be affecting a term of "employment" when it denies staff privileges to a physician with the result that the physician may not treat his patients at the hospital. *Alexander v. Rush North Shore Medical Ctr,* 101 F.3d 487 (7th Cir. 1996). In determining when the treatment of a worker involves a condition of "employment," the courts have rejected a standard that relies primarily on the "economic realities" of the relationship, and hold that the common law "right of control" standard is used to determine whether "employment" terms or benefits have been denied. *See, Clackamas Gastroenterology Assoc. v. Wells, supra,* 4.02(d). Even when an individual has economic dependence on the covered "employer," if the employer lacks the "right to control" the means and manner of a worker's performance, the relationship is not "employment" and the treatment of the worker is outside the scope of the statutes. For example, a musician who performed for a symphony orchestra and received much of his income for this work was deemed to be an "independent contractor" even though the employer determined what music would be performed, when and where it was rehearsed and performed, with the music director directing plaintiff how the music should be played. *Lerohl v. Friends of Minn. Sinfonia,* 322 F.3d 486 (8th Cir. 2003). A television personality who worked exclusively for a covered television station developing and presenting public interest stories aired by the "employer" was an independent contractor, and thus her termination was not a discharge from an "employment" relationship with station. *Alberty–Velez v. Corporacion de Puerto Rico Para La Difusion Publica,* 361 F.3d 1 (1st Cir. 2004). Note, however, *Price Waterhouse v. Hopkins,* 490 U.S. 228 (1989), stated "[D]ecisions pertaining to advancement to partnership, are, of course, subject to challenge under Title VII".

B. FORMER EMPLOYMENT

Covered "employers" that adversely affect "employment" of their former employees at other "employers" are subject to the statutes. Thus, providing a poor reference for a former employee in retaliation for the employee having filed discrimination charges is actionable. *Robinson v. Shell Oil Co.,* 519 U.S. 337 (1997). Actions of an agency of a state government in denying a teacher certification necessary for employment have been held actionable. *Ass'n of Mexican–American Educators v. California,* 231 F.3d 572 (9th Cir. 2000) (en banc). *Contra: Woodward v. Virginia Bd. of Bar Examiners,* 598 F.2d 1345 (4th Cir. 1979).

C. TEMPORARY, SHARED, OR SEASONAL WORKERS

Employers often rely upon temporary workers to meet seasonal, flexible, or temporary staffing needs. Other employers are in the business of supplying such workers for a fee paid either by the client or the worker. The temporary nature of the relationship between the workers and the "client" firm has resulted in the argument that temporary or seasonal workers are "independent contractors" for both entities. However, where the client firm effectively directs the means and manner of the day-to-day work, the worker will be deemed an employee of the client employer. *Vizcaino v. Microsoft,* 120 F.3d 1006 (9th Cir. 1997). However, when the staffing agency exercises significant responsibility for the worker's on-job performance, is responsible for the salary and benefits of the worker, and assignments to clients are relatively short in duration, the staffing firm may be deemed the "employer." Employment may be "joint," subjecting both firms to liability for discrimination by either, if key responsibilities for the worker's performance are shared. *Redd v. Summers,* 232 F.3d 998 (D.C. Cir. 2000).

D. "AGENTS" AND INDIVIDUAL LIABILITY

While the statutes define "employer" to include "any agent of an employer" (*e.g.,* 42 U.S.C. 2000e–(b)), courts have determined that only the covered "employer," not its agents or supervisors, are liable for discrimination attributed to employers. Individual supervisors who may have caused the discriminatory treatment are not personally liable under the core federal statutes. *Miller v. Maxwell's Int'l Inc.,* 991 F.2d 583 (9th Cir. 1993). However, State non-discrimination law may impose individual liability.

E. RECONSTRUCTION ERA CIVIL RIGHTS ACT

42 U.S.C. 1981 broadly prohibits race discrimination in the making and enforcing of *contracts.* The party discriminating need *not* be an "employer" and the discrimination need *not* involve an "employment" relationship. Discrimination in both employment contracts and the treatment of independent contractors on the basis of *race* is proscribed. Similarly, claims against governments for violating rights protected by the Constitution are not dependent on an employee/employer relationship and may be enforced through 42 U.S.C. 1983.

5.02: "TERMS, CONDITIONS, OR PRIVILEGES OF EMPLOYMENT"

"Employer" treatment of the "employee" must reach the level of adversely affecting "the individual's status as an employee" as to his/her "terms, conditions, or privileges of employment." 42 U.S.C. 2000e–(a)(1) and (2). This language is "not limited to economic or tangible discrimination * * * but strikes at the entire spectrum of disparate treatment." *Meritor Savings Bank, FSB v. Vinson,* 477 U.S. 57 (1986). Nonetheless, while the adverse treatment need not cause physical or psychological injury nor affect adversely the employee's job performance (*Harris v. Forklift Systems,* 510 U.S. 17 (1993)), the statutes "do not reach genuine but innocuous difference" in treatment. *Oncale v. Sundowner Offshore Services, Inc.,* 523 U.S. 75 (1998). *Infra,* 24.01.

5.03: "TO DISCRIMINATE"—EMPLOYERS

A. GENERALLY

The statutes require that the employer's adverse action "discriminate." "Discriminate" is frequently, but mistakenly, construed to require some subjectively invidious element. At the basic level "to discriminate" means the objective act of treating persons differently; nothing more. When an employer selects one job applicant over another the employer has "discriminated" between the two applicants. Liability, however, is established only when it is shown that the "discrimination" was "because of" classifications or actions proscribed by the statutes (*e.g.,* race, color, national origin, religion, sex, age, disability, etc.).

B. ACTIVE VS. PASSIVE DISCRIMINATION

"Discrimination" requires action that denies "equal employment *opportunity*." "Discrimination" does not consist of a passive failure to insure equality of *outcome,* or "fairness," between classes, nor impose *obligations* to remedy past societal patterns of discrimination. *AFSCME v. State of Washington,* 770 F.2d 1401 (9th Cir. 1985) (while recognizing that women had been past victims of unfairness in the pay structure, state had no obligation to implement reform plan that would have provided equal pay for work of "comparable worth").

C. INDIVIDUAL VS. CLASS DISCRIMINATION

The concept of discrimination is analyzed in terms of the treatment of individuals, not groups. When individuals in fact are treated differently, this is "discrimination" even if the employer does not discriminate against the *class* of individuals to which the plaintiff belongs. In *City of Los Angeles Dep't of Water and Power v. Manhart,* 435 U.S. 702 (1978), the employer had required female employees to make greater monthly contributions than male employees to the employer's defined benefit pension plan. This was discrimination against individual women based on sex, and was not justified by the actuarial fact that as a class woman had a longer life expectancy than men, and thus women, as a class, would draw from the retirement fund for more years than men.

D. UNIFORMLY APPLIED PRACTICES

It is an appealing oversimplification to assume that treating all employees alike is not "discrimination." Ostensibly neutral rules or policies applied equally to all employees are "discriminatory" against the individuals actually affected by the policy. Standing alone, that "discrimination" does not violate the statutes. The "discrimination" must be "because of" class membership. Thus, a job related employment test given to all applicants resulting in the rejection of some, is discrimination against those who fail the test. The discrimination will violate Title VII if plaintiff can demonstrated that the test was adopted for the purpose of disadvantaging minority applicants. *Albemarle Paper Co. v. Moody,* 422 U.S. 405 (1975). Setting aside the results of a test is discrimination against those who passed it. If "discrimination" was "because of race," it violates Title VII. *Ricci v. DeStefano,* 557 U.S. 557 (2009). Moreover, if the test has an adverse impact on a class protected by the statutes and is not justified as being "job related and consistent with business necessity" it will be deemed discrimination "because of" protected class membership. *Griggs v. Duke Power Co.,* 401 U.S. 424 (1971); 42 U.S.C. 2000e–2(k)(1)(A).

It has been held that a supervisor who is an "equal opportunity abuser," harassing all employees equally has not "discriminated" against any one of them. *See, Smith v. Hy–Vee,* 622 F.3d 904 (8th Cir. 2010). Rarely, if ever, is this a reality. Invariably there will be differences in actual treatment of individuals or protected classes, and abusive treatment of one class cannot be negated by abusing equally other classes. Cursing black employees as "niggers" is not negated simply because the supervisor calls white employees "honkies" and white female employees "bitches." *See, Steiner v. Showboat Operating Co.,* 23 F.3d 1459 (9th Cir. 1994). As the statutes also reach "discrimination" that produces an adverse *effect* on a protected class (*Griggs v. Duke Power Co., supra*), "equal treatment" may have differing effects on different classes, and on this basis constitute "discrimination." A male supervisor who subjects all employees to abusive, aggressive behavior will have discriminated illegally against women because such "masculine" aggressiveness has a greater impact on women than on men. *EEOC v. NEA, Alaska,* 422 F.3d 840 (9th Cir. 2005). *Infra,* 25.04(d).

5.04: "LABOR ORGANIZATION" DISCRIMINATION

Labor organizations that have the requisite number of employees will be covered as an "employer" subject to the same restraints in the organization's relationship to its employees as any other employer.

In its capacity as a *representative* of workers, the statutes specify three kinds of union discrimination: (1) excluding or expelling from union membership or otherwise discriminating in the *internal affairs* of the organization such as eligibility for union office, voting rights, etc.; (2) *referrals* for employment or segregating or classifying individuals in a way that tends to deprive individuals of employment opportunities; (3) causing or attempting to cause "employers" to discriminate in a way that violates the statues. 42 U.S.C. 2000e–2(c).

The statutes implicitly prohibit unions from refusing or failing to process grievances an employee has against an employer on the basis of the proscribed classifications. *Goodman v. Lukens Steel Co.,* 482 U.S. 656 (1987). The *Lukens* Court was divided on the question of whether a labor organization had a positive duty to actively oppose discrimination practiced by an employer. Lower courts have rejected union liability based solely on the union's failure to oppose employer discrimination. *EEOC v. Pipefitters Ass'n Local 597,* 334 F.3d 656 (7th Cir. 2003).

However, a union in a bargaining relationship with an employer has an implicit "duty of fair representation" that is imposed by labor relations statutes. That duty not only prohibits invidious discrimination in the negotiation and administration of collective agreements (*Steele v. Louisville & Nashville R.R. Co.,* 323 U.S. 192 (1944)); it imposes an affirmative obligation on unions to attempt to eliminate discriminatory practices of employers with which the union has a bargaining relationship. *Local Union No. 12 United Rubber, Cork, Linoleum & Plastic Workers v. NLRB,* 368 F.2d 12 (5th Cir. 1966).

Where unions have joined with employers in a collective decision found to violate the statutes, union and employer will be severally and jointly liable. *Northwest Airlines, Inc. v. Transport Workers Union,* 451 U.S. 77 (1981).

5.05: "EMPLOYMENT AGENCY" DISCRIMINATION

Similar to labor organizations, employment agencies with the requisite number of employees will be subject to the obligations of an "employer" in its relationship with its "employees." The statutes proscribe agency *referral* actions in their: (1) failure or refusal to refer for employment, otherwise discriminate, or classify individuals in a manner that would interfere with employment; (2) honoring discriminatory requests by an employer; and (3) segregation of files in a way that permits others to discriminate. 42 U.S.C. 2000e–2(b). However, so long as the agency refers individuals on a non-discriminatory basis and takes no action to aid discrimination by an employer, the agency has no affirmative duty to police the hiring practices of employers to which it refers individuals. *Kaplowitz v. Univ. of Chicago,* 387 F.Supp. 42 (N.D. Ill. 1974).

5.06: "BECAUSE OF"

The core statutes require that "discrimination" by covered entities be "because of" an individual's protected class. There are three situations where the "because of" requirement is found:

A. FACIAL DISTINCTIONS

When defendants have expressed policies that deny positions to members of a protected class and apply that policy to a member of that class, the discrimination is clearly "because of" the victim's class membership. For example, having and applying a policy that denies positions to women, but not men, with pre-school aged children is discrimination "because of sex." *Phillips v. Martin Marietta Corp.*, 400 U.S. 542 (1971). A policy applied to a 60 year old employee that requires retirement is discriminating "because of" the employee's age. *Western Air Lines, Inc. v. Criswell*, 472 U.S. 321 (1985). *Infra*, Chapter 12.

B. DISPARATE TREATMENT

Discrimination with an improper but undisclosed motive is known as "disparate treatment." In such cases a factual issue is presented as to defendant's state of mind and whether that state of mind motivated the discriminatory treatment. "A disparate treatment claim cannot succeed unless the employee's protected trait actually played a role in that process and had a determinative influence on the outcome." *Hazen Paper Co. v. Biggins.* 507 U.S. 604 (1993). *Infra*, 14.02.

C. DISPARATE IMPACT

The seminal case of *Griggs v. Duke Power Co.*, 401 U.S. 424 (1971), held that under Title VII:

[G]ood intent or absence of discriminatory intent does not redeem employment procedures or testing mechanisms that operate as 'built in headwinds' for minority groups and are unrelated to measuring job capability. * * *

What is required by Congress is the removal of
artificial, arbitrary, and unnecessary barriers
to employment when the barriers operate
invidiously to discriminate on the basis of racial
or other impermissible classification. * * * The
touchstone is business necessity. If an
employment practice which operates to exclude
Negroes cannot be shown to be related to job
performance, the practice is prohibited.

This *Griggs* standard of liability based on the
unjustified impact of facially neutral devices was
codified by amendments to Title VII in 1991. 42
U.S.C. 2000e–2(k).

The ADA expressly adopted an impact basis for
liability, but added language more specifically
addressing issues arising when the impact of a
selection device is upon persons with disabilities. 42
U.S.C. 12112(b)(6). *Infra,* Chapter 18.

The ADEA, unlike Title VII and the ADA, has no
specific language creating liability based on impact.
Smith v. City of Jackson, 544 U.S. 228 (2005),
recognized that the rationale of *Griggs v. Duke
Power Co., supra,* was applicable to neutral policies
having an adverse impact on a protected age class.
However, as the ADEA specifically allows employers
to make distinctions based on "reasonable factors
other than age," defendant's burden in justifying a
device having an adverse impact is significantly
lighter than demonstrating the device's "business
necessity." *Mecham v. Knolls Atomic Power Lab.,*
554 U.S. 84 (2008). *Infra,* 18.04.

The Reconstruction Era Civil Rights Acts require proof of proscribed motive. Liability cannot be established by proving that the discrimination had only an adverse impact on one race. *General Bld. Contr. Ass'n v. Penn.,* 458 U.S. 375 (1982).

PART 2

PROTECTED CLASSES

The statutes are not general "civility codes" designed to reach "every bigoted act or gesture that a worker might encounter in the work place." *Thompson v. Mem. Hosp. of Carbondale,* 625 F.3d 394 (7th Cir. 2010). Discrimination must be because of membership in one of the classes protected by the statutes. Other forms of discrimination, no matter how offensive, are outside their scope. *Oncale v. Sundowner Offshore Services, Inc.,* 523 U.S. 75 (1998). This Part defines the classes, or the "status," receiving statutory protection.

CHAPTER 6
RACE AND COLOR

6.01: TITLE VII

A. "RACE"

Eradicating racial discrimination in the workplace was perhaps the key purpose behind the enactment of Title VII. The term "race" has been broadly construed to reach perceived racial origins such as Africa, Asia, Middle East, Pacific Islands, and the Americas, including Native Americans ("Indians"). "Race" is not limited to so-called racial minorities. Individuals with European ancestry ("whites") are protected under the same standards as are racial minorities. *McDonald v. Santa Fe Trail Transp. Co.,* 427 U.S. 273 (1976). Discriminating against a person because of perceived immutable physical characteristics of a racial class, such as hair texture or eye color, is "race" discrimination. However, discriminating on the basis of an individual's clothing or hair *styling* is not race discrimination simply because a particular style currently is favored by an identifiable racial group. *Rogers v. American Airlines,* 527 F.Supp. 229 (S.D.N.Y. 1981)(prohibiting corn row hair style worn by black employee was not "race" discrimination).

Discrimination against a white job applicant because of the black race of the applicant's *spouse* is racial discrimination against the applicant in that had plaintiff been of a different race (*i.e.,* the race of the spouse), he would not have been rejected. *Parr v. Woodmen of the World Life Ins. Co.*, 791 F.2d 888 (11th Cir. 1986). Similarly, harassment of a white employee based on his perceived inter-racial *friendships* is proscribed race discrimination. *Barrett v. Whirlpool Corp.*, 556 F.3d 502 (6th Cir. 2009).

Employer segregation of its *customers* by race may create a psychologically hostile atmosphere for employees who are forced to serve only members of their racial group. *Rogers v. EEOC*, 454 F.2d 234 (5th Cir. 1971).

B. "COLOR"

Color discrimination is also proscribed by Title VII. "Color" is ill-defined, but has been applied to discrimination by a supervisor who does not discriminate against blacks generally, or against whites, but favors persons of African heritage with dark skin over persons of African heritage with lighter skin. *Walker v. Secretary of Treasury*, 713 F.Supp. 403 (N.D.Ga. 1989). The prohibition of discrimination because of skin "color" eliminates the need for plaintiffs to identify the precise racial origins upon which the alleged discrimination was based.

6.02: RECONSTRUCTION ERA CIVIL RIGHTS ACTS: 42 U.S.C. 1981

This 1866 Act provides that "all persons shall have the same right to make and enforce contracts as is enjoyed by white citizens." Its origins are in the

13th Amendment which outlawed slavery and authorized implementing legislation to remove "badges and incidents" of slavery. Its broad language was expanded and clarified in 1991 to make it applicable to all aspects of the employment contract—hiring, promotion, discharge, compensation, and harassment. While originally intended to guaranty newly freed slaves equal contract rights as "enjoyed by white citizens," it has been construed to prohibit racial discrimination against whites. *McDonald v. Santa Fe Trail Transp. Co.,* 427 U.S. 273 (1976).

While not facially limited to race discrimination, (*"all persons"* shall have the same right to make and enforce contracts), as its roots are in the 13th Amendment, section 1981 has been construed narrowly to apply *only* to racial discrimination. However, the conception of "race" was construed to encompass the very broad, mid–19th Century notions of "race." At that time "race" was considered to be "identifiable classes of persons * * * [based on] their ancestry or ethnic characteristics" (*e.g.*, "Irish race," "German race," "Jewish race", etc.). *St. Francis College v. Al–Kharaji,* 481 U.S. 604 (1987) (Iraq/Arab is "race"); *Shaare Tefila Congregation v. Cobb,* 481 U.S. 615 (1987) (Jewish or Hebrew origins, as opposed to Judaism the religion, is "race"). Hispanics, and so-called hyphenated Americans, such as Polish–Americans, Irish–Americans, are protected under 1981 against discrimination based on their distinct ethnic characteristics or origins.

The distinction between religion and "national origin," neither of which are within the scope of 1981, and the broad protection 1981 gives to "race" can be confusing. Discriminating against an Hispanic could be considered "national origin," and thus not protected by 1981, but it will also be considered protected as "race" under 1981. *See, Manzanares v. Safeway Stores, Inc.,* 593 F.2d 968 (10th Cir. 1979). Disparaging remarks about the nation of Israel were sufficient to uphold a finding that discrimination was because of plaintiff's Jewish "race." *Sinai v. New England Tel. & Tel. Co.,* 3 F.3d 471 (1st Cir. 1993).

This Act allows for a broader range of remedies than does Title VII, including compensatory and punitive damages without statutory caps. Moreover, it imposes no administrative exhaustion obligations on claimants and has more generous time limitations on filing an enforcement suit. Accordingly, complaints of race discrimination should pursue both Title VII and 1981 remedies.

CHAPTER 7
NATIONAL ORIGIN

7.01: DEFINED: GENERALLY

"National origin" discrimination is proscribed, but not defined, by Title VII. *Espinoza v. Farah Mfg. Co.*, 414 U.S. 86 (1973), defined "national origin" to mean "the country from which you or your forebearers came." The term has been interpreted to include ethnic distinctions broader than strict nationality, such as Latino or Middle–Eastern, as well as to narrower, distinct cultural heritages, even when no current country or nation exists, such as the Roma ("gypsies"), Cajuns, Puerto Ricans, or Kurds. *Pajic v. Hughes Helicopters, Inc.*, 840 F.2d 667 (9th Cir. 1988). However, discrimination in favor of residents of a particular state, region, or city in the United States is not based on "national origin."

Discrimination against Native Americans ("Indians") will be considered race discrimination. However, if the discrimination is based solely upon tribal membership this may constitute national origin discrimination in that native American tribes are recognized as semi-sovereign "nations." *Dawavendewa v. Salt River Project Ag. Imp. & Power Dist.*, 154 F.3d 1117 (9th Cir. 1998) (non-tribal employer discriminating against Native Americans because they were not members of a particular tribe). (*Cf.* 42 U.S.C. 2000e-(b), which excludes Indian *tribes* from the definition of "employer", and 42 U.S.C. 2000e–2(i) which allows businesses on or near Indian reservations to grant preferential treatment to "Indians" living on or near the reservation.).

7.02: CITIZENSHIP AND "ALIENAGE"

A. TITLE VII

Espinoza v. Farah Mfg. Co., supra, held that "national origin" did not encompass discrimination based on *lack* of U.S. citizenship (or "alienage"). Lower courts have found that discrimination because of U.S. citizenship, that is discrimination against U.S. citizens in favor of citizens of another nation, is proscribed "national origin" discrimination. *MacNamara v. Korean Airlines,* 873 F.2d 1135 (3d Cir. 1988).

B. THE IMMIGRATION REFORM AND CONTROL ACT (IRCA) (8 U.S.C. 1324(A))

IRCA mandates employer discrimination against "undocumented" aliens and requires employers to verify the employment eligibility under U.S. law of all new hires, but it also prohibits discrimination against "protected individuals" because of national origin or "citizenship status." "Protected individuals" include: (1) citizens of the U.S., (2) lawfully admitted "aliens" who are (a) permanent residents, (b) temporary residents admitted under specified amnesty provisions, or (c) residents granted asylum.

Non-citizen residents will lose their "protected individual" status if they fail to apply for naturalization within six months of becoming eligible to apply, or after having applied in a timely fashion, have not been naturalized within two years, unless the immigrant can establish active pursuit of naturalization.

IRCA is not enforced through EEOC procedures, but requires aggrieved persons to file charges with the Special Counsel in the U.S. Department of Justice within 120 days of the discriminatory action.

C. LANGUAGE

The primary language one speaks has been seen as an immutable characteristic of the country or region from which the speaker or his/her forebears came. Thus, using language as a basis for discrimination may be considered *per se* "national origin" discrimination. Just as hair texture is an immutable characteristic of race, the Spanish language is seen as an immutable characteristic of Latino "national origins." *Hernandez v. New York,* 500 U.S. 352 (1991) (non-Title VII), 29 C.F.R. 1606.7. In this view, discrimination based on one's "foreign accent and restrictions on language use, such as requirements that employees speak only English, are facial national origin discrimination justified only if defendant establishes that the policy is a bona fide occupational qualification. *Rodriguez v. FedEx Freight East, Inc.,* 487 F.3d 1001 (6th Cir. 2007). The BFOQ defense is discussed, *infra,* Chapter 12. Other courts are reluctant to reach a *per se* conclusion, and view enforcement of restrictive language rules merely as evidence of invidious "national origin" motivation. *Garcia v. Spun Steak Co.* 998 F.2d 1480 (9th Cir. 1993). Such rules also may be shown to create a hostile working environment for persons of other origins or when enforced, such rules may produce an adverse impact on persons of a particular national origin, and on this basis violate Title VII unless the employer demonstrates the "business necessity" of the rule. 29 C.F.R. 1606.7 Work place language rules are discussed *infra* 25.02(c).

CHAPTER 8

SEX

8.01: GENERALLY: DEFINED

Aside from the 1978 Pregnancy Discrimination Act amendment to Title VII which states that "sex" includes "pregnancy, childbirth, and related medical conditions," Title VII provides no definition of the word "sex." Moreover, the legislative history provides little guidance. "Sex" was inserted into the House Bill during debates in an unsuccessful effort to defeat the statute. The "poison pill" amendment was accepted without significant debate, and without discussion, "sex" became a class protected by Title VII.

The courts have tended to limit the term "sex" to the physical, biological differences that distinguish males and females. *General Electric Co. v. Gilbert,* 429 U.S. 125 (1976). Males are protected against discrimination because they are male under the same standards as applied to women. *Oncale v. Sundowner Offshore Services,* 523 U.S. 75 (1998).

In analyzing "sex" discrimination courts have used the terms "sex" and "gender" interchangeably. *See, e.g., Price Waterhouse v. Hopkins,* 490 U.S. 228 (1989). Social scientists draw a distinction. "Sex" is the biological difference between males and females based almost exclusively upon the difference in physical organs. "Gender" is broader and includes all the things that an individual does to outwardly manifest his or her status or identification as a male or female. It is unclear whether courts are using "sex" and "gender" interchangeably when they mean the narrow physical difference, or whether Title VII prohibits the broader concept of "gender" discrimination.

8.02: GENDER STEREOTYPING

Price Waterhouse v. Hopkins, supra, accepted the concept that "gender stereotyping" was a form of "sex" discrimination. Plaintiff, a female employee, was denied a promotion to a partnership in defendant's accounting firm. The evidence disclosed numerous evaluative comments by decision-makers, such as that plaintiff "overcompensated for being a woman," she was "macho," and that a "lady" shouldn't use such "foul language." Plaintiff was advised that she would improve her chances for future promotion if she "took a course in charm school," would "walk more femininely, dress more femininely, wear make-up, have her hair styled, and wear jewelry." The Court affirmed that Ms. Hopkins was being evaluated on the basis of outward characteristics typically associated with the respective sexes, and that such gender "stereotyping" constituted sex discrimination.

The most broad interpretation of the decision is that all stereotyping that imposes burdens based on different gender characteristics is forbidden. It should also be noted that the stereotype engaged in by Price Waterhouse was largely an immutable characteristic, perhaps of women, but most certainly Ms. Hopkins, namely her "non-female" personality, manner, and behavior. Thus, one could interpret the case as applying only to those stereotypes as to immutable characteristics, but not simply to choice of clothing or hair styles.

The most narrow interpretation of *Price Waterhouse* is that use of a stereotype is simply "some evidence" of a sex-motivated decision, which taken together with other evidence, supported the lower court finding that sex motivated the decision. In addition to the expressions of gender stereotypes, the Court noted the near absence of female partners at Price Waterhouse, its disproportionate rejection of female applicants, and direct, sex-based commentaries by decision-makers.

This ambiguity produced confusion as *Jesperson v. Harrah's Operating Co.,* 444 F.3d 1104 (9th Cir. 2006)(en banc), demonstrates. The employer imposed on all its employees a "Personal Best" grooming code that made distinctions between male and female workers that admittedly were based on stereotypes as to personal appearance. Men's hair must be short, women's must be "down," "teased, curled, or styled." Men may not wear facial make-up; women must, specifically including a requirement of face blush, mascara, and lip coloring.

The court uniformly agreed that plaintiff was subjected to gender stereotyping that distinguished between men and women. However, the majority held that this, standing alone, did not constitute actionable sex discrimination. The distinction must burden women to the level that the rule adversely affected plaintiff's "terms or conditions of employment." The majority held that plaintiff had failed to prove that these grooming distinctions rose to that level. It noted that unlike Ms. Hopkins the distinction drawn by the employer did not affect her ability to get and hold the job. That is, this employer did not rely on a stereotype that effectively denied plaintiff employment at Harrah's. Plaintiff could change her grooming preferences. Ms. Hopkins could not change her basic personality. The majority also noted that men, too, had obligations under the "personal best" code and the absence of evidence that the employer harbored a bias against women.

The four judge dissent read *Price Waterhouse* more broadly to reach stereotypes as to how women should dress and present themselves. The dissent suggested that, at the least, this stereotyping was "direct evidence" of sex motivated rules, sufficient to avoid the summary judgment granted to the employer by the trial court. Finally, the dissent contested the factual finding by the court that the grooming policy did not place a time and expense burden on women not suffered by men.

Price Waterhouse was given a broad application in *Lewis v. Heartland Inns of America, LLC,* 591 F.3d 1033 (8th Cir. 2010). A hotel admissions desk clerk was dismissed because she had a "tomboyish" rather than a "pretty, Midwestern girl" appearance. The court held that such a stereotype constituted sex discrimination. In *Chadwich v. Wellpoint, Inc.,* 561 F.3d 38 (1st Cir. 2009), plaintiff was denied a promotion because she was the mother of four children, including triplets in kindergarten. Relying on *Price Waterhouse,* the court held that plaintiff was a victim of sex stereotyping based on the assumption that she, as a woman, would be "overwhelmed" by the new job and her inevitable child care responsibilities.

8.03: SEXUAL ORIENTATION

A. GENERALLY

The laws of at least 29 states and hundreds of municipalities specifically proscribe discrimination based on sexual orientation. Presidential Order 13160 prohibits such discrimination against federal employees. However, the courts agree that discrimination based on sexual orientation, practices, or preferences is not facial sex discrimination under Title VII. *Etsitty v. Utah Transit Auth.*, 502 F.3d 1215 (10th Cir. 2007). Thus, harassing a worker because he is perceived to be homosexual does not, on its face, constitute sex discrimination. *Kalich v. AT & T Mobility LLC,* 679 F.3d 464 (6th Cir. 2012). These courts have rejected as "bootstrapping" the argument, accepted in race discrimination cases, that discriminating against an individual because of the sex of a spouse, companion, or friends is "sex" discrimination. *DeSantis Co., Inc. v. Pacific Tel. & Tel. Co.,* 608 F.2d 327 (9th Cir. 1979). *See, supra,* 6.01.

B. TRANSSEXUALITY

"Transsexuality" is the process by which one has changed or is changing their biological sex through surgery, drug treatments, and psychological adjustments. Discriminating against transsexuals has been distinguished from unprotected sexual orientation discrimination, as, unlike orientation, transsexuality involves an actual physical and biological change. Accordingly, discrimination against one undergoing such a sex transformation has been deemed facial "sex" discrimination. *See, Schroer v. Billington,* 577 F.Supp.2d 293 (D.D.C. 2008); *Glenn v. Brumby,* 693 F.3d 1312 (11th Cir. 2011) (constitutional analysis). Others have reached a similar outcome by reasoning that discrimination on the basis of one's changing sexuality is a proscribed form of gender stereotyping. *Smith v. City of Salem,* 378 F.3d 566 (6th Cir. 2004).

C. HOMOSEXUALITY AND BISEXUALITY

While facial discrimination against lesbians, gays, and bisexual individuals is not directly prohibited by Title VII, the concept of gender stereotyping, as developed in *Price Waterhouse v. Hopkins, supra,* has provided indirect, but incomplete, protection for individuals in the lesbian, gay, bisexual and transsexual (LGBT) community. Relying on *Price Waterhouse,* the courts have uniformly found that it is sex discrimination when distinctions are based on an individual exhibiting gender characteristics normally associated with members of the opposite sex. *Nichols v. Azteca Restaurant Enterprises,* 256 F.3d 864 (9th Cir. 2001). This draws a narrow but critical distinction between discrimination against a person because he/she is perceived to be homosexual—which is not proscribed by Title VII— and discrimination against the person because of his or her masculine or feminine gender characteristics—which is. *Hamm v. Weyauwega Milk Products, Inc.,* 332 F.3d 1058 (7th Cir. 2003).

8.04: "SEX" AS A VERB: SEXUAL CONDUCT

The term "sex," on its face, does not include sexual activity, behavior, or relationships. Thus, discriminating against a woman because she had a pre-marital sexual relationship was not, on in its face, sex discrimination. However, if the sexual relationship resulted in her pregnancy, she could not be discriminated against because of that pregnancy, which is defined by Title VII to be "sex." *Hamilton v. Southland Christian School, Inc.,* 680 F.3d 1360 (11th Cir. 2012).

An argument once made, but rejected, was that sexual advances toward an individual because of a desire to have a sexual relationship was not because of sex, but because of a desire to form a physical relationship. As the sex (male or female) of the employee played a critical role in motivating the employer's denial of a tangible job benefit, such as a promotion, a salary increase, or continued employment, the individual's refusal to consent to a sexual relationship is actionable "sex discrimination." *Meritor Savings Bank, FSB v. Vinson,* 477 U.S. 57 (1986).

If the employee rejects a single employer proposition and the employer takes no tangible job action against the employee, the single proposition of trading sex for favorable job benefits is unlikely to be actionable "discrimination." However, if such threats or propositions are repeated, they can reach

a level creating an abusive or hostile work
environment that affects a "term or condition of
employment." At this point the harassing treatment
becomes actionable sex discrimination. *Meritor
Savings Bank v. Vinson,* 477 U.S. 57 (1986). *See,
infra,* 25.04.

Nevertheless, Title VII generally will not reach
claims of non-harassed "bystander" employees based
simply on favoritism shown to another employee
because the favored employee has a sexual
relationship with the employer. *Ackel v. National
Communications,* 339 F.3d 376 (5th Cir. 2003). The
discrimination is seen as discrimination based on a
"special place" the favored person has in the heart of
the employer that equally disadvantages all other
employees regardless of their sex. *Womack v.
Runyon,* 147 F.3d 1298 (11th Cir. 1998). Not only is
favoritism for a paramour not "sex" discrimination,
complaints by female co-workers about such
favoritism has been held not to be protected
"opposition" to perceived illegal discrimination.
Kelly v. Shapiro & Assoc., 716 F.3d 10 (2d Cir.
2013). Some authority suggests, however, that a
male employee should have a claim of sex
discrimination when female employees are favored
because of the female employees' sexual relationship
with the employer in that such decision-making
excluded male employees of "employment
opportunities" because they were male. *King v.
Palmer,* 778 F.2d 878 (D.C. Cir. 1988).

At some point rampant sexual favoritism and
pervasive, welcomed as well as unwelcomed sexual
advances in the workplace can create a hostile

atmosphere that negatively affects the terms and conditions of employment even for employees not directly subjected to the advances. *Miller v. Dep't of Corrections,* 115 P.3d 77 (Cal. 2005); 29 C.F.R. 1604.11(a)(2) & (3). *Infra,* 25.04. In sum, discrete favoritism of a paramour generally is not sex discrimination; flagrant sexual promiscuity can be. *Priest v. Rotary,* 634 F.Supp. 571 (N.D. Cal. 1986).

8.05: PREGNANCY, CHILDBIRTH AND CHILDCARE

A. TITLE VII GENERALLY

In response to a Supreme Court decision holding that pregnancy was not "sex," Congress enacted the Pregnancy Discrimination Act of 1978 (PDA) which amended Title VII to define "sex" to include "pregnancy, childbirth, and related medical conditions." A second clause provides that "women affected by pregnancy, childbirth and related conditions shall be treated the same for all employment-related purposes, including receipt of benefits under fringe benefit programs, as other persons not so affected but similar in their ability or inability to work." 42 U.S.C. 2000e–(k). The first clause is general and makes it "sex" discrimination to refuse to hire a woman, to discharge her, or require that she take leave because of her pregnancy, childbirth, or related medical conditions. The second clause is more specific. It requires employers to provide benefits to a woman related to her childbirth and pregnancy that are equal to those provided for similar medical conditions affecting the ability to work.

The question is whether there is a negative implication in the second clause that there is no actionable sex discrimination if a worker's pregnancy or childbirth results in her being denied "benefits" that are similarly denied to employees with other similar medical conditions. *Nashville Gas Co. v. Satty,* 434 U.S. 136 (1977), a pre-PDA case, distinguished between denial of "extra *benefits*" for pregnant women, which then would not constitute sex discrimination, from policies affecting pregnancy that impose a disproportionate burden on women, which would be "sex" discrimination. Accordingly, a uniformly applied policy resulting in loss of seniority for taking extended leave was found to impose a burden on women who needed to take medical leave for their pregnancy and childbirth. As the employer's leave and seniority policy was not a denial of a *benefit* to pregnancy, but imposed a disproportionate burden suffered only by women, the loss of seniority for extended leave policy constituted "sex" discrimination.

It would seem doubtful that in enacting the PDA Congress intended to overrule *Nashville Gas. See, Newport News Shipbuilding & Dry Dock Co. v. EEOC,* 462 U.S. 669, n. 14(1983) ("The meaning of the first clause is not limited by the specific clause."). Nonetheless, many courts hold that the treatment of pregnancy and childbirth no differently than other conditions is not sex discrimination simply because of its burden on women. *Troup v.*

May Department Stores Co., 20 F.3d 734 (7th Cir 1994). *See, infra,* Chapter 24.

B. PROCEDURES TO END PREGNANCY: ABORTION

It is pregnancy, and thus "sex," discrimination to refuse to hire, to dismiss, or to otherwise discriminate against a woman because she has had, or refuses to have, an abortion. *Doe v. C.A.R.S. Protection Plus,* 527 F.3d 358 (3d Cir. 2008). Testing women for pregnancy or fertility itself may be sex discrimination. *Norman–Bloodsaw v. Lawrence Berkeley Lab.,* 135 F.3d 1260 (9th Cir. 1998).

If an employer has a health care plan, the plan may exclude medical care benefits for voluntary abortions not necessary to preserve the life of the woman, but must include equal benefits for treatment of complications flowing from her abortion. 42 U.S.C. 2000e–(k).

If the employer has a policy or informal practice of granting leaves for illnesses or to secure medical treatments, denial of leave to secure an abortion would be sex discrimination. However, if medical leaves were regularly denied or limited in time, under the "equal treatment" application of the second clause of the PDA, similarly denying or limiting leave to women to secure an abortion or to treat its complications is not sex discrimination *See, Troup v. May Department Stores Co., supra.*

C. PROCEDURES TO PREVENT PREGNANCY: CONTRACEPTION

The EEOC's position is:

Contraception is a means by which a woman controls her ability to become pregnant. The PDA's prohibition on discrimination against women based on their ability to become pregnant thus necessarily includes a prohibition related to a woman's use of contraceptives. EEOC Dec. 14, 2000, 2 EPD Guide Para. 6878.

Accord: Erickson v. Bartell Drug Co., 141 F.Supp.2d 1266 (W.D.Wash.2001).

The EEOC's position is that exclusion of contraception coverage from an employer's prescription drug benefit program is sex discrimination because it interferes with a woman's decisions relating to pregnancy, and because such an exclusion imposes on women additional, out-of-pocket health financial costs and unique health care risks, not faced by men. State or federal policies mandating inclusion of contraceptives in employee health care plans does not violate the constitutional rights of religious organizations engaged in secular activities. *Catholic Charities of Sacramento v. Superior Court,* 109 Cal.Rptr.2d 176 (2001), *aff'd* 85 P.3d 67 (2004). *Priests for Life v. Sebelius* (E.D. N.Y. 2013), 81 USLW 1513. Some authority is to the contrary. *In re Union Pacific R.R.,* 479 F.3d 936 (8th Cir. 2007), held that excluding contraception from a health care coverage plan was not sex discrimination because the "contraception" exclusion applied to both men and women. Proposed regulations under the federal Affordable Health Care Act would mandate inclusion of contraception in health care plans.

D. FERTILITY AND PROCEDURES TO BECOME PREGNANT

Saks v. Franklin Covey Co., 316 F.3d 337 (2d Cir. 2003), held that discrimination against a woman to secure *fertility* treatments was neither "pregnancy" nor sex discrimination in that reproductive capacity is a condition common to both men and women. However, when a female employee was dismissed for an absence to undergo in vitro *fertilization* procedures in order to make her pregnant, this was pregnancy, and thus sex, discrimination. The inability of a woman to become pregnant, and the procedure to produce such a pregnancy, is "sex" within the meaning of the PDA. *Hall v. Nalco Co.,* 534 F.3d 644 (7th Cir. 2008).

E. UNWED PREGNANCY

Discrimination against a woman who is pregnant but unwed is sex discrimination. The employer's concerns about the morality of unwed mothers, when none are raised about the morality of unwed fathers, is a "double standard" imposed on women but not on men. *Cline v. Catholic Diocese of Toledo,* 206 F.3d 651 (6th Cir. 2000).

F. "RELATED MEDICAL CONDITIONS"

The PDA also prohibits discrimination based on "related medical conditions" directly associated with pregnancy, such as cramping, dizziness, "morning sickness" nausea, the birth itself, and the necessary post-delivery recovery. A pregnant woman thus may not be denied employment based on any such pregnancy-related conditions. Menstruation, "a normal aspect of the female physiology," is sufficiently related to pregnancy that discrimination based on a woman's post-pregnancy menstrual cycle may constitute sex discrimination. Similarly, in reversing a trial court decision to the contrary, *EEOC v. Houston Funding II,* 717 F.3d 425 (5th Cir. 2013), held that lactation, the natural production of milk, was a "related medical condition" of being pregnant and bearing a child. Consequently, terminating the employee based on her *request* to use a breast pump while at work was prima facie discrimination based on pregnancy and childbirth. (The court reserved the question of whether the employer would be required to make an accommodation for the actual use of the breast pump.)

The PDA does not protect or require leave for *care* for infants, as opposed to their "birth." *Piatanida v. Wyman Ctr.,* 116 F.3d 340 (8th Cir. 1997). "Related medical conditions" in the PDA refers to the conditions relating to the employee's pregnancy, not to medical conditions of the employee's children. *Fleming v. Ayers & Assoc.,* 948 F.2d 993 (6th Cir. 1991). The Family and Medical Leave Act does require covered employers to provide 12 weeks of unpaid leave for "eligible employees." *Infra,* 8.07. Leaves and job assignment adjustments that must be made to accommodate pregnancy, childbirth and related medical conditions are discussed *infra,* 24.02.

8.06: MARRIAGE AND PARENTING

A. GENERALLY

Title VII does not extend protection to marriage or parental status. The refusal to hire married *persons* or *persons* with families does not violate Title VII. However, it will be sex discrimination if an employer refuses to hire married women or women with children but does not disqualify men for the same reason. *Phillips v. Martin Marietta Corp.,* 400 U.S. 542 (1971).

Employers may impose nepotism rules that prohibit marriage, intimate and other social relationships between employees. *EEOC v. Rath Packing Co.,* 908 F.2d 318 (8th Cir. 1986). Conversely, favoring employees who have a relationship by blood, marriage, or friendship does not, on its face, violate Title VII. *Thomas v. Washington County School Bd.,* 915 F.2d 922 (4th Cir. 1990).

B. CHILD CARE RESPONSIBILITIES

It may be sex discrimination, based on stereotyping, to deny a female applicant a position based on an assumption that her childcare responsibilities would interfere with her job performance. *Chadwick v. Wellpoint, Inc.,* 561 F.3d 38 (1st Cir. 2009). This would be particularly true if the employer expressed no such concerns regarding male applicants. Title VII does not prohibit an

employer from discriminating on the basis of a
medical condition of a child or family member if the
disqualification is applied to both sexes. *Fleming v.
Ayers & Assoc.,* 948 F.2d 993 (6th Cir. 1991).

While the PDA requires leave for the mother's
childbirth, it does not require that similar leave be
granted to fathers, or extend to mothers the right to
a period of leave beyond that which is required to
give birth and recover medically. *Piantanida v.
Wyman Ctr.* 116 F.3d 340 (8th Cir. 1997).

Employers may grant employees childbirth leave
beyond that medically required for the birth, and
also allow leave for post-delivery *childcare* not
required by law. Some states mandate leave
requirements that exceed those required by the
federal statutes. However, to the extent an employer
provides leave to mothers for purposes *not required*
by federal law, it is sex discrimination to deny
similar childcare leave to fathers. *Schafer v. Bd. of
Public Educ., Pittsburgh,* 903 F.2d 243 (3d Cir.
1990).

8.07: THE FAMILY AND MEDICAL LEAVE ACT, (FMLA), 29 U.S.C. 2601

The FMLA requires granting "eligible employees,"
male and female, unpaid leave for childbirth and
childcare, as well as for all "serious health
conditions." An uncomplicated pregnancy, however,
is not considered a "serious health condition" that
requires the grant of leave until such time as the
pregnancy of the employee renders her unable to
perform essential functions of her particular job. At

this point, and after giving the employer proper notice, the pregnant employee is entitled to take up to 12 weeks of *unpaid* leave prior to or after the child's delivery. This leave may be taken at one time, intermittently, or on a reduced work week basis. Thus, when a pregnant employee could work for no more than 8 hours a day, the employer must grant requested "leave" from working in excess of 8 hours. *Whitaker v. Bosch Braking Systems div.,* 180 F.Supp.2d 922 (W.D.Mich. 2001).

"Eligible" male employee also are entitled to unpaid leave to care for a spouse who has a "serious health condition," which would include a spouse who is no longer able to work because of her pregnancy, as well as leave to provide care for his infant child. *See,* Chapter 24, *infra.*

CHAPTER 9

RELIGION

9.01: TOWARD A DEFINITION

Title VII does not define "religion" other than to specify that it includes "all aspects of religious observance and practice, as well as belief." 42 U.S.C. 2000e–(j). "Religion" implicitly includes the teachings or traditions of established faiths, such as Roman Catholic, Judaism, Islam, Hindu, or Buddhist, subdivisions and schisms, such as Orthodox, Sunni, Eastern, and the various branches of Protestantism, such as Methodist, Baptist, Lutheran. "Religion" includes non-traditional faiths and practices that are sincerely held with the strength of traditional religious views, such as Native American spiritualism, and even the unorthodox such as Wicca ("witchcraft"). *Van Koten v. Family Health Management, Inc.,* 134 F.3d 375 (7th Cir.1998). Discrimination against atheists or agnostics is religious discrimination as it is based on the absence of religious belief. *Reed v. Great Lakes Companies,* 330 F.3d 931 (7th Cir. 2003).

The EEOC and courts generally apply the extremely broad definition adopted by the Supreme Court in defining the scope of religion protected by the First and Fourteenth Amendments. Thus, "religion" includes an individual's sincerely held "moral or ethical beliefs as to what is right or wrong * * * with the strength of traditional religious views." 29 C.F.R. 1605.1; *Wilson v. U.S. West Communications,*

58 F.3d 1337 (8th Cir. 1995). That no religious group espouses such belief or practice, or the fact that the religious group to which the individual professes to belong does not accept such belief, is not determinative of whether the individual's sincere beliefs are protected "religion." *Id.*

9.02: RELIGIOUS/SECULAR DISTINCTION

While secular beliefs and practices are not protected, the broad definition of "religion" can make it difficult to distinguish protected "religion" from unprotected personal preferences, political beliefs, secular ideas, and social activities. In making this distinction courts have considered five factors. *See, e.g., Alvarado v. City of San Jose,* 94 F.2d 1223 (9th Cir. 1996):

• *Shared or individual?* Idiosyncratic beliefs are less likely to be considered "religious" than widely shared ethical views. For example, one's dietary preferences, divorced from established religious direction, are unlikely to be protected "religion." *Brown v. Pena,* 441 F.Supp. 1382 (S.D.Fla. 1977), *aff'd* 589 F.2d 1113 (5th Cir. 1979). An individual's desire to a transfer to a different location may be seen as a personal aspiration rather than a religious belief. *Vetter v. Farmland Indus. Inc.,* 120 F.3d 749 (8th Cir. 1997).

• *Element of a comprehensive system?* "Religion" suggests beliefs that are a part of a broader, comprehensive belief or values system. Narrow, single issue concerns, even if widely shared, are less likely to be classed as "religious." Protesting obscenity or bawdy behavior, at the workplace for example, is unlikely a religious practice. *Rivera v. Puerto Rico Aqueduct & Sewer Auth.,* 331 F.3d 183 (1st Cir. 2003).

• *Structure?* Shared ethical beliefs within a comprehensive ethical system often are channeled in some form of organization such as a name, a hierarchy, regular meetings, leaders or teachers, publications, etc. Membership in the "World Church of the Creator" was protected even though this group espoused an extreme view of white supremacy, denied the Holocaust, advocated driving Jews from their "control over the nation," and preached that blacks were "savages" that should be "shipped back to Africa." *Peterson v. Wilmur Communications,* 205 F.Supp.2d 1014 (E.D. Wis. 2002). The "Nation of Islam" movement (aka "Black Muslims"), was a defined "religion" even though the organization advocated political and economic justice that included attacks on whites and Jews. *Ali v. Southeast Neighborhood House,* 519 F.Supp. 489 (D.D.C. 1981). In each case the "political" beliefs were channeled through a structure with strong religious overtones.

• *Supreme being:* An earmark of religion is a reference to an extra-human ordering of human behavior that is similar to a "god" in traditional religions. The absence of any such reference indicates an organizational structure that is more social or political than religious. Displaying a Confederate flag cannot be considered a religious practice no matter how strongly held even a large group feels about "the lost cause." *Storey v. Burns Int'l Security Servs.,* 390 F. 3d 760 (3d Cir. 2004).

• *Significance of ethical activity:* Even if the organization employs religious trappings such as prayers, crosses, reliance upon Biblical scriptures, and the "word of God," when the thrust of the organization is a political or social goal, it will be classed as secular. *Bellamy v. Mason's Stores Inc.,* 368 F.Supp. 1025 (E.D.Va. 1973), *affd* 508 F.2d 504 (4th Cir. 1974) (membership in the KKK).

Balancing these factors courts have held that sincerely held ethical beliefs opposing war, abortion, homosexual lifestyles, and similar social issues are protected "religion." *Wilson v. United States West Communications,* 58 F.3d 1337 (8th Cir. 1995) (abortion), *Shahar v. Bowers,* 114 F.3d 1097 (11th Cir. 1997) (same sex marriage). As it is more difficult to classify as "religious" beliefs that *favor* such issues, the generous definition of "religion" provides Title VII protection only to one side of essentially political debates.

9.03: SECULAR ACTIVITIES OF RELIGIOUS ORGANIZATIONS

Attending religious services, observing the Sabbath or religious holidays, wearing symbols of the faith including attire, attending church conventions, and teaching a Bible study class are protected religious practices, even if not required by the religion. *Redmond v. GAF Corp.,* 574 F.2d 897 (7th Cir. 1978). Participation in a social welfare project as part of a church's ministry is a protected religious practice. *Dorr v. First Kentucky Nat. Corp.,* 796 F.2d 179 (6th Cir. 1986). However, purely social activities sponsored by a church such as playing on a church sponsored sports team, attending a church picnic, and decorating the church for the Christmas holiday may be considered unprotected secular activities. *Westerling v. Kroger Co.,* 554 F.Supp. 548 (E.D.Mich. 1982).

9.04: DISCRIMINATION BY RELIGIOUS ORGANIZATIONS

As discussed *supra,* 4.09, Title VII specifically permits religious organizations to discriminate on the basis of religion in all of its activities, religious as well as secular. *Corp. of Presiding Bishop v. Amos,* 483 U.S. 327 (1987). This exemption is limited to *religious* discrimination. By its terms Title VII prohibits religious organizations from discriminating on all other grounds proscribed by the statutes. However, this prohibition constitutionally can be applied only to the religious organization's *secular* employees. *Hosanna–Tabor Evangelical Lutheran Church and School v. EEOC,* ___ U.S. ___, 131 S.Ct. 1783 (2011) (Courts lack constitutional authority to regulate discrimination by a church against its recognized "ministers").

9.05: ACCOMMODATION OF "OBSERVANCES AND PRACTICES"

A. GENERALLY

An employer's obligation not to discriminate because of religious observances and practices goes beyond non-discrimination, but requires *affirmative* steps to accommodate uniformly applied rules to the employee's religious observances and practices. 42 U.S.C. 2000e–(j). The most common forms of religious observances and practices where accommodation is requested are the adjustment of work schedules to enable the employees to observe their Sabbath or Holy days, modification of the employer's dress or grooming codes to permit employees to wear clothing (such as head covering) or hair styles (such as beards) required by their religious beliefs, or to permit employees to display at their work-place symbols of their faith (such as a scripture, a Christian cross, or star of David).

B. BONA FIDES

Employees have the initial obligation to demonstrate the sincerity of their religious belief. Token "conversions of convenience" to avoid employer rules will not suffice. The employee must notify the employer of the belief, note the conflict between the belief and the employer's work rule, and suggest an accommodation. The employee may not simply follow the religious practice without first giving the employer notice of the conflict and allowing the employer an opportunity to make or suggest accommodations. *Goldmeier v. Allstate Ins. Co.,* 337 F.3d 629 (6th Cir. 2003).

C. "REASONABLE ACCOMMODATION" AND "UNDUE HARDSHIP"

The employer can justify discrimination based on the employee following sincerely held religious beliefs or practices if the employer demonstrates that it "is unable to reasonably accommodate to an employee's religious observance or practice without undue hardship on the conduct of the employer's business." 42 U.S.C. 2000e–(j).

Trans World Airlines, Inc. v. Hardison, 432 U.S. 63 (1977), held that the general reduction of Saturday work to that necessary to maintain operations and allowing voluntary trading of week-end shifts provided a reasonable accommodation to plaintiff's Sabbath. Refusal to modify the contractual seniority provisions to require shift changes that would require workers senior to plaintiff to be assigned Saturday work would impose an "undue hardship" on the employer and co-workers. Reasonable accommodation, the Court held, cannot require the employer "to bear more than *de minimis* cost," and concluded that it would constitute an "undue hardship" to require the employer to offer premium overtime pay to induce workers to accept week-end work.

The *de minimis* standard established by *Hardison* is the talisman for measuring reasonable accommodation and whether hardships are "undue." *Harrell v. Donahue,* 638 F.3d 975 (8th Cir. 2011). While an accommodation will not be "reasonable" if it places a significant hardship on co-workers, moving a staff appreciation day to accommodate one employee's religious observances is reasonable and does not constitute religious discrimination against other employees who are asked to attend the rescheduled meeting simply because the timing may be inconvenient. *Ross v. Colorado Dep't of Transp.,* (D.Colo. 2012) 96 EPD 44,681. *See, infra* 24.05.

CHAPTER 10

AGE: THE AGE DISCRIMINATION IN EMPLOYMENT ACT (ADEA)

10.01: THE PROTECTED CLASS: AGE 40 AND OVER

Using operative language similar to Title VII, discrimination because of "age" is proscribed by the Age Discrimination in Employment Act of 1967 (ADEA), 29 U.S.C. 621 et seq. The statute qualifies the prohibition by providing that only individuals *age 40 and over* are protected. Thus, employers may refuse to hire workers *under* the age of 40, or favor an applicant who is age 20 over one who is 35. No longer does the ADEA place upper age limits on protection for those over age 40. The Act further specifies that seniority systems or employee benefit plans may not require or permit involuntary retirement because of age or justify the failure to hire an individual over age 40 because of age. 29 U.S.C. 623(f)(2)(A) and (B).

10.02: "AGE" DEFINED

A. PASSAGE OF TIME

In *Hazen Paper Co. v. Biggins,* 507 U.S. 604 (1993), the employer-provided pension plan vested retirement benefits upon ten years of service. The sixty-two year old plaintiff, who had been employed for over nine years, was dismissed. The lower court found as a matter of fact that defendant dismissed the plaintiff to avoid vesting of plaintiff's pension rights, and held that since both years of service necessary for vesting and one's chronological age were based on the *passage of time,* the employer was motivated by plaintiff's age. The Court reversed. "[A]ge and years of service are analytically distinct * * * and it is incorrect to say that a decision based on years of service is necessarily age based." The Court distinguished plans that vest upon one reaching a certain chronological age (*e.g.,* age 55). In such cases the employee's age is the motivating factor.

Smith v. City of Jackson, 544 U.S. 228 (2005), held that pay raises to employees with less than five *years of service* that exceeded raises granted to those with more than five *years of service* were not facial age discrimination even though those with less than five years of seniority usually were younger than workers with more than five years of service. Similarly, using "reverse seniority" to determine order of lay-off, laying off first the workers who had been employed the longest, is not age discrimination unless this reverse "seniority system" was implemented in order to dismiss older workers. *Allen v. Highlands Hosp. Corp.,* 545 F.3d 387 (6th Cir. 2008).

Replacing a higher paid worker, who happened to be older, with a younger worker who was paid less was not age discrimination. "Wage rates," like years in service, are "analytically" distinct from an employee's age. *Anderson v. Baxter Healthcare Corp.,* 13 F.3d 1120 (7th Cir. 1994). Similarly, it is not age discrimination to offer higher salaries to

entry level workers (who tend to be younger), based
on the economic demands of the marketplace, than
the salaries currently paid to incumbent workers
(who tend to be older). *Davidson v. Board of Gov. of
State Colleges & Universities,* 920 F.2d 441 (7th Cir.
1990).

If plaintiff can demonstrate that the non-age factor
was a pretext to disadvantage older workers
because of age, that would establish proscribed age
motivation. Or, if plaintiff can demonstrate
statistically that a policy has an adverse effect on a
distinct age class of older workers, the employer
would be required to prove that the age-neutral
factor was "reasonable." However, relative seniority
or genuine economic demands will be "reasonable
factors other than age" that would justify an
economic-based response that produces an adverse
impact. *Meacham v. Knolls Atomic Power Lab.,* 554
U.S. 84 (2008). Chapter 18 *infra,* discusses liability
based on unjustified adverse impact.

B. "AGED"

In *General Dynamics Land Systems v. Cline,* 540
U.S. 581 (2004), the employer facing financial
problems removed health benefits for younger
employees when they retired, while retaining
existing health care benefits upon retirement for
workers over age 50. Lower courts concluded that
this discrimination against workers between ages
40 and 50 in favor of workers over 50 was proscribed
age discrimination. The Court disagreed reasoning
that the word "age" was ambiguous. It could mean,
as the lower courts held, an individual's

chronological age, the years since birth. Or, it could mean "older age" or *"aged."* The Court resorted to legislative history to resolve the perceived ambiguity. While legislative comments suggested that younger workers would be protected against age discrimination under the same standards as older workers, the Court concluded that the problem identified and addressed by the ADEA was discrimination against older workers, and thus the statute should not be construed to prohibit discrimination that *favored* older workers. Only discrimination *against* older workers, or ageism, is proscribed.

10.03: EXCEPTIONS

A. EXECUTIVES

The ADEA allows mandatory retirement of "bona fide executives" who have reached age 65, have vested, non-forfeitable pension benefits *from this employer* that exceed a given annual amount ($44,000), excluding government benefits (*e.g.,* social security*)*, the employee's private savings or retirement plans, or benefits from other employers. This executive exemption does not apply to "low level supervisors" or middle management employees regardless of the pension benefits provided. *Passer v. American Chem., Soc.* 935 F.2d 322 (D.C. Cir. 1991).

B. PUBLIC SAFETY

State and local governments may establish programs that set maximum hiring and mandatory retirement ages for public safety positions (*e.g.,* firefighters, police, and corrections officers) provided that such programs include job performance tests through which older workers can qualify for employment if they demonstrate their physical fitness for duty. However, if the program allows exceptions, which often are granted, a refusal to re-hire a 42 year old former police officer because he was above the maximum hiring age, could not be justified as part of a bona fide plan. *Davis v. Indiana State Police,* 541 F.3d 760 (7th Cir. 2008).

In language similar to that of Title VII, age may be used by an employer in limited instances were age is a "bona fide occupational qualification." This defense, to be discussed in Chapter 12.02, has been used in private sector safety-sensitive jobs such as commercial aircraft crew and bus drivers where the risks of sudden cardio-vascular events impose unacceptable risks on third parties which cannot be reduced to acceptable levels through individual evaluations of the older worker's health. *Western Air Lines, Inc. v. Criswell,* 472 U.S. 400 (1985). *See, Usery v. Tamiamiami Trail Tours, Inc.,* 531 F.2d 224 (5th Cir. 1976) (demonstrably higher risk of accidents by older workers justified refusing to hire bus drivers over age 40).

Federal regulations have set maximum retirement ages for certain safety-sensitive positions such as t commercial pilots and air traffic controllers. Such congressionally authorized regulations implicitly are authorized by the ADEA, but do not implicitly sanction similar age-based regulations by state or local governments. *Johnson v. City Council of Baltimore,* 472 U.S. 353 (1985).

CHAPTER 11

DISCRIMINATION BASED ON "IMPAIRMENTS:" THE AMERICANS WITH DISABILITIES ACT

11.01: GENERALLY

Discrimination against persons with disabilities is proscribed by the Americans With Disabilities Act. 42 U.S.C. 12101 et. seq. (ADA). Employment rights of individuals with disabilities is but one part of the ADA, with other parts establishing a broad range of rights including public facilities and transportation access, education, rehabilitation services, etc. The ADA, as it relates to employment, has two thrusts. First, similar to Title VII and the ADEA, the ADA simply prohibits discrimination against persons with mental and physical *"impairments."* Second, and most significantly, it imposes an obligation on employers to make "reasonable accommodations" for "individuals with *disabilities,"* 42 U.S.C. 12102(A), which will be discussed *infra,* 24.06. Persons who do *not* suffer from an impairment have no claim under the ADA if an employer favors, or makes accommodations for, persons with perceived impairments regardless of whether the adjustment is required by the statute.

11.02: "INDIVIDUAL WITH A DISABILITY"

A person is a protected "individual with a disability" if he has: "(A) a physical or mental impairment that substantially limits one or more major life activities;

(B) a record of such an impairment, or (C) is being regarded as having such an impairment." "An individual meets the requirement of 'being regarded as having such an impairment' if the individual establishes that he or she has been subjected to an action prohibited * * * because of an actual or perceived physical or mental *impairment,* whether or not the *impairment* limits or is perceived to limit a major life activity."

By making it a violation to discriminate because of an individual's real or perceive mental or physical *"impairment,"* the ADA severs the concept of "impairment" from "disability." The employer's obligation to make a "reasonable accommodation" to the individual's "impairment" arises only if the "impairment" reaches the heightened level of substantially limiting "one or more major life activities." The concept of "substantial limitation" on "major life activities" is not relevant in evaluating whether a person is "regarded as having such an impairment." 29 C.F.R. 1630.2(*l*) App.

11.03: "IMPAIRMENT"

A. GENERALLY

The ADA, as amended effective 2009, directed that the term "impairment" be construed broadly and expansively to reach not only actual medical conditions, but also "unfounded concerns, mistaken fears, myths, and prejudices" regarding persons with mental or physical conditions even when the impairments have no actual disabling effects. *School*

Bd. of Nassau County v. Arline, 480 U.S. 273 (1987) (recited with approval in legislative history).

Physical "impairments" include manifested physical conditions such as broken bones, "bad backs," chronic pain, limitations on walking, lifting, seeing, hearing, migraine headaches, and sleeping. *Arrieta–Colon v. Wal–Mart, Inc.,* 434 F.3d 75 (1st Cir. 2006). It also includes asymptomatic diseases or conditions such as diabetes, cancer, cardio-vascular conditions, and HIV, affecting internal organs which impair normal bodily functions. It is an "impairment" even if the condition is being successfully treated with medication or corrective medical devices.

Mental impairments include recognized disorders such as retardation, organic brain syndrome, bipolar disorders, dyslexia, learning disorders, such as ADD, and clinical depression. *See,* 29 C.F.R. 1632.2(j)(3)(iii) for a non-exclusive list of conditions considered by the EEOC to be "impairments."

B. "CHARACTERISTIC" VS. "IMPAIRMENT"

"Impairment" does not include *characteristics* that are within a "normal" range that are not the result of a medically recognized disorder. Eye or hair color, baldness, left-handedness, height and weight variations within "normal" ranges, and physical attractiveness (not involving disfigurement) are traits, not protected "impairments." Personality "problems" such as timidness, aggressiveness, poor judgment, and quick temper are not "impairments" if the trait is not a symptom of a medically recognized disorder. *Doebele*

v. *Spirit/United Mgt., Co.,* 342 F.3d 1117 (10th Cir. 2003). The ADA does not protect obnoxious "jerks." "Impairment" does not include variations in intelligence or aptitude that fall within "normal" ranges, that are not attributable to a defined medical condition. Variations in ability to master or perform certain tasks, such as mathematics, art, or foreign languages, are not "impairments." Nor are environmental, cultural, or economic disadvantages caused by poverty or lack of education.

Normal pregnancy is not an "impairment." However, medical conditions related to pregnancy that are sufficiently severe in themselves to affect bodily systems or abnormally limit the victim's activity can be "impairments." When the medical condition associated with pregnancy is disabling, the employer may be required to provide a "reasonable accommodation." *Mayorga v. Alorica, Inc.* (S.D.Fla. 2012), 2012 WL 3043021. *Infra,* 24.02. Similarly, while aging itself is not an "impairment," hearing loss, osteoporosis, or arthritis, often associated with aging, are "impairments." *Appel v. Inspire Pharm. Inc.,* 428 Fed.App'x 279 (5th Cir. 2011).

The line between an unprotected trait and a protected impairment can be unclear. For example, in one case an "overweight" plaintiff five feet, four inches tall and weighing over three hundred pounds was held not to suffer from an "impairment." *Cassista v. Community Foods, Inc.,* 856 P.2d 1143 (Cal. 1993). In another, the plaintiff with a similar height and weight was considered to meet the medical definition of "morbidly obese," and thus discrimination against her was prohibited. *Cook v. State of R.I. Dep't of Mental Health,* 10 F.3d 17 (1st Cir. 1993). A person who has some difficulty reading or following instructions may suffer from a medically recognized learning "impairment" such as dyslexia or ADD and thus be protected. Or, he may simply be a "slow learner," with a "trait" that is unprotected.

C. "TRANSITORY AND MINOR"

Excluded from the definition of "impairment" are conditions that are *both* transitory in time *and* minor in seriousness. Minor *and* short term impairments such as head colds, minor rashes, and tooth aches will be both transient and minor, and thus unprotected.

(1) "Transitory:"

Transitory impairments are those with actual or expected durations of six months or less." 42 U.S.C. 12102(C)(B). Thus, a chronic condition lasting more than six months will be a protected impairment even though the impairment is relatively "minor." (*e.g.,* disfiguring scar, a limp, "tennis elbow," chronic back pain, a chronic cough, or minor hearing or speech deficiencies). *Arrieta–Colon v. Wal–Mart, Inc.,* 434 F.3d 75 (1st Cir. 2006). A chronic condition is an impairment even though there are long periods of remission and the onset of the condition is manifested only for short periods of time. Accordingly, migraine headaches, shingles, and epilepsy are impairments. 29 C.F.R. 1630(j)(l)(i).

(2) "Minor"

As serious impairments are protected even if they have less than six months in duration, heart attacks, major trauma, surgery for conditions that require hospitalization all are serious impairments, protected even though the impairment may be "transitory" in that it may last for less than six months. 29 C.F.R. 1630.15(f) App. *Katz v. City Metal Co.,* 87 F.3d 26 (1st Cir. 1996). Diseases which adversely affect bodily functions, but which may have no outward symptoms, or be in long term remission, such as HIV, cancer, tuberculosis, hypertension, and diabetes all are "serious" medical conditions.

Ambiguity exists as to whether a short term condition is "minor" and unprotected, or "serious" and protected. Minor but painful muscle strains, fatigue from an occasional sleepless night (as opposed to long term sleep apnea), common colds, are "minor," unprotected impairments. However, influenza, may be sufficiently "serious" to constitute an impairment. *Lewis v. Florida Default Law Group,* (M.D.Fla. 2011), 2011 WL 4527456. It is unclear whether broken bones, serious muscle strains, or tissue ruptures that require medical treatment and may totally disable the victims temporarily would be considered sufficiently serious to be protected impairments.

D. "REGARDED AS"

The relevant inquiry is whether the actual or perceived impairment on which the employer's action is based is objectively 'transient and minor,' not whether the employer claims it subjectively believed the impairment was transitory and minor. 29 C.F.R. 1630.15(f) App.

An employer that terminates an employee because of a minor condition, such as a superficial cut, which in fact is "transitory and minor," based on a mistaken belief that the employee's minor injury may be a symptom of a "serious" or long term condition such as leukemia or HIV infection, has illegally discriminated against the employee because the employee was "regarded as" suffering from a defined impairment. An employee with minor angina pain, or a temporary "shortness of breath" but is believed by the employer to be suffering from heart disease is "regarded as" having an impairment. Similarly, an employee with an unusual personality but who is perceived, mistakenly, by the employer to have a bi-polar disorder, and discharged for this reason, is a victim of disability discrimination.

11.04: EXCLUDED

The ADA specifically excludes certain disorders even though they may be based on medical conditions: kleptomania, pyromania, pedophilia, compulsive gambling, exhibitionism, voyeurism, transvestism, and other sexual behaviors, as well as substance abuse disorders resulting from current illegal use of drugs. 42 U.S.C. 12211(b)(1), (2) and (3). The ADA recognizes that homosexuality and bisexuality are not "impairments" and thus are outside the protection of the ADA. 42 U.S.C. 12211(a). .

11.05: DRUG AND ALCOHOL ADDICTION

Medically diagnosed addiction to drugs or alcohol (alcoholism) are protected impairments. *Bailey v. Georgia–Pacific Co.,* 306 F.3d 1162 (1st Cir. 2002). Discrimination based on one's participation in an alcohol or drug rehabilitation program is expressly prohibited, provided that the individual enrolled in the program is not currently using illegal drugs. 42 U.S.C. 12114(b).

Protected "addiction" is distinguished from unprotected overuse or abuse of drugs or alcohol. A worker with a "drinking problem" does not have a protected "impairment," unless the employer "perceives" the worker to be addicted. *Kozisek v. County of Seward,* 539 F.3d 930 (8th Cir. 2008).

The Act excludes from protection even addicts "currently engaging in the illegal use of drugs when the covered entity acts on the basis of such use." 42 U.S.C. 12114(a). Moreover, the ADA specifically permits a covered entity to: (1) prohibit the use of illegal drugs or any use of alcohol at the workplace, (2) require employees not be under the influence of alcohol or illegal drugs while at the workplace (even if consumed while not at work and are the result of addiction), and (3) hold the person who is an alcoholic or an addict "to the same qualification standards for employment or job performance and behavior that such entity holds for other employees, even if any unsatisfactory performance or behavior is related to the drug use or alcoholism of such employee * * *." 42 U.S.C. 12114(c).

To be considered not "currently engaging in illegal use of drugs," and thus unprotected, the addict must have been drug free for a significant period of time. An addict in a rehabilitation program and who was drug free for the five preceding weeks was considered "currently using" illegal drugs. *Zenor v. El Paso Healthcare Systems, Ltd.,* 176 F.3d 847 (5th Cir. 1999).

The ADA allows employers to administer tests for illegal drug use and to implement the Drug Free Workplace Act of 1988 (41 U.S.C. 701). 42 U.S.C. 12114(c)(3) and (d). Employers may rely on test results indicating current illegal use in taking adverse employment actions, even when the disclosed use has no adverse effect on the employee's job performance. *Lopez v. Pacific Maritime Ass'n,* 657 F.3d 762 (9th Cir. 2011).

In *Raytheon Co. v. Hernandez,* 540 U.S. 44 (2003), plaintiff had been legally dismissed for his failure to pass an employer-administered drug test. Plaintiff, admittedly an addict, successfully completed a drug rehabilitation program, remained drug free for an extended period of time, and thereafter applied for reinstatement. Defendant denied plaintiff's application, allegedly based on a long-standing policy not to rehire any former employee who had been dismissed "for cause." The lower court concluded that such a policy was directly, or indirectly discrimination because of plaintiff's impairment as an addict. The Court reversed, holding that reliance on defendant's "no-rehire" policy, even when applied to persons with disabilities, was a legitimate reason, absent evidence that the policy itself was instituted for the purpose of excluded individuals with disabilities or that it was used in this case as a pretext to exclude the plaintiff because of his particular impairment.

11.06: "QUALIFIED"

A. GENERALLY

Unlike race or sex where one's class membership rarely has any relationship to one's ability to perform the job, it is not uncommon for a physical or mental impairment potentially to inhibit the ability to perform certain job duties. Accordingly, the ADA specifically requires the plaintiffs to prove that they are "qualified," and defines "qualified" to mean possess the requisite skill, experience, and educational requirements for the position *and* the ability to perform *essential* functions of the job. 42 U.S.C. 12111(8) and 12201. "It is rather a common sense idea that if one is unable to be at work, one cannot be a qualified individual." *Samper v. Providence St. Vincent Medial Ctr.,* 975 F.3d 1233 (9th Cir. 2012) (An intensive care nurse who had an ongoing pattern of failure to report for her shift was not "qualified," and her dismissal did not violate the ADA).

B. OBJECTIVE CREDENTIALS

An individual is not "qualified" if she lacks the credentials required for the job. For example, if the job involves driving a commercial vehicle, the individual is not qualified if he/she cannot secure the necessary driver's licenses, even though the inability to secure the license is the result of an impairment. An individual who lacks an employer-required educational credential such as a high school diploma, a college degree, or a given grade average, is not qualified even though a mental impairment, such as a bipolar disorder, precluded securing the required credential. *Albertson's Inc. v. Kirkinburg,* 527 U.S. 555 (1999); *Johnson v. Bd. of Trustees,* 666 F.3d 561 (9th Cir. 2011).

Liability may be established, however, if the individual who has a disability can demonstrate that the challenged credential which she does not possess screens out individuals with her disability, and defendant cannot demonstrate that the required credential is "job related and consistent with business necessity." 42 U.S.C. 12112(b)(6). Impact liability is discussed, *infra,* 18.07.

C. "ESSENTIAL" JOB DUTIES

In addition to the ability to come to work, the individual must demonstrate an ability to actually perform the "essential" elements of the job. For example, an amputee or person with arthritis may not be able to climb. If climbing is an essential duty of the job, the impaired individual is not "qualified" and thus need not be hired. *Skerski v. Time Warner Cable Co.,* 256 F.3d 273 (3d Cir. 2001). A job requires operating a computer and navigating the internet. An individual suffering from a physical or mental impairment which makes him unable to do this is not "qualified." A morbidly obese person unable to perform essential lifting tasks is not "qualified." *Cook v. State of R.I. Dep't of Mental Health,* 10 F.3d 17 (1st Cir. 1993).

Employers are under no obligation to make adjustments to *essential* job duties unless the impairment is proved by plaintiff to "substantially limit" one or more of the individual's "major life activities," in which case the employer is placed under an affirmative obligation to make a "reasonable accommodation" that would enable the disabled person to perform these duties unless the accommodation would impose on this employer an "undue hardship." 42 U.S.C. 12112(a). Liability based on an employer's failure to reasonably accommodate an individual's "disability" is discussed, *infra,* 24.06.

D. "NON-ESSENTIAL"

The individual with an impairment who possesses the required objective prerequisites, and who can perform "essential" duties, but is unable, because of the impairment, to perform duties deemed *non-essential,* is "qualified." The impairment and resulting inability to perform non-essential job duties cannot be used as a basis for discrimination, with the result that such secondary duties must be assigned to other, non-impaired workers. To illustrate this critical distinction: the ability to lift certain weights may be "essential" for a particular nursing job (*e.g.* intimate patient care or emergency room), and thus the inability to lift renders the individual not qualified. However, for other nursing positions (*e.g.,* pharmacy or surgical), the need to lift may be secondary or incidental. This impaired nurse is "qualified" for the particular position. *Deanne v. Pocono Med. Ctr.*, 142 F.3d 138 (3d Cir. 1998). Similarly, lifting will be necessary for an airline baggage handler, but may not be essential for an airport gate attendant who only occasionally must lift heavy luggage. Occasional lifting must be assigned to another worker. *Summerville v. Trans World Airlines, Inc.*, 220 F.3d 855 (8th Cir. 2000). The ability to drive will be essential for a job centered on delivering products, but non-essential for an office manager who only occasionally needs to drive to make bank deposits. *Lovejoy v. NOCO Motor Fuel, Inc.*, 263 F.3d 208 (2d Cir. 2001).

The EEOC has set forth a non-exclusive list of factors the fact finder may consider in determining whether job duties are essential, no one of which is dispositive: (1) the employer's consistent judgment as to what duties are "essential" to the job, (2) written and advertised job descriptions defining essential and non-essential duties, (3) amount of time spent performing the alleged essential duty, (4) consequences of not performing the function, (5) terms of any collective bargaining agreement, (6) past experiences, and, (7) work of incumbents at similar jobs. 29 C.F.R. 1630.2(n)(2). The level of skill or training required to perform the duty also can be important. Duties requiring a specialized skill tend to be "essential." Another factor is the number of employees able perform the disputed duty. When there are few, if any, other employees available to perform the duty plaintiff cannot perform, suggests that *to this employer,* the duty is "essential." Conversely, a simple duty that can be performed by a number of other employees, suggests that the duty is non-essential. *Skerski v. Time Warner Cable Co.,* 257 F.3d 273 (3d Cir. 2001). A blind teacher/librarian who could perform her classroom duties, but because of her blindness could not monitor hall and playground activity, was "qualified" because the unskilled secondary duties could be assigned to others. *Norcross v. Sneed,* 755 1113 (8th Cir. 1985). Finally, the risk of injury posed by the inability to perform a seldom required duty is a factor. *Cremeens v. Montgomery,* 427 F.3d 855 (11th Cir. 2011), held that an essential element of the job of fire "investigator" was an ability to perform in an extreme emergency firefighting and lifesaving duties, even though such duties would need to be performed rarely, if ever.

As the issue of "essential" varies with the job and the organization of the employer, and is a fact issue to be resolved by the jury (*Miller v. Ill. Dep't of Trans.,* 643 F.3d 190 (7th Cir. 2011)), generalizations are impossible. *Kellogg v. Energy Safety Serv., Inc.,* 544 F.3d 1121 (10th Cir. 2008). Even indistinguishable facts produce different, sustainable jury verdicts. *Compare, Kuehl v. Wal–Mart Stores, Inc.,* 909 F.Supp. 794 (D.Col. 1994) *with EEOC v. Wal–Mart Stores, Inc.* 477 F.3d 561 (8th Cir. 2007).

E. BURDEN

Courts are divided on the question of which party is responsible for proving that the plaintiff is "qualified." One view is that if the individual with the impairment proves that she possesses the objective credentials required for the position, defendant must carry the burden of proving that plaintiff cannot actually perform the on-job duties found to be "essential." *Hamlin v Charter Twsp. of Flint,* 165 F.3d 426 (6th Cir. 1999). Another applies a shifting burden approach. The employer has the initial burden of going forward with the evidence of the essential nature of the duties and presenting creditable evidence that plaintiff cannot perform these duties. The burden then shifts to plaintiff to persuade the fact finder that the functions plaintiff cannot perform either are not "essential" or that plaintiff is able to perform them. *Fenny v. Dakota, Minn. & Eastern R. Co.,* 327 F.3d 707 (8th Cir. 2003).

11.07: DIRECT THREAT TO HEALTH OR SAFETY

The ADA allows employers to exclude those with impairments, who because of the impairment, would "impose a direct threat to the health or safety of other individuals in the workplace." 42 U.S.C. 12113(b). The structure of the ADA suggests that individuals are not "qualified" for the position if they impose a "direct threat." Nonetheless the "direct threat" provision is a defense that must be established by the employer. 42 U.S.C. 12113(b).

The determination of whether an individual poses such a direct threat to health and safety must be based on a medical judgment that relies on the most current medical knowledge which in turn must balance four factors: (1) duration of the risk, (2) nature and severity of the potential harm (3) likelihood of the potential harm, and (4) the imminence of the potential harm. 29 C.F.R. 1630.2(r). *Bragdon v. Abbott,* 524 U.S. 624 (1998), held that the "direct threat" standard required more than a showing of good faith and even a reasonable belief of the degree of danger and proximity of possible harm, but the belief must be supported by objective, prevailing expert opinion as to the degree of risk balanced against the probability of harm. Thus, absent supporting medical evidence, a medically unsupported fear that a dreaded disease may be communicated by casual contact cannot be a defense for an employer's refusal to hire an infected waiter or school teacher. *School Bd. of Nassau County v. Arline,* 480 U.S. 273 (1987). However, if the job requires regular intimate physical contact with bodily fluids, or surgical procedures make transmission of the infection possible, even if reasonable precautions make the risk of infection remote, the severity of the potential risk is sufficient to constitute a "direct threat." *Mauro v. Borgess Medical Center,* 137 F.3d 398 (8th Cir. 1998).

The "direct threat" defense was been relied upon to exclude past, non-current drug abusers from "safety sensitive" jobs or jobs where they have ready access to controlled substances. In *Altman v. New York City Health Hospitals Corp.,* 903 F.Supp. 503 (S.D.N.Y. 1995), *affd.,* 100 F.3d 1054 (2d Cir. 1996), a physician had successfully completed an alcohol rehabilitation program (*See,* 42 U.S.C. 12114(b)), and there was no evidence of the physician's "current use" of alcohol. (*See,* 42 U.S.C. 12114(a)). Nonetheless, based on the danger of relapse, the difficulty of detecting a relapse, and the danger a relapse would impose on patients, the hospital was justified in concluding that reinstating the doctor would pose a "direct threat to the health and safety of others."

In *Chevron U.S.A. Inc., v. Eschzabal,* 536 U.S. 73 (2002), plaintiff's lung condition allegedly made it dangerous for him to be exposed to chemicals at the work place, but his potential incapacity posed no threat to others. Notwithstanding the language of the statute (poses a "direct threat to the health and safety *of others"*), the Court held that a direct threat to the health of the *employee* alone justified use of the defense. On remand the lower court concluded that defendant had failed to support with objective, medical evidence that the exposure was a "direct threat" even to the health of the plaintiff. *Echazabal v. Chevron USA, Inc.,* 336 F.3d 1023 (9th Cir. 2003).

PART 3

SELECTING THE WORKFORCE: ESTABLISHING DISCRIMINATORY HIRING, PROMOTIONS, AND DISMISSALS

Regardless of the nature of the discrimination violation of the statutes require application of the basic principles discussed in Chapter 5 ("discrimination" in "terms or conditions of employment" "because of"), and membership in one of the protected classes which were defined in PART 2. PART 3 will focus on applying these principles to the practical problems of *selecting* employees. Hiring, promotion, discipline, and discharge all present similar models of proof. Workplace discrimination *among* employees, including compensation, assignments, leaves, and miscellaneous intangible "terms and conditions of employment" involve distinct issues of proof that will be the focus of PART 4 *infra*.

Hiring, promotion and dismissal discrimination falls within one of three categories: (1) Facial classifications and their justifications (Chapters 12–14), (2) Improperly motivated discrimination ("disparate treatment") (Chapter 15–17), and (3) Discrimination produced by neutral policies that have an adverse impact on a protected class ("disparate impact") (Chapter 14).

CHAPTER 12

FACIAL EXCLUSIONS AND THE BONA FIDE OCCUPATIONAL QUALIFICATION DEFENSE

12.01: FACIAL DISCRIMINATION

A classification that on its face excludes from employment members of a protected class truncates any need to prove motivation or impact. The classification establishes that discrimination brought about by the policy's application is "because of" plaintiff's class membership. Examples: an airline refuses to employ flight crew members over age 60. *Western Air Lines, Inc. v. Crisswell,* 472 U.S. 400 (1985). An employer denies women, but not men, jobs that expose them to toxic chemicals. *UAW v. Johnson Controls, Inc.,* 499 U.S. 187 (1991). An employer refuses to hire a non-Muslim to work in an Islamic nation. *Abrams v. Baylor College of Medicine,* 805 F.2d 528 (5th Cir. 1986). An employer requires women and older applicants, but not males or younger applicants, to pass a physical stamina test. *EEOC v. Brown & Root, Inc.,* 688 F.2d 338 (5th Cir. 1982). Even though Title VII does not prohibit discrimination based on sexual orientation, rejecting gay men but not lesbians is a distinction between men and women and thus constitutes "sex" discrimination. *See, Valdes v. Lumbermen's Mut. Cas. Co.,* 507 F.Supp. 10 (S.D.Fla. 1980).

12.02: THE BONA FIDE OCCUPATIONAL QUALIFICATION (BFOQ): GENERALLY

Defendant's exclusion of a protected class, or sub-class, is permitted if the employer can establish that an employee's religion, sex, national origin, or age "is a bona fide occupational qualification reasonably necessary to the normal operation of that particular business or enterprise." (BFOQ). 42 U.S.C. 2000e–2(e). Note the conspicuous absence of "race" in the defense. Presumably this omission is based on the assumption that racial classifications could never be "reasonably necessary to the normal operation" of an enterprise.

The BFOQ defense found in both Title VII and the ADEA use the same standards and analysis under each statute as is applied to the other. *UAW v. Johnson Controls, Inc., supra* (Title VII); *Western Air Lines, Inc. v. Criswell, supra,* (ADEA). The ADA has no expressed BFOQ defense, but because the ADA requires that the individual with an "impairment" must be "qualified" to perform essential job duties notwithstanding their "impairment," a similar outcome can be expected. *Supra,* Chapter 11.06—.07.

The BFOQ defense is strictly construed to reach only "special circumstances. *UAW v. Johnson Controls, Inc., supra.* It places the burden on defendant to establish two elements: (1) the exclusion of the protected class is directly related to an identified employer *business purpose,* and (2) the exclusion is *"reasonably necessary"* to serve that *business* purpose.

12.03: BUSINESS PURPOSE

UAW v. Johnson Controls, Inc., supra, involved an employer that denied fertile women, but not men, positions that exposed the employee to toxic substances. The employer justified this exclusion of fertile women based on a concern for the reproductive health of female employees and the health of their future children. The Court held that this concern for the welfare of the employee and her future children did not qualify for the BFOQ defense because it did not relate to a *business purpose* or legitimate concern of the employer. Thus, the BFOQ defense does not allow employers to deny women jobs simply because the jobs are "dangerous" (*e.g.,* police officers, firefighters, or prison guards), (*Henry v. Milwaukee County,* 539 F.3d 573 (7th Cir. 2008)), or would place women in heightened danger of assault, as might occur by working at night, in remote locations, or in high crime areas. *Weeks v. Southern Bell Tel. & Tel. Co.,* 408 F.2d 228 (5th Cir. 1969).

Dothard v. Rawlinson, 433 U.S. 321 (1977), recognized, however, that in rare cases the BFOQ could be established if the employer demonstrates that the heightened risk of injury or attack to the employees because of their class imposes a significant risk on *third parties* or to the employer's core "business." *Dothard* involved a maximum security, all male prison where violent sex offenders were not segregated. The prison refused to hire female guards in this prison asserting sex as a BFOQ. It was uncontested that an inmate attack on any guard jeopardized the safety of other guards, inmates, and to some degree the public at large. The Court assumed that a woman guard in this unique atmosphere is more likely to be attacked than a male guard, which, in turn heightened the risk to third parties and the employer's interest in safe confinement of prisoners. *Compare, Abrams v. Baylor College of Medicine,* 805 F.2d 528 (5th Cir. 1986) (concern over safety of Jewish *employee* being assigned to Muslim region does not justify BFOQ), *with Kern v. Dynalectron Corp.,* 577 F.Supp. 1196 (N.D.Tex. 1983), *aff'd* 746 F.2d 810 (5th Cir. 1984) (Non–Muslim employees would be unable to safely perform *essential job duties* of taking Muslims into holy places, thus the Muslim religion permitted to be a BFOQ).

12.04: "ALL OR SUBSTANTIALLY ALL"

"To exclude a class of applicants because of their sex, national origin, or religion the employer must have * * * a factual basis for believing that *all or substantially all* [members of the excluded class] would be unable to perform safely and efficiently the duties of the job involved." *Western Airlines v. Criswell,* 472 U.S. 400 (1985) (ADEA). Accordingly, statistical demonstrations of differences between the sexes (i.e., stereotypes) cannot sustain a BFOQ. For example, if a job requires muscle strength for lifting, the employer may not use sex as a proxy for strength simply because more men than women can lift the necessary weight. Unless the employer could demonstrate that "all or substantially all" women could not lift the necessary weight the employer could not assert that the male sex is a BFOQ. In such cases the employer is required to make individual evaluations of each applicant's ability to lift the necessary weight. *See, City of Los Angeles Dep't of Water and Power v. Manhart*, 435 U.S. 702 (1978) (use of statistically sound sex-based mortality tables to set retirement contributions violates Title VII); *Chadwick v. Wellpoint, Inc.*, 561 F.3d 38 (1st Cir. 2009) (rejecting a woman because childcare responsibilities would hinder job performance is based on an impermissible assumption that women could not perform as well as men).

12.05: SUBSTANTIAL RISKS TO SAFETY

If the employer cannot establish that "all or substantially all" members of the excluded class could not safely perform essential job duties, the employer may exclude members of the protected class when it introduces substantial evidence that: (1) "Some members of the discriminated-against class possess a trait precluding safe and efficient job performance that cannot be ascertained by means other than knowledge of the applicant's membership in the class" and (2) "It is impossible or highly impractical to deal with members of that class on an individualized basis" in a way that would reduce the safety risk to acceptable levels through individual evaluations of fitness. In *Western Airlines, Inc. v. Criswell*, 472 U.S. 400 (1985), the employer disqualified certain non-pilot airline flight crew members who reached the age of 60. The employer justified the rule as being a reasonable safety precaution. The Court found that notwithstanding the "reasonableness" of the exclusion, the employer had failed to establish that being younger than age 60 was a BFOQ. First, it could not be said that "all or substantially all" persons in the over–60 age group presented a heightened risk to safety. Second, the airline failed to demonstrate the "substantiality" of the risk this particular non-pilot job would present in the event this crew member was incapacitated. Third, even if there was a substantial safety risk in retaining crew members over the age of 60, the airline failed to establish that it was impracticable to reduce any risk to acceptable levels through individual evaluations of the cardio-vascular fitness of each employee.

Similarly, pregnancy at some point limits the physical activity of most women. However, until that physical condition prohibits her from safely or effectively performing essential job duties, non-pregnancy cannot be a BFOQ. An employer may not disqualify pregnant women based on an assumption that all pregnant women will be unable to perform job duties. In safety-sensitive positions where an unanticipated disabling event, such as a miscarriage, could render the woman unable to perform duties that would put *others at risk*, a BFOQ would exist at the point where the increased risk of harm to third parties is substantial and that risk cannot be reduced to acceptable levels through individual evaluations of the woman's fitness. *Burwell v. Eastern Airlines, Inc.,* 633 F.2d 361 (4th Cir. 1980).

12.06: "REASONABLY NECESSARY"

A. "NECESSARY" MEANING "ESSENTIAL"

The statutory term "reasonably necessary" means "essential." *Western Airlines v. Criswell, supra.* The mere inability of the excluded class to perform peripheral, secondary job duties is insufficient to establish the "reasonable necessity" of the exclusion. For example, even if female airline flight attendants offer a more "soothing cabin atmosphere" than would male attendants, the element of "soothing atmosphere" is tangential to the essential job duties of safely and efficiently transporting passengers, and thus the female sex cannot be a BFOQ for the job of a flight attendant. *Diaz v. Pan American World Airways, Inc.,* 442 F.2d 385 (5th Cir. 1971). Assuming that language fluency is a form of national origin discrimination, the ability to communicate with supervisors, co-workers, or customers may make fluency essential, and thus a BFOQ. *Fragante v. Honolulu,* 888 F.2d 591 (9th Cir. 1989). Speaking English without a "foreign" accent is national origin discrimination and rarely can be considered "essential." *See, Rodriguez v. FedEx Freight East, Inc.,* 487 F.3d 1001 (6th Cir. 2007). However, for jobs such as language teachers and radio announcers, "accent-free" speech may be a BFOQ. *Bina v. Providence College,* 39 F.3d 21 (1st Cir. 1994).

B. INCREASED COSTS

Expenses entailed in hiring the excluded class, such as providing sanitary and changing facilities necessary to insure health and privacy, and the cost of providing new uniforms or protective clothing cannot serve as the basis of a BFOQ. *Henry v. Milwaukee County,* 539 F.3d 573 (7th Cir. 2008).

C. "CUSTOMER PREFERENCE"

As a general proposition, customer preferences for, or prejudice against, members of a protected class cannot be a BFOQ. That predominately male airline passengers may prefer female flight attendants does not justify exclusion of males. *Diaz v. Pan American World Airways, Inc.,* 442 F.2d 385 (5th Cir. 1971). That businessmen from foreign cultures would prefer dealing with males, does not establish the male sex as a BFOQ for such jobs. *Fernandez v. Wynn Oil Co.,* 653 F.2d 1273 (9th Cir. 1981). The Muslim faith is not a BFOQ for a job requiring work with Muslims in an Islamic region that might treat persons of other faiths with suspicion or hostility. *Abrams v. Baylor College of Medicine,* 805 F.2d 528 (5th Cir. 1986).

Nonetheless, in extreme situations the customer "preference" may be so strong, or be of such a nature, that class members are prohibited from performing, as where persons of a different faith would be prohibited by law from entering a place where the employee must enter in order to perform her job. *Kern v. Dynalectron Corp.,* 577 F.Supp. 1196 (N.D.Tex. 1983). Established privacy rights of "customers" may require limiting access of one sex to jobs that would compromise those rights, such as providing intimate care or full body searches to members of the opposite sex or having a necessary presence in baths or locker rooms. *Torres v. Wisconsin Dep't of Health & Soc. Serv.,* 859 F.2d 1523 (7th Cir. 1988). A particular religion can be a BFOQ for teacher of that religion at a religiously oriented, but secular, academic institution. *Pime v. Loyola University of Chicago,* 803 F.2d 351 (7th Cir. 1986). One court allowed non-pregnancy to be a BFOQ when applied to a pregnant, unmarried female employee of a girls club on the dubious grounds that unmarried pregnancy for a counselor was an inappropriate "role model" for impressionable young women. *Chambers v. Omaha Girls Club,* 854 F.2d 697 (8th Cir. 1987).

As the BFOQ does not apply to race discrimination, it would seem to violate Title VII to honor demands of customers or patients not to be served by members of a particular race, if such discrimination reaches the level of affecting adversely a "term or condition of employment." *Rogers v. EEOC,* 454 F.2d 234 (5th Cir. 1971) (customer segregation). Even demands of nursing home patients to be tended by persons of their race did not justify segregation of black workers. *Chaney v. Plainfield Healthcare Ctr.,* 612 F.3d 908 (7th Cir. 2010). *See, Johnson v. California,* 534 U.S. 499 (2005) (segregating prisoners by race in a penitentiary violates 14th Amendment).

D. "AUTHENTICITY"

The concept of "authenticity" for dramatic roles, to enhance a theme or atmosphere at restaurants was recognized in the legislative history as a basis for sex or national origin being a BFOQ. 110 Cong.

Rec. 7213; 29 C.F.R. 1604.2. (*e.g.,* Italian waiters in an Italian themed restaurant).

However, sex or national origin is not a BFOQ when the class membership does not go to the essence of the service being provided, but is merely a marketing tool to attract customers. Thus, the female sex would be a BFOQ for the position of exotic dancer, even if food and drink are sold in the establishment, in that the primary product being sold is "sex." However, an airline attempting to lure male business travelers with a theme of sexiness, could not use the female sex as a BFOQ to exclude male flight attendants. *Wilson v. Southwest Airlines, Co.,* 517 F.Supp. 292 (N.D. Tex. 1981). The distinction can be narrow. Presumably a roadside cafe serving traditional food and beverages could not use the female sex as a BFOQ because the cafe was trying to attract as customers predominately male truck drivers. However, a seafood restaurant attempting to create an "old world" atmosphere hiring only tuxedo wearing male waiters was allowed to rely on "authenticity" to establish the male sex as a BFOQ. *EEOC v. Joe's Stone Crab, Inc.,* 220 F.3d 1263 (11th Cir. 2000).

12.07: REASONABLE ALTERNATIVES

The BFOQ requires that exclusion of the class be *"reasonably necessary."* Thus, even where members of the excluded class are unable to perform a duty deemed "essential," when reasonable adjustments or alternatives are available, the exclusion of the class from the job is not "reasonably *necessary.*" *Hardin v. Stynchomb,* 691 F.2d 1364 (11th Cir. 1982). For example, exclusion of females from certain counselor positions at a juvenile detention center that housed predominately male juveniles based on privacy and safety concerns could be justified only if the employer could show that alternatives such as an altered alarm system, more surveillance cameras, more frequent patrols, or minor job realignments were unreasonable. *Henry v. Milwaukee County,* 539 F.3d 573 (7th Cir. 2008).

This obligation to make job duty adjustments as an alternative to exclusion is required only if to do so is "reasonable." Reasonable does not demand restructuring of the work place, moving employees into different job duties, or assignment of the excluded worker to a job requiring different skills or training. Thus, when a pregnant airline flight attendant could not continue flight duties, the employer need not reassign her to the job of ticket agent. *Levin v. Delta Airlines, Inc.,* 730 F.2d 994 (5th Cir. 1984).

CHAPTER 13

AFFIRMATIVE ACTION

13.01: DEFINED

"Affirmative action" was a remedial power granted under the National Labor Relations Act. Title VII grants similar authority to the courts to remedy found violations of the Act. 42 U.S.C. 2000e–5(g)(1). *Infra,* 28.09. "Affirmative action," as understood today consists of positive, pro-active steps to remedy underrepresentation of women or minorities even absent past illegal conduct. Title VII contains no expressed authorization for employers to use race or sex to make employment decisions. On the contrary, there are many markers suggesting that to do so violates Title VII. Understanding "affirmative action" under Title VII requires an appreciation of the context in which the issue and concept evolved.

13.02: "INDIANS"

Title VII provides:

> Nothing contained in this Title shall apply to any business or enterprise on or near an Indian reservation with respect to any publically announced employment practice * * * under which preferential treatment is given to any individual because he is an Indian living on or near a reservation. 42 U.S.C. 2000e–(2)(i).

This authorization of "affirmative action" that favors "Indians" demonstrates that Congress was aware of the affirmative action concept and chose to sanction only this limited use of it.

13.03: "REQUIRED" USE OF RACE OR SEX

Title VII has a proviso that might appear to prohibit use of race or sex based on numerical underrepresentation of these classes in the employer's work force:

> Nothing contained in this Title shall be interpreted *to require* any [covered entity] to grant preferential treatment to any individual or to any group * * * on account of an imbalance which may exist with respect to the total number or percentage of persons of any race, color, religion sex, or national origin employed by any employer * * * in comparison with the total number or percentage of [such persons] * * * in the available work force. 42 U.S.C. 2000e–(2)(j).

13.04: EXECUTIVE ORDER 11246

Presidential E.O. 11246, and implementing Department of Labor Regulations, impose on employers having significant service or supply contracts with federal agencies or who receive federal financial support to undertake affirmative action which consists of identifying job classifications where women and minority employees are underrepresented in light of their availability in the area workforce, and when significant underrepresentation is identified to craft a plan to remedy the underrepresentation.

Regulations require that the remedial plan must contain fixed "goals and timetables" that include the use of sex or race in making hiring decisions in order to reach the set goal. 41 C.F.R. Part 60–2. The program is administered by the Department of Labor, Office of Federal Contract Compliance Programs (OFCCP). Private enforcement of the Order and its regulations is not authorized. *Jackson v. FKI Logistex,* 608 F.Supp.2d 705 (E.D.N.C. 2009). Enforcement depends upon the OFCCP enforcing the employer's contractual obligations to implement the affirmative action commitment in its government contract through a breach of contract action, contract cancellation, or debarment of the breaching contractor from future government contracts. Enforcement has not been vigorous.

E.O. 11246 has been held not to violate either equal protection concepts of the 5th Amendment or impose on contracting employers an obligation that would cause them to violate Title VII. *Contractors Ass'n of Eastern Penn. v. Secretary of Labor,* 442 F.2d 159 (3d Cir. 1971).

13.05: THE EMPLOYER'S DILEMMA

A. WHITE MALES ARE PROTECTED

McDonald v. Santa Fe Trail Transp., 427 U.S. 273 (1976), held that discrimination against whites because of their white race is to be measured under the same standards as discrimination against racial minorities. Had the Court held otherwise, there could have been no effective legal challenge by white males when private employers undertook "affirmative action" that gave preferences to racial minorities or women. *McDonald* provided standing under Title VII for white males to challenge the "affirmative action" use of race or sex that benefited other classes.

B. LIABILITY BASED ON UNDERREPRESENTATION

Int'l Br'hd of Teamsters v. U.S., 431 U.S. 324 (1977), established that plaintiff could establish race or sex motivation of defendant's decision-making process based largely on statistically significant underrepresentation of women and minorities in the employer's workplace when compared to the demographics of the area's available labor pool. *Infra,* Chapter 17. As a consequence, if employers who have workforces with few women and minorities are prohibited from using race or sex in making future hiring decisions employers will be "on a tight rope without a net." If they take no action to remedy the imbalance, they risk liability on suit of women or minority plaintiffs. If they attempt to remedy the imbalance to avoid potential liability, they face liability on suit of white male plaintiffs under *McDonald v. Santa Fe Trail Transp., supra.* This dilemma is magnified for employers required by E.O. 11246, *supra,* 13.04, to adopt affirmative action plans contractually committing them to use race and sex to remedy found underrepresentation.

13.06: THE DILEMMA RESOLVED: *STEELWORKERS V. WEBER*

United Steelworkers of America v. Weber, 443 U.S. 193 (1979), provided a roadmap out of the employer's dilemma by allowing circumscribed use of race or sex pursuant to a structured affirmative action plan reasonably designed to remedy documented "conspicuous imbalances" in job categories that had been "traditionally segregated." It reached this result largely by ignoring the literal wording of Title VII, in favor of the underlying purpose and "spirit" of the statute.

Weber's employer was located in an area that had 39% black population, but had a skilled work force less than 2% black. Defendant had not been charged with illegally discriminating against black applicants, although the Court noted a history of pervasive segregation in the industry and in the state where defendant was located. Defendant employer had entered federal government contracts subject to E.O. 11246, *supra,* that required adoption of an affirmative action plan to remedy the underrepresentation of black workers in the skilled trades. The plan committed defendants to admit into a union/employer apprenticeship training program equal numbers of black and white trainees until the documented underrepresentation of blacks in the skilled job category was remedied.

Weber, the plaintiff, who was white, was not one of the six white applicants selected into the apprenticeship program. It was not contested that given Weber's seniority and credentials had he been black he would have been selected. Weber sued alleging that his rejection was race discrimination specifically prohibited by *McDonald v. Santa Fe Trail Transp. Co., supra.* The lower court agreed. The Supreme Court reversed.

The Court was faced with those markers indicating that Weber was a victim of proscribed race discrimination. First was the proviso in Title VII prohibiting the requirement of "preferential treatment" based on racial imbalances in the work force. 42 U.S.C. 2000e–2(j), *supra,* 13.03. The Court narrowly and literally construed this proviso as applying only to the *required* use of race, and thus was inapplicable to *voluntary* affirmative action efforts. Moreover, the use of the term "require" implied a negative pregnant that the proviso implicitly authorized such "voluntary" preferential treatment if based on racial imbalances in the employer's workforce. (The Court assumed that the defendants acted "voluntarily" in implementing the plan even though it was imposed on them by E.O 11246, *supra*).

Plaintiff and the dissent relied upon *McDonald v. Santa Fe Trails Transp. Co. supra,* and forcefully argued that extensive legislative history made Title VII applicable to the "reverse discrimination" practiced by defendants. Conceding that these arguments were "not without force," the Court nonetheless found that the pervasive underlying "spirit" behind Title VII was to increase the employment opportunities of minorities which would be undermined if the literal language were applied to prevent reasonable voluntary attempts to increase job opportunities for minorities. Looking to other Titles of the 1964 Civil Rights Act, the Court opined that it would be of little use to have access to restaurants, housing, and public accommodations if racial minorities had no job allowing them to pay for such access.

The concurring opinion, while sympathizing with the dissent, noted that the majority outcome was a practical compromise that provided a necessary "net" that allowed employers to avoid possible liability on suit of black plaintiffs without imposing liability for "reverse discrimination" against disappointed white employees.

As *Weber* did not overrule *McDonald v. Santa Fe Trail Transp. Co. supra,* *McDonald* must be distinguished: (1) The discrimination against the white plaintiff there, unlike *Weber,* was not made pursuant to any pre-existing plan to remedy identified underrepresentation of black workers, but was merely an *ad hoc* response to a particular event with at most only vague affirmative action concerns, and (2) *McDonald* involved the *discharge* of an employee. The plaintiff in *Weber* was an applicant frustrated in his hope to fill a vacant position. The impact on the white plaintiff discharged in *McDonald* was much greater than the impact on Mr. Weber and other disappointed white applicants.

13.07: *WEBER* EXPANDED AND CLARIFIED

Johnson v. Transportation Agency, Santa Clara County, 480 U.S. 616 (1987), reaffirmed, applied, and extended the principles of *Weber.* (1) The analysis of *Weber* would apply to plans designed to remedy underrepresentation of females. (2) Plans can remedy significant imbalance of women in the employer's work force by using the female sex of applicants as a "tie breaking" factor between similarly qualified applicants. (3) "Affirmative action" is not a true defense. Rather the asserted use of "affirmative action" is a "legitimate, non-discriminatory" basis for making a sex or race-based decision that need only be articulated by the employer, leaving to plaintiff the burden to establish that the employer's plan failed to meet the standards articulated in *Weber* and refined in *Johnson*.

13.08: THE *WEBER/JOHNSON* STANDARDS

A. A PLAN

To warrant defendant's use of race or sex, the decision must be made pursuant to a pre-existing, presumably publicly announced plan. The plan need not be mandated by E.O. 11246. Indeed, a premise of *Weber* was that affirmative action should be "voluntary." However, *ad hoc* discrimination against white males does not qualify simply because the actions are subsequently labeled "affirmative action."

B. JUSTIFICATION FOR THE PLAN

To warrant adoption of an affirmative action plan *Weber* teaches and *Johnson* confirms, that the employer must document a "conspicuous imbalance in a traditionally segregated job category."

(1) "Imbalance"

An imbalance that justifies adoption of a plan requires first identifying and documenting: (1) the race or sex demographics of the geographic area from which the employer reasonably would draw its work force (*i.e.,* available labor pool), and then (2) refining, if necessary, the gross population numbers. If the underrepresentation occurs, as it did in *Weber,* in a position that is semi- or unskilled, or requires skills that could be acquired with minimal on-the-job training, the unrefined demographics of the geographic area will suffice. However, if the job requires particular skills, education, training, or experience, the data must be refined to reflect those within that general population who possess the required credentials. Thus, for example, if the underrepresentation is of school teachers, the degree of underrepresentation is shown only by comparing the percentage of persons by class in the area population who have teaching credentials with the percentage of teachers employed by defendant. General population data in such cases does not reflect the necessary "underrepresentation."

(2) "Conspicuous"

The identified imbalance must reach the level of being "conspicuous." The dissent in *Weber* argued that, at most, only proven *illegal* behavior could justify racially conscious remedies. The concurring opinion suggested that racially conscious affirmative action needs to be premised on an imbalance sufficient to create a *prima facie case* of illegal discrimination. The majority specifically rejected the standard of a prima facie illegality in favor of the imprecise term of "conspicuous imbalance," which presumably means that the imbalance must be clear, but need not reach the level of being statistically "significant."

(3) "Traditionally Segregated Job Category"

Documented underrepresentation will not suffice absent some evidence of past segregation or exclusion. The Court made it clear that conspicuous underrepresentation must in some way be the product of a "tradition" of past segregation or societal prejudices. Thus, it would be difficult to justify affirmative action plans that favored white males in that only rarely would current underrepresentation be the product "traditional segregation" that had excluded white males.

C. PLAN CONTENT

The plan, if justified, must set reasonable ends, must utilize reasonable means to reach the set end, must be remedial, and thus temporary, in nature.

(1) Ends

The plan must set an ultimate goal in terms of a percentage ratio in the employer's job category that reflects with some precision the degree of underrepresentation in that job compared to workers available in the area's labor pool. An employer's work place goal may not exceed the percentage of women or minorities available in the area's labor pool. *Cygnar v. Chicago,* 865 F.2d 287 (7th Cir. 1989).

(2) Means

The plan adopted to remedy the imbalance must be reasonable. A plan is unreasonable if the means to achieve the articulated goal "unduly trammels" the interests of white males.

(a) Firing

In reaffirming its precise holding in *McDonald v. Santa Fe Trails Transp., Weber* implied that firing workers to achieve its set goal would be an unreasonable trammeling of white worker interests. Similarly, using the race of current employees to determine order of lay off "unduly trammels" the interest of incumbent workers. Laying off of employees has a greater personal and financial impact than does failing to make a job offer to a hopeful applicant. *Taxman v. Bd. of Edu. of Tp of Piscataway,* 91 F.3d 1547 (3d Cir. 1996).

(b) Qualified

It is reasonable to use race or sex of applicants only when the applicants from different classes are similarly "qualified" for the vacant position. An affirmative action plan is unreasonable if it committed the employer to hire minority applicants regardless of their qualifications. *See,* 41 C.F.R. Part 60–2.

(c) Ratio or Factor

In *Weber* the use of a 1–1 hiring ratio was reasonable in that it did not exclude white plaintiffs from the position. Equal numbers of white and black applicants would be hired. However, a plan that reserved certain positions to minorities is unreasonable. Thus, if a black retires from a position, a plan cannot provide that the vacant position will be filled by a black applicant. *Hill v. Ross,* 183 F.3d 586 (7th Cir. 1999).

The employer in *Johnson* used sex as a "tie breaking" factor to be weighed with other credentials. The plan set the percentage goal of women in various job categories ranging as high as 36% women. Supervisors were directed to make efforts to achieve that goal by using sex as a factor in selecting among equally qualified applicants, with the caution that supervisors would be evaluated, in part, by their success in achieving the set goals. Relying on the constitutional case of *Wygant v. Jackson Bd. of Ed.,* 476 U.S. 267 (1986), *Johnson* held that a plan directing the use of sex as factor, or as tie-breaker between similarly qualified applicants, was reasonable. *Accord, Grutter v. Bollinger,* 539 U.S. 244 (2003). Thus, the use of either fixed hiring ratios or the use of race or sex as a factor in making each decision was held to be "reasonable."

(3) Remedial and Temporary

The program must be remedial in nature, designed to go no further than achieving a work force that reflects the set balanced work force goal. Once that goal is reached the plan must become inoperative. Attempts to maintain a balanced work force after the set goal has been achieved by continuing the use of race or sex no longer is remedial in nature but akin to a permanent, and thus impermissible, quota. *See, Taxman v. Bd. of Ed. of Tp of Piscataway, supra.*

Failure to set a specific termination condition on the face of the plan is not necessarily fatal if the plan, in its totality, prescribes that it will be operative only until the underrepresentation goal has been remedied. *Johnson v. Transp. Auth., Santa Clara County, supra.*

13.09: TESTING: 703(*L*) AND *RICCI*

Affirmative action plans typically include a commitment to evaluate selection devices for their adverse impact on minority applicants, and where such devices have an adverse impact, determine the job relatedness/business necessity of their continued use. However, specific statutory language limits the employer's ability to alter post-testing results:

> It shall be an unlawful employment practice for a [covered entity] in connection with the selection or referral of applicants or candidates for employment or promotions, to adjust the scores of, use different cutoff scores for, or otherwise alter the results of, employment related tests on the basis of race, color, religion, sex or national origin. 42 U.S.C. 2000e–(2)(*l*).

The impact of this section, added in 1991 after the *Weber* and *Santa Clara County* decisions, is unclear. For example, pursuant to a plan committed to filling vacancies on a 50–50 ratio the employer selects the five highest scoring whites and the five highest scoring blacks. This use of different cut off scores by race could be construed to conflict with the above provision. However, section 116 of the 1991 Amendments provides, "Nothing in the amendments shall affect * * * affirmative action * * * that [is] in accordance with the law." This suggests that use of different cut off scores on a test to meet a ratio sanctioned by *Weber* would be permitted. *See, Officers for Justice v. Civil Serv. Comm.,* 979 F.2d 721 (9th Cir. 1991); 29 C.F.R. pt. 1608 to the effect that the 1991 Amendments did not affect the standards of affirmative action programs.

Ricci v. DeStefano, 557 U.S. 557 (2009), injected additional uncertainty. This case involved a public employer refusing to implement the results of an objective test to select among firefighters who would be eligible for promotion to officer positions. The disproportionately higher performance of white applicants on the qualifying test resulted in a pool from which the officers would be selected that virtually excluded black firefighters from being considered for the promotion. The white firefighters made eligible for promotion based on their test performance, but who would not now be considered for promotion, sued alleging that disregarding the test results was illegal race discrimination.

The Court held first, that the decision not to make the appointments from the eligibility pool produced by the test scores was race motivated and thus actionable. Second, relying on the 42 U.S.C. 2000e–2(*l*) proviso, *supra,* held that a race-centered basis for setting aside the test results was not justified by a general affirmative action concern. Nor could it be based on the possibility that implementing the test results would result in a lawsuit and potential liability toward black firefighters based on the adverse impact of the test on black applicants. The Court then announced a new defensive concept; that an employer could disregard test scores, but only if the employer produced a "strong basis in the evidence" that use of the test results would result in its Title VII liability toward underrepresented minority applicants. The Court concluded with a finding that the employer was liable in this case because it had no "strong basis in the evidence" to believe that the test lacked the "job relatedness" necessary to validate the test results. (*See,* Chapter 18 discussing liability based on the adverse impact of testing devices.) The Court noted, however, that it was not addressing formal affirmative action plans that involved an evaluation of the racial impact of testing devices.

United States v. Brennan, 650 F.3d 65 (2d Cir. 2011), held that Ricci did not make it illegal race discrimination for an employer to alter its seniority system to implement an affirmative action plan goal, even if to do so disappointed the expectations of some white workers, suggesting that ranking test results by race or sex to achieve goals set forth in a formalized plan would not violate Title VII.

13.10: THE CONSTITUTION

Government entities using race or sex to make decisions raises the issue of whether use of race or sex violates the constitutional rights of non-minorities under the 5th and 14th Amendments. The argument that the Constitution requires governments to be absolutely "color blind" has been rejected. Nonetheless, all governmental race distinctions (and to some degree sex distinctions) are accorded "strict judicial scrutiny." Applying the "strict scrutiny" standard, the Court has sustained limited, narrowly circumscribed use of such factors when they are shown to be "necessary" to serve directly "compelling" governmental interests. A "compelling interest" can include a need to remedy past patterns of segregation resulting in significant underrepresentation of women or minorities. Narrowly drawn remedial programs, such as using race or sex as one factor to make selection, have been sustained. "Quotas" that essentially guarantee selection of black over white applicants have been struck down. *Grutter v. Bollinger,* 539 U.S. 306 (2003) (law school admissions). *See also, Adarand Constructors, Inc. v. Pena,* 515 U.S. 200 (1995) (government contracts); *Parents Involved v. Seattle School Dist. No. 1,* 551 U.S. 701 (2007) (education).

The required "compelling interest" also is present when a defendant employer has been found to have engaged in "pervasive" or "egregious" illegal discrimination. Judicial imposition on guilty employers of a requirement to use race or sex in making future hiring decisions based on a reasonable hiring or promotion ratio similar to the 1–1 ratio sanctioned in *Weber,* does not violate the equal protection rights of disappointed white applicants. *U.S. v. Paradise,* 480 U.S. 140 (1987).

As public employers also are prohibited from using race and sex classifications by Title VII, when they adopt voluntarily affirmative action programs to increase women and minority employment in the public sector, the challenge to the programs invokes Title VII as well as the Constitution. While legal analysis differs, outcomes under Title VII and the Constitution appear to be similar. *See e.g., U.S. v. Paradise, supra; Wygant v. Jackson Bd. of Educ.,* 476 U.S. 267 (1986).

CHAPTER 14

"BECAUSE OF:" MOTIVE–BASED DISPARATE TREATMENT LIABILITY

14.01: INTRODUCTION

The core statutes proscribe discrimination "because of" a protected class. This Chapter addresses application of that term to discrimination in hiring, promotion, discipline, and discharge where there is no facially discriminatory policy. In such cases, plaintiff's ultimate burden is to prove the fact of defendant's motivation in making the decision by a "preponderance of the evidence." *Texas Dep't of Comm. Affairs v. Burdine,* 450 U.S. 248 (1981). "A disparate treatment claim cannot succeed unless the employee's protected trait actually played a role in that process and had a determinative influence on the outcome." *Hazen Paper Co. v. Biggins,* 507 U.S. 604 (1993).

> Proof of [illegal motive] is always difficult. Defendants of even minimal sophistication will neither admit animus nor leave a paper trail demonstrating it; and because most employment decisions involve an element of discretion, alternative hypotheses (including that of simple mistake) will always be possible and often plausible. Only the very best workers are completely satisfactory, and they are not likely to be discriminated against—the cost of discrimination is too great. The law tries to protect average and even below average

workers against being treated more harshly than would be the case if they were of a different race, sex, religion, or national origin, but it has difficulty in achieving this goal because it is so easy to concoct a plausible reason for not hiring, or firing, or failing to promote or denying a pay raise to a worker who is not superlative. *Riorian v. Kempiners,* 831 F.2d 690 (7th Cir. 1987).

14.02: DEFINING ILLEGAL MOTIVATION

A. "BECAUSE OF" NOT "IN SPITE OF"

Mere awareness that a distinction or practice may adversely affect members of a protected class is not the discriminatory purpose required to establish proscribed motive. For example, in spite of the foreseeable impact on women of granting preferences for military veterans, if the intent was to benefit veterans, not to harm women or benefit men, the distinction lacked the required discriminatory motivation. *Personnel Administrator v. Feeney,* 442 U.S. 256 (1979). Similarly, setting salaries for jobs dominated by women at a rate lower than for different but comparable jobs held predominately by men could be foreseen to be "unfair" to women. This fact did not establish illegal sex motivation. *AFSCME v. State of Washington,* 770 F.2d 1401 (9th Cir. 1985). In *Ricci v. DeStefano,* 557 U.S. 557 (2009), an employer refused to implement the results of an objective test because of its adverse effect on racial and ethnic minorities. The employer argued that it was not motivated "because of the race" of those who had passed the test (whites), but to avoid Title VII litigation and potential liability based on the outcome of the test. The Court nonetheless held that setting aside the test because of its racial outcomes was "because of race."

B. "GOOD FAITH"

Discrimination "because of" an individual's protected trait does not require an invidious purpose to harm or disadvantage. *Goodman v. Lukens Steel Co.,* 482 U.S. 656 (1987), accepted that union "leaders were favorably disposed toward minorities" and that the union's decision not to process racial discrimination claims of black employees was a good faith attempt to better serve all workers—including racial minorities—by not antagonizing the employer with charges of racism. Nonetheless, because the union made decisions based on the race of the employee, this was discrimination "because of race."

C. "SOLELY?"

Phillips v. Martin–Marietta, 400 U.S. 542 (1971), addressed an employer that disqualified women, but not men, who had pre-school-aged children. The lower court had held that distinctions based on "sex plus" a legitimate, non-proscribed factor (pre-school children) was not unlawful. The proscribed factor must be the *sole* basis for the employer's distinction. The Court reversed, holding that it was sex discrimination for an employer to have one policy for men and a different, more stringent policy that disqualified only women. This analysis was confirmed in *UAW v. Johnson Controls, Inc.* 499 U.S. 187 (1991), which held that it was facial sex discrimination for an employer to disqualify fertile women, but not fertile men, from jobs requiring exposure to toxic substances.

D. "JUST CAUSE"

The ADEA specifically allows employees to be disciplined for "just cause." 29 U.S.C. 623(f). Notwithstanding this cautionary proviso, found only in the ADEA, applying legitimate rules differently to protected classes is not justified simply because there was "cause" for the treatment of the employee actually disciplined. In *McDonald v. Santa Fe Trail Transp. Co.,* 427 U.S. 273 (1976), the employer discharged a white employee for theft while similarly situated black employees were retained. The Court stated:

> While [the employer] may decide that participation in a theft of cargo may render an employee unqualified for employment, this criterion must be applied alike to members of all races. * * * [W]hat ever factors the mechanisms of compromise may legitimately take into account in mitigating discipline of some employees, under Title VII, race may not be among them.

Similarly, penalizing a female employee because of her aggressive or abrasive behavior, while tolerating or even rewarding similar aggressive behavior by male employees, is discrimination because of sex. *Price Waterhouse v. Hopkins,* 490 U.S. 228 (1989).

While the employer may not use the race or sex of the offenders in allocating differences in discipline, the employer is free to make distinctions based on the relative gravity of the employees' misconduct, the degree of their culpability, or their past work history. *Gray v. Toshiba America Consumer Products, Inc.,* 263 F.3d 595 (6th Cir. 2001).

E. NATIONAL SECURITY

Section 703(g) of Title VII, (42 U.S.C. 2000(e)-2(g)) provides:

[I]t shall not be an unlawful employment practice for an employer to fail or refuse to hire any individual for any position, for an employer to discharge any individual from any position * * * if (1) the occupancy of such position, or access to the premises upon which any part of the duties of such position is performed * * * is subject to any requirement imposed in the interest of the national security of the United States under any security program in effect pursuant to any statute * * * or Executive order * * * and (2) such individual has not fulfilled or has ceased to fulfill that requirement.

Rattigan v. Holder, 643 F.3d 975 (D.C.Cir. 2011), held that an individual has a claim against an employer who, because of proscribed motivation, provided false or misleading information for the purpose of causing the employee to be denied a necessary clearance. The motive was not lack of a security clearance, but the victim's protected class. However, *Toy v. Holder,* 714 F.3d 881 (5th Cir. 2013), held that the proviso protects even improperly motivated denial of a clearance. National security concerns, as reflected in the proviso, "trumped" the employee's right to be free from improperly motivated sex discrimination.

14.03: CAUSATION: CONNECTING MOTIVE TO DISCRIMINATION

A. "AFTER ACQUIRED EVIDENCE"

The critical point for determining motivation is at the time of the discriminatory decision. While the fact that the employer would (or might) have made the same decision on legitimate grounds discovered *after* the discriminatory act does not affect liability. In *McKennon v. Nashville Banner Pub. Co.,* 513 U.S. 352 (1995), plaintiff filed a suit alleging age motivated discrimination. In preparing its defense of plaintiff's claim, the employer discovered that before she was discharged plaintiff had copied and removed confidential documents. The lower court granted summary judgment for defendant on grounds that defendant had proved that plaintiff would have been discharged for her misconduct. The Court reversed, holding that as defendant's motivation for dismissing plaintiff was plaintiff's age, plaintiff had established a violation of the ADEA. Whether defendant would have made the "same decision anyway" is irrelevant to the issue of defendant's liability. The Court remanded the case for determination of remedy, but directed that if the employer established that "the employee would have been terminated on those [legitimate] grounds alone if the employer had known of it at the time of the discharge," the employer should be relieved of an obligation to reinstate the plaintiff and the obligation to provide plaintiff full back wage monetary relief.

A related issue arises where an employee is discharged for illegitimate reasons after which the employer discovers that the employee had engaged in misconduct *prior* to being hired. A common example is so-called "resume fraud" where the employee misstates information on his/her application, such as educational background, experience, or criminal record. Courts have applied the reasoning of *McKennon*. The key issue is defendant's motivation *at the time of the decision,* not whether it would have hired the plaintiff had it known the truth. Whether defendant can establish that it would have dismissed the plaintiff upon discovery of the "fraud" simply goes to the extent of plaintiff's remedy. *Wallace v. Dunn Const. Co., Inc.,* 62 F.3d 374 (11th Cir. 1995). The issue in determining whether the successful plaintiff is entitled to reinstatement and recovery of full back pay is not whether he would not have been *hired* had the truth been known, but whether, upon discovery of the misstatements, plaintiff would have been *discharged. Shattuck v. Kinetic Concepts, Inc.,* 49 F.3d 1106 (5th Cir. 1995). Minor misstatements in the application process or those not material to job performance (*e.g.,* age, marital status, or number of dependents) may not serve as a basis for denying a successful plaintiff full remedial relief. *See, Calloway v. Partners Nat'l Health Plans,* 986 F.2d 44230 (11th Cir. 1993).

Misconduct by a former employee *after he has been discharged* provides no basis for an employer to avoid liability for improperly motivated discharge. Again, such evidence goes only to the extent of plaintiff's remedy. *Carr v. Woodbury County Juvenile Detention Ctr,* 905 F.Supp. 619 (N.D.Iowa 1995), *aff'd per curiam,* 97 F.3d 1456 (8th Cir. 1996). For discussion of reinstatement and back pay remedies *see, infra,* 28.02–.05.

B. "CAT'S PAW:" CONNECTING MOTIVE TO THE DECISION–MAKER

Illegally motivated discrimination consists of two factual elements: (1) an actor's state of mind, and (2) whether that state of mind *caused* the challenged action. *Staub v. Proctor Hospital,* ___ U.S. ___, 131 S.Ct. 1186 (2011), involved the Uniformed Services Employment and Reemployment Act (38 U.S.C. 4301), which uses operative language similar to the core statutes. Plaintiff claimed that his discharge was motivated by hostility to his ongoing military service obligations. Plaintiff's immediate supervisor had expressed such hostility, but did not disclose this hostility in recommending that plaintiff be discharged. The supervisor's recommendation allegedly gave false, but facially legitimate, reasons for recommending discharge, hoping that his negative recommendation would be accepted by the decision-maker. The decision-maker considered the recommendation, but also reviewed plaintiff's personnel file and made some independent inquiries. Ultimately the decision-maker accepted the supervisor's recommendation to discharge the plaintiff. The decision-maker held no anti-military bias and was unaware of the alleged bias of the supervisor. The court of appeals held, as a matter of law, that plaintiff could prevail only if the immediate supervisor making the tainted recommendation "exercised such 'singular influence' over the decision-maker that the decision to terminate was the product of 'blind reliance.'" The Court reversed. "[T]he ultimate decision-maker's exercise of judgment does not automatically render[] the link to the supervisor's bias 'remote' or 'purely contingent.'" "[I]f a supervisor performs an act motivated by [proscribed] animus that is *intended* by the supervisor to cause an adverse employment action, and if that act is a proximate cause of the ultimate employment action, then the employer is liable * * *." In such cases the supervisor's improperly motivated action has become the "cat's paw" to effectuate discrimination.

14.04: FACIALLY NEUTRAL POLICIES IMPROPERLY MOTIVATED

Albemarle Paper Co. v. Moody, 422 U.S. 405 (1975), held that even if a selection device (a pen and paper test) was "job related" and a "business necessity," it would be illegal if the plaintiff proved that its adoption or use was a pretext for discriminatory motive. *Raytheon Co. v. Hernandez,* 540 U.S. 44 (2003), addressed an employer's policy of not rehiring employees who had been dismissed. The Court held that *if* the policy was adopted for the purpose of not rehiring former employees with disabilities the policy would violate the ADA. A seniority system amended for the purpose of protecting male employees at the expense of female employees, if challenged in a timely fashion, would violate Title VII. *See, Lorance v. AT & T Technologies,* 490 U.S. 900 (1989) (challenge time barred). If the employer imposes a rule requiring all employees to speak only English at work because of hostility toward workers of different national origins, the discrimination would be "because of" national origin. *Maldonado v. City of Altus,* 433 F.3d 1294 (10th Cir. 2006). Even in a work force consisting solely of one class of workers, adopting a rule or policy because of the class of that work force is "because of" the protected classification. *Gerdom v. Continental Airlines,* 692 F.2d 602 (9th Cir. 1982) (burdensome grooming standards imposed on all-female job category).

CHAPTER 15

PROVING MOTIVE THOUGH EXPRESSIONS OF PREJUDICE

15.01: INTRODUCTION

Written or spoken indications of animus against a protected class ("smoking gun evidence") present evidentiary issues on four levels that intertwine rules of evidence with principles of employment discrimination. First, is the proffered evidence admissible? Issues of relevance and other evidence rules such as hearsay, "best evidence," document authentication, etc. must be addressed. Second, credibility? If plaintiff alleges that a decision maker (or one influencing a decision maker) made statements indicating hostility toward plaintiff's class, and the alleged speaker denies having made such statements, there will be a threshold factual issue of witness credibility as to whether the words were actually spoken. This critical preliminary issue must be resolved by the fact finder. *EEOC v. Alton Packaging Corp.,* 901 F.2d 920 (11th Cir. 1990). Third, are defendant's expressions sufficient to *support* a verdict for plaintiff? This is an issue of law for the court to resolve that will arise before trial on a motion for summary judgment, at the close of testimony on a motion for directed verdict, or after a jury verdict on a motion of the non-prevailing party for judgment notwithstanding the verdict (JNOV). Finally, is plaintiff's evidence so strong that no reasonable jury could render a verdict for defendant, requiring a court-directed verdict for plaintiff?

15.02: ANIMUS REVEALED: "EVALUATIVE" VS. "DESCRIPTIVE"

To have probative value words attributed to defendant must be "evaluative" of a protected class, not merely "descriptive." Identifying an employee as a "bright young man" was merely "descriptive" and thus was not evidence of sex or age animus. *Beshears v. Asbill,* 930 F.2d 1348 (8th Cir. 1991). By contrast, a comment, "looking for a bright young star," is an evaluative indication of prejudice favoring younger applicants. *Woody v. Covenant Health,* (E.D. Tenn. 5/8/13) 81 USLW 1632. Reporting that an incident involved "a large, strong, muscular black man" attempting to intimidate "three smaller white men" was merely "descriptive" of the event and not indicative of a racial animus against the black plaintiff. *Evans v. McClain of Georgia, Inc.,* 131 F.3d 957 (11th Cir. 1997). Noting an applicant's age on a formal application carries little inference that age motivated his subsequent discharge. General references, such as "good ole' boy network," "oldtimers," and "deadwood" have been held to be more descriptive than evaluative and were insufficient to support an inference of age discrimination against an older worker. *Pottenger v. Potlatch,* 329 F.3d 740 (9th Cir. 2003). Even referring to plaintiff as "an old fart" was found to be a descriptive colloquialism, not significant evidence of an age bias. *Montgomery v. John Deere & Co.,* 169 F.3d 556 (8th Cir. 1999). Similarly, describing the female plaintiff as a "bitch" was seen as a colloquial personality description, rather than evidence of an evaluative prejudice against women! *Neuren v. Adduci, Mastriani, Meeks & Schill,* 43 F.3d 1507 (D.C. Cir. 1995).

By contrast, unambiguous slurs such as "nigger," "wetback," "chink," or "wop" uniformly are found to be "evaluative" of the insulted class and thus strong evidence of proscribed motivation. *DiCarlo v. Potter,* 358 F.3d 408 (6th Cir. 2004).

15.03: CONTEXT

Ash v. Tyson Foods, 546 U.S. 454 (2006), emphasized the importance of evaluating the context in which the words were used. An employer regular referred to his black male workers as "boys." The lower court held that without modifiers, such as "black," the word "boy," standing alone, was not evidence of racial bias. The Court reversed, holding that in many circumstances in some geographical regions the term "boy," when used to describe adult black males, would indicate the speaker's animus against blacks and thus should have been admitted into evidence. Similarly, during a termination discussion with a black employee his supervisor referred to "your kind" not being allowed to exit through a particular door. This reference to "your kind" in this context was evidence of race motivation. *Crump v. NBTY, Inc.,* 847 F.Supp.2d 388 (E.D.N.Y. 2012).

15.04: WEIGHING VERBAL EVIDENCE: FROM "DIRECT EVIDENCE" TO "STRAY REMARKS"

A. GENERALLY

Verbal evidence may be so weak that it is excluded from consideration or so powerful that no reasonable jury could conclude that defendant did not have a discriminatory motive. The verbal evidence ranges from "direct evidence" of motivation to "stray remarks" which, even if admitted, will not support a finding of illegal motive. In between are verbal statements that indicate a prejudice, but an inference is required to establish that the express prejudiced motivated the decision. The weight of such verbal evidence varies with the role of the speaker in making the decision, the temporal proximity between the expression and the decision, whether the words were directed at the plaintiff or used generally, the context in which the words were used, and the intensity of the prejudice they revealed.

B. DIRECT EVIDENCE

Comments made by the actual decision maker which, if credited, establish the issue in question *without reliance upon an inference or presumption* is considered "direct evidence" of an illegally motivated decision. Such statements demonstrate both prejudice and that the prejudice played a role in the challenged decision. The words, in effect, are an admission by the defendant that proscribed animus caused the adverse action. *Shorter v. ICG Holdings, Inc.,* 188 F.3d 1204 (10th Cir. 1999).

"Direct" evidence was presented by plaintiff in *Price Waterhouse v. Hopkins,* 490 U.S. 228 (1989). The decision-makers made written and oral evaluations of the female plaintiff, stating that their decision not to promote her was based, at least in part, on an expressed gender stereotype ("too macho," needs to "walk more femininely, talk more femininely, dress more femininely, wear make-up, have her hair styled, and wear jewelry"). Having expressed a sexual reason to explain their action no inference was needed to infer that defendant's action was motivated by plaintiff's sex. Similarly, an Hispanic worker has presented direct evidence that his national origin motivated defendant's decision to deny him a promotion when plaintiff was told by the decision-maker that it was "because of his Hispanic accent." *In re Rodriguez,* 487 F.3d 1001 (6th Cir. 2007).

Since the words themselves established the motivation for the action, unambiguous direct evidence not only permits, but may require a judgment for the plaintiff. *Van Voorhis v. Hillsborough County,* 512 F.3d 1286 (11th Cir. 2008) (notation on interview file that the rejected plaintiff was "too old for this job; we need a younger person" compels a finding of age discrimination.). *Cf. Lewis v. City of Chicago,* 496 F.3d 645 (7th Cir. 2007) (jury verdict for defendant upheld in spite of the decision maker's statement that plaintiff was not hired because she was female, and that the "job was too dangerous for a woman."

C. "STRAY REMARKS"

Expressions made by persons who played no role in the challenged decision have little, if any, probative value (*Price Waterhouse v. Hopkins, supra*), and may be excluded from jury consideration. For example, various ageist comments directed over time at plaintiff by non-decisionmaker co-workers such as "pops," "grandpa," "old man," and "the old fart," were dismissed as "stray remarks." *Reed v. Neopost, USA.,* 701 F.3d 434 (5th Cir. 2012). Utterances by a decision-maker (or one influencing a decision) made at a time or in a context sufficiently removed from the challenged employment decision that their probative value, balanced against the potential to unduly inflame the jury, may be so weak that the trial court, in its discretion, may exclude them from jury consideration. For example, defendant uttering a single racial curse four years prior to the challenged decision was so remote that the inflammatory curse was seen as a "stray comment" that could be excluded from evidence. *Manning v. Chevron Chemical Co., LLC,* 332 F.3d 874 (5th Cir. 2003). A single critical, even blasphemous, reference to an employee's religion may be dismissed as "stray," and thus insufficient to support an inference of religious motivation. *EEOC v. Witel, Inc.*, 81 F.3d 1508 (10th Cir. 1996) ("I don't like Ellie because she is into all that Jesus shit.").

D. "INDIRECT"

Verbal evidence that is sufficient to establish that the speaker harbors an animus against a protected class, but requires an inference that the animus influenced the challenged decision is considered "indirect" evidence of an illegally motivated decision. For example, use of racial slurs indicates a racial animus. However, if the slurs were general in nature, not directly connected to the challenged decision, it is necessary to draw an inference that the unambiguous prejudice expressed in fact played a role in a subsequent decision. Indirect evidence may be sufficiently strong to *permit* a fact finder to draw such an inference of illegal motivation from repeated use of racist slurs. For example, use of the term "nigger" and commenting that plaintiff was "paid a lot for a black man" was sufficient to support a verdict for the plaintiff. *Ayissi-Etoh v. Fannie Mae* 712 F.3d 572 (D.C. Cir. 2013). Rarely is indirect evidence strong enough to *require* a judgment for plaintiff. *DiCarlo v. Potter,* 358 F.3d 408 (6th Cir. 2004). However, repeated indiscriminate use of such pejorative insults that establish deep-seeded racism, particularly when the insults are directed at the plaintiff, can be sufficiently strong evidence of a racist motivation for the subsequent treatment of the plaintiff that a directed verdict for plaintiff is required. *Brown v. East Mississippi Electric Power Ass'n,* 989 F.2d 858 (5th Cir. 1993).

In *Reeves v. Sanderson Plumbing Products, Inc.,* 530 U.S. 133 (2000), the decision-maker described plaintiff as being "so old that he must have come over on the Mayflower" and on another occasion opined that plaintiff was "too damned old to do his job." The Court concluded that this evidence, coupled with the lack of credibility of the proffered reason for defendant's termination, and evidence that younger workers, generally, had received favorable treatment was sufficient to support the verdict for plaintiff. Because the Court re-instated the jury verdict for plaintiff the Court did not need to resolve whether the evidence was sufficiently strong to require a judgment for the plaintiff. Nevertheless, the Court opined that even this massive amount of indirect and circumstantial evidence of age motivation may not have *required* a directed verdict for the plaintiff.

The inconsistency in outcomes as to when indirect evidence is sufficient to support a jury verdict is illustrated by two cases. One held that an angry outburst, "I hate having fucking women in the office" was insufficient to support a finding that a female plaintiff was a victim of sex discrimination, (*Heim v. State of Utah,* 8 F.3d 1541 (10th Cir. 1993)), while another held that the comment, "women are the worst thing that ever happened to [this company]" was sufficient to support a jury finding of sex discrimination. *Stacks v. Southwestern Bell Yellow Pages, Inc.,* 27 F.3d 1316 (8th Cir. 1994). *King v. Hardesty,* 517 F.3d 1049 (8th Cir. 2008), further illustrates. The decision maker's statement—that "white people teach black kids better than someone from their own race," was evaluative evidence sufficient to support a verdict that the removal of the black *teacher* was racially motivated. However, this negative evaluation of the abilities of black teachers coupled with numerous racially "insensitive" comments made over time that included referring to African–American males as "big black bucks" and "boys," the use of "ho" "and "whore" to describe black female students, derogatory statements about black parents, and reference to blacks as "slaves" was insufficient to support a jury finding that there was race discrimination in plaintiff's pay and denial of assignments to vacant non-teaching positions.

CHAPTER 16

PROVING MOTIVE WITH CIRCUMSTANTIAL EVIDENCE

16.01: GENERALLY

An objective fact from which one can reasonably draw an inference as to the existence of another fact is known as circumstantial evidence. *McDonnell Douglas Corp. v. Green,* 411 U.S. 792 (1973), held that discriminatory motivation may be established solely through circumstantial evidence. "Smoking gun" verbal evidence is not required. Circumstantial evidence of illegally motivated action can consist of suspicious disparate treatment of plaintiff coupled with the lack of credible legitimate reasons to explain plaintiff's treatment or through presentation of a mosaic of circumstantial evidence such as discriminatory treatment of others and suspicious numerical imbalances.

16.02: THE MCDONNELL DOUGLAS MODEL

To bring order into the evaluation of circumstantial evidence *McDonnell Douglas Corp. v. Green, supra,* established a three step model of shifting evidentiary burdens: (1) plaintiff can establish a prima facie case of improperly motivated disparate treatment if the evidence eliminates the most common *legitimate* reasons for disparate treatment; (2) defendant then *must* "articulate a legitimate, non-discriminatory reason" for its disparate treatment of plaintiff; (3) thereupon plaintiff must present additional evidence sufficient to show that defendant's articulated reason was but a "pretext" for illegal motivation. The ultimate burden of persuasion on the issue of motive is with the plaintiff. *Texas Dep't of Comm. Affairs v. Burdine,* 450 U.S. 248 (1981). This model has been applied in the three core statutes. *Reeves v. Sanderson Plumbing Products, Inc.,* 530 U.S. 133 (2000) (ADEA).

The *McDonnell Douglas* model is not intended to be rigid, but is a flexible guide that may be adapted to varying facts. *Texas Dep't of Community Affairs v. Burdine, supra.* The elements need not be precisely pleaded, nor need they be submitted to the jury as distinct issues. *Swierkiewicz v. Sorema N.A.,* 534 U.S. 506 (2002).

16.03: PLAINTIFF'S PRIMA FACIE CASE: HIRING AND PROMOTION

A. GENERALLY

McDonnell Douglas Corp. v. Green, supra, addressed a complaint of a black former employee of defendant who applied for and was denied re-employment. In this context the Court stated:

The complainant in a Title VII trial must carry the initial burden under the statute of establishing a prima facie case * * *. This may be done by showing (i) that he belongs to a racial minority, (ii) that he applied and was qualified for the job for which the employer was seeking applicants; (iii) that despite his qualifications, he was rejected; and (iv) that after his rejection the position remained open and the employer continued to seek applicants from persons of complainant's qualifications.

Absent significant verbal or statistical evidence of improper motivation, the failure of plaintiff to establish a prima facie case will result in judgment for defendant.

B. ELEMENTS OF THE PRIMA FACIE CASE

(1) "Racial Minority" = "Protected Class"

The *McDonnell Douglas* model is not limited to "racial minorities," but has been applied to allegations of sex, national origin, religious, age, and disability discrimination. White males are protected under the same standards as racial minorities, and discrimination against them is not immunized where the decision-maker is of the same class as the plaintiff. *Oncale v. Sundowner Offshore Services, Inc.,* 523 U.S. 75 (1998). Nevertheless, when the decision-maker is of the same race or sex as plaintiff, some courts require plaintiff's prima facie showing to include some additional evidence to suggest that defendant is one of those "unusual employers that discriminates against its own class." *Mattioda v. White,* 323 F.3d 1288 (10th Cir. 2003). "Special circumstances" include statistical patterns of favoritism toward minorities, an ill-defined, *ad hoc* affirmative action goal, verbal expressions of animus, or evidence that the white male plaintiff had qualifications clearly superior to those of the favored minority person. *Sutherland v. Michigan Dep't of Treasury,* 344 F.3d 603 (6th Cir. 2003).

"Age" presents another variation. A prima facie showing requires plaintiff to demonstrate that favoritism was shown to persons "significantly younger" than the over–40 plaintiff. *O'Connor v. Consolidated Coin Caterers Corp.,* 517 U.S. 308 (1996) (difference between the 56 year old plaintiff who was dismissed and the 40 year old who was retained established a prima facie case). The fact that the favored person was over 40 is not relevant. "[T]he fact that a replacement is substantially younger than the plaintiff is a far more reliable indicator of age discrimination than the fact that the plaintiff was replaced by someone outside the protected class." *Id.*

It is unclear what age differential is sufficiently "significant" to establish a prima face showing. *Balderston v. Fairbanks Morse Engine,* 328 F.3d 309 (7th Cir. 2003) held that a 6 year age difference is not "significant." *Fabrizio v. UPMC,* 96 EPD 44,461 (W.D.Pa. 2012), held that 6 years, 9 months was sufficient. That the decision-maker was the same age or older than the disadvantaged workers should not undermine an initial inference that age motivated the favoritism toward "significantly younger" individuals. *Kadas v. MCI Systemhouse Corp,* 255 F.3d 359 (7th Cir. 2001).

While a prima facie case of religious discrimination will be established where plaintiff is a member of an historically victimized faith (*e.g.,* Jewish) or one that is subject to political *hostility* (*e.g.,* Muslim) (*Hasan v. Foley & Lardner, LLP.,* 552 F.3d 520 (7th Cir. 2008)), mere distinctions by a secular employer between persons of different "mainstream" religions (*e.g.,* Lutheran vs. Methodist) may be insufficient, standing alone, to suggest a religious motivation. *Shapolia v. Los Alamos Nat. Lab.,* 992 F.2d 1033 (10th Cir. 1993). In such cases plaintiff must present evidence of the employer's strongly held religious practices which conflict with those of the plaintiff, a pattern of favoritism toward a particular religion, or expressions of disfavor toward plaintiff's religion. *Fischer v. Forestwood, Inc.,* 525 F.3d 972 (10th Cir. 2008).

(2) Knowledge

Unlike race or sex, a person's religion, age or national origins rarely are self-evident. Physical or mental impairments may not have obvious manifestations. In such cases plaintiff must present evidence that defendant was aware of plaintiff's protected class. *Norman–Nunnery v. Madison Area Tech. College,* 625 F.3d 422 (7th Cir. 2010). *Hunter v. United Parcel Service, Inc.,* 697 F.3d 397 (8th Cir. 2012) (No prima facie case of sex discrimination where plaintiff failed to establish that defendant was aware that the male plaintiff was transgender). If such information is in defendant's files or was on a submitted application, knowledge of plaintiff's status is presumed. *See, Nieman v. Grange Mut. Cas. Co.,* (C.D. Ill. 2012), 2013 WL 173466, where the employer was held to know plaintiff's age by virtue of it being disclosed in plaintiff's LinkedIn-posted resume.

(3) "Applied for" and "Vacancy"

"Vacancy" is established by evidence that defendant has formally posted job openings, advertised vacancies, or informally has solicited or welcomed applications. "Application" includes any reasonable effort by plaintiff to convey to the employer a specific interest in filling existing vacancies, such as sending e-mails or letters of interest in being informed of vacancies as they arise. If the employer uses informal, word-of mouth hiring, plaintiff will have "applied" by making it clear to the employer that he/she was interested in being considered for such vacancies. Nevertheless, "application" requires more than informal inquiries about possible future vacancies. *Lockridge v. Bd. of Trustees, Univ. of Ark.,* 315 F.3d 1005 (8th Cir. 2003).

(4) "Rejected"

Formal notice of rejection is not required when a vacancy is filled by a person of a class different from plaintiff, or where plaintiff did not receive an offer within a reasonable period of time and defendant continues to seek applicants. *McDonnell–Douglas Corp. v. Green, supra.* However, if the vacancy for which plaintiff applied is filled by a person of the same class, this defeats any inference that plaintiff's rejection was motivated by her class membership. *Jones v. Western Geophysical Co.,* 669 F.2d 280 (5th Cir. 1982).

(5) "Qualified"

In cases of hiring or promotion "qualified" means that plaintiff possessed the announced, objective job requirements in terms of education, experience, licenses, training, test scores, certificates, etc. Plaintiffs who possess the required credentials need not present evidence that they could actually perform up to the employer's expectations. Defendant's subjective evaluation of plaintiff's inability to perform does not undermine plaintiff's demonstration that he is "qualified." *Nicholson v. Hyannis Air Serv., Inc.* 580 F.3d 1116 (9th Cir. 2009). The ADA does require that plaintiffs present evidence that, notwithstanding their physical or mental impairment, they possess the required credentials, *and* are able to perform "essential" duties. *Supra* 11.06.

Even if plaintiff does not possess posted job qualifications, plaintiff's demonstration that she had previously performed the job successfully establishes that plaintiff is "qualified" (*McDonnell Douglas Corp v. Green, supra*), as will a showing by plaintiff that defendant regular hires persons who lack the posted requirements. *Scheidenantle v. Slippery Rock Univ.,* 470 F.3d 535 (3d Cir. 2006).

"Qualified" is non-comparative. Plaintiff's prima facie showing need not include evidence that her qualifications were superior to those of the person selected. *Patterson v. McLean Credit Union,* 491 U.S. 164 (1989). That the person selected may be "more qualified" ultimately is relevant, but must be articulated by defendant. *Turner v. Honeywell Fed. Mfg. & Tech.,* 336 F.3d 716 (8th Cir. 2003).

16.04: DISCHARGE AND DISCIPLINE: VARIATIONS ON THE THEME

The *McDonnell Douglas* model for establishing a prima facie showing has been applied, in a modified form, to the discipline of workers for misconduct. *Reeves v. Sanderson Plumbing Products, Inc.,* 530 U.S. 133 (2000), set the standard:

> First, plaintiff must establish a prima facie case of discrimination. It is undisputed that petitioner satisfied this burden here: (i) at the time he was fired, he was a member of the class protected by the ADEA ('individuals who are at least 40 years of age'), (ii) was otherwise qualified for the position, (iii) he was discharged by respondent, and (iv) respondent successively hired three persons in their thirties to fill petitioner's position.

Some courts, however, have required plaintiff to present additional evidence in his prima facie showing that up until the adverse action, plaintiff had been performing up to the employer's legitimate expectations. This is satisfied by plaintiff showing adequate performance ratings, regular salary increases, long term employment with absence of criticisms, etc. A burden of showing ongoing satisfactory job performance is not satisfied solely by plaintiff's self-evaluation ("I was doing a good job"), or by imprecise, non-expert conclusions by plaintiff's co-workers. In the absence of evidence indicating the employer's ongoing satisfaction with the plaintiff's work, the disciplined plaintiff can satisfy this burden by presenting expert testimony that compares the employer's general performance expectations with the expert's evaluation of plaintiff's on-job performance. *King v. Rumsfeld,* 328 F.3d 145 (4th Cir. 2003). Even where plaintiff's formal performance ratings were favorable, defendant's showing that it had made informal oral criticisms of plaintiff's job performance can indicate that plaintiff was not performing satisfactorily and thus was not "qualified" for retention. *Lucas v. PyraMax Bank, FSB,* 539 F.3d 661 (7th Cir. 2008).

Some courts hold that even the adequately performing plaintiff must further demonstrate in her prima facie showing that employees of other classes had engaged in misconduct of "comparable seriousness" and were not similarly disciplined. Plaintiff must show that the circumstances of plaintiff and those of the retained employees "closely resemble each other in all relevant aspects." *Garcia v. Bristol–Myers Squibb Co.,* 535 F.3d 23 (1st Cir. 2008). Accordingly, evidence that the retained employee had better job evaluations, less tardiness, or had greater responsibility than the plaintiff will defeat plaintiff's prima facie case. *Knight v. Baptist Hosp. of Miami,* 330 F.3d 1313 (11th Cir. 2003). Conversely, it would seem that even if plaintiff fails to prove that his work had been "satisfactory," a demonstration that retained workers with equal or inferior work records were retained should establish the disparate treatment necessary to create a prima facie showing. *McDonald v. Santa Fe Trail Transp. Co.* 427 U.S. 273 (1976).

Imposing the burden of showing "satisfactory" job performance as part of plaintiff's prima facie case appears inconsistent with Supreme Court statements in *Texas Dep't of Community Affairs v. Burdine*, 450 U.S. 248 (1981), and *Reeves v. Sanderson Plumbing Products, Inc.*, *supra.* Articulating plaintiff's unsatisfactory job performance or plaintiff's greater culpability would seem to be defendant's burden, not an element of plaintiff's prima facie case. *Haigh v. Gelita, USA, Inc.*, 632 F.3d 464 (8th Cir. 2011).

16.05: REDUCTIONS-IN-FORCE

When the plaintiff is laid off there is no issue of whether plaintiff is "qualified" to perform the job. Presumably no adverse action would have been taken were it not for the economic adjustments. *Reeves v. Sanderson Plumbing Products, Inc., supra,* and some lower courts have held that when a person or persons in the protected age group are laid off while significantly younger persons are retained this is sufficient, standing alone, to create a prima face case of age discrimination. *Currier v. United Techs. Corp.*, 393 F.3d 246 (1st Cir. 2004). Some circuits, however, require that plaintiffs present "additional evidence" of age motivation or demonstrate that persons of other classes, not only were retained, but also were performing at a level lower than plaintiff. *Burks v. Wisconsin Dep't of Transp.*, 464 F.3d 744 (7th Cir. 2006). *Cf. Fabrizio v. UPMC,* (W.D.Pa. 2012), 2012 WL 3929213, (similarly situated comparator not required when job duties of laid off older worker are reassigned to a significantly younger co-worker). Any obligation of plaintiff to present "additional evidence" of age motivation is not satisfied simply by demonstrating other incidents where older workers were laid off. *Schoonmaker v. Spartan Graphics Leasing, LLC,* 595 F.3d 261 (6th Cir. 2010).

Defendant, not the plaintiff, possesses information of the performance of *retained* employees. Thus, imposing a burden on plaintiff to demonstrate, as part of a prima facie case, that retained employees were performing at a lower level seems inappropriate. *See, Lighter v. City of Wilmington,* 545 F.3d 260 (4th Cir. 2008).

16.06: DEFENDANT'S BURDEN: "LEGITIMATE, NONDISCRIMINATORY REASON"

When plaintiff succeeds in making a prima facie showing, "if the employer remains silent in the face of the presumption, the court must enter a judgment for the plaintiff because no issue of fact remains in the case. The burden that shifts to the defendant, therefore is to rebut the presumption [created by plaintiff's prima facie showing]." *Texas Dept' of Comm. Affairs v. Burdine,* 450 U.S. 248 (1981). The burden shifted to the defendant is to "articulate a legitimate non-discriminatory reason" for the employee's rejection. *McDonnell Douglas Corp. v. Green, supra.*

[The articulated reason] is sufficient if the defendant's evidence raises a genuine issue of fact as to whether it discriminated against the plaintiff. To accomplish this, the defendant must clearly set forth, through admissible evidence, the reasons for plaintiff's rejection. An articulation not admitted into evidence will not suffice. Thus the defendant cannot meet this burden merely through an answer to the complaint or argument of counsel. * * *

Placing this burden of production on the defendant [should] * * * frame the factual issue with sufficient clarity so that the plaintiff will have a full and fair opportunity to demonstrate pretext. The sufficiency of the defendant's evidence should be evaluated by the extent to which it fulfills [this] function." *Texas Dep't of Comm. Affairs v. Burdine, supra.*

Thus, defendant must identify with "relative clarity," a reason, and support with evidence that defendant relied on this reason in its treatment of the plaintiff. *Furnco Constr. Corp. v. Waters,* 438 U.S. 567 (1978). The articulated "reason" need not meet a high standard of being "job related." *Raytheon Co. v. Hernandez,* 500 U.S. 44 (2003) (ADA). That the reason may have an adverse impact on plaintiff's class and lesser discriminatory alternatives may exist does not deprive the articulated reason of its legitimacy. *Furnco Constr. Corp. v. Waters, supra.* Reasons may be "legitimate" even if they violate other laws. *Hazen Paper Co. v. Biggins,* 507 U.S. 604 (1993) (discharging plaintiff to avoid a pension obligation met defendant's burden under the ADEA even if such a discharge violated a federal pension protection statute.)

Because rational employers make decisions based on personal reasons, such as friendship or family relationships, non-business related reasons can be "legitimate." *Foster v. Dalton,* 71 F.3d 52 (1st Cir. 1995). However, reasons so vague, strange, bizarre, or idiosyncratic that no rational employer would utilize them in making employment decisions should not carry defendant's burden. Such reasons do not meet the *Burdine* standard for refuting the inference of improper motive raised by plaintiff's proof of suspicious disparate treatment because they are inadequate to give plaintiff a "full and fair opportunity to demonstrate pretext." *Barber v. CI Truck Driver Training, LLC,* 656 F.3d 782 (8th Cir. 2011). *Cf. Balderston v. Fairbanks Morse Engine,* 328 F.3d 309 (7th Cir. 2003) (That defendant "did not like" the plaintiff sufficed as a "reason" even if "foolish" and "trivial").

Subjective judgments are legitimate where the job itself is not amenable to objective measurements and performance involves unquantifiable, subjective elements (*e.g.*, executives, professionals). *Watson v. Fort Worth Bank & Trust,* 487 U.S. 977 (1988). Unduly subjective reasons for most jobs would not seem to meet the *Burdine* standard because a subjective reason is "easily fabricated" to cloak conscious or unconscious bias (*Barber v. CI Truck Driver Training, LLC, supra*), and, like bizarre or idiosyncratic reasons, often denies plaintiff the "full and fair opportunity" to frame a meaningful response. *Robbins v. White–Wilson Medical Clinic,*

Inc., 660 F.2d 1064 (5th Cir. 1981) (plaintiff's "yucky attitude" not a legitimate reason).

Conclusions without supporting facts also should be suspect. It would seem that the conclusion "personality problems" would be legitimate reason only if the employer identified those personality traits that the employer found objectionable. "Conflicts" should isolate the disagreements warranting defendant's conclusion. "Appearance" should detail the aspects of plaintiff's grooming that defendant disliked. *Chapman v. AI Transport,* 229 F.3d 1012 (11th Cir. 2000) (en banc).

Many courts, however, have allowed defendants to meet their burden by articulating extremely non-specific, subjective conclusions. *Sabinson v. Trustees of Dartmouth College,* 542 F.3d 1 (1st Cir. 2008) (acting in a "manner damaging to department" without specifying the "damaging" activity). *Loeb v. Best Buy, Inc.,* 537 F.3d 867 (8th Cir. 2008) (lack of "people skills, leadership, and decision-making"). Even incompetence of the decision maker was a legitimate reason for plaintiff's rejection. *Hill v. Miss. State Emp. Serv.,* 918 F.2d 1223 (5th Cir. 1990). *Autry v. Fort Bend Ind. Sch. Dist.,* 704 F.3d 344 (5th Cir. 2013), upheld as legitimate a largely unstructured ranking of applicants based on interviews by a committee (a member of which had expressed some level of racial prejudice), which resulted in the rejection of a black applicant who possessed the posted objective education and experience credentials which the white female who was selected lacked.

Should defendant fail to present credible evidence of a "legitimate, non-discriminatory reason" a judgment is required for plaintiff. However, defendant's burden goes no further than presenting evidence of the reason; defendant has no burden to prove the actual existence of the reason, nor that the reason motivated defendant's action. *St. Mary's Honor Center v. Hicks,* 509 U.S. 502 (1993).

16.07: PLAINTIFF'S REPLY: EVIDENCE OF "PRETEXT"

If, but only if, defendant articulates and supports with evidence a legitimate, non-discriminatory reason" for the treatment of plaintiff, the burden re-shifts to plaintiff to come forward with evidence that tends to demonstrate that the articulated reason was but a pretext for proscribed motive. Such evidence can be a "direct" attack on the reason itself with proof that the articulated reason did not exist, and thus could not have motivated the defendant. Or, plaintiff's pretext evidence can be "indirect," which may consist of bits and pieces of circumstantial evidence which together are sufficient to support a finding that the articulated reason, even if it existed, was not the true reason for defendant's action. The trial court need not follow the *McDonnell Douglas* three step dance, but may require plaintiff initially to present all evidence of illegal motive.

A. DIRECT EVIDENCE OF PRETEXT

St. Mary's Honor Center v. Hicks, 509 U.S. 502 (1993), involved a "direct" attack on defendant's articulated reason, which was plaintiff's alleged "failure to investigate a fight" between inmates. Plaintiff's pretext evidence convinced the fact finder that plaintiff acted properly, and thus established that the reason articulated by defendant did not exist. This, the Court held, met plaintiff's burden of going forward with the evidence, and that such proof would support a jury verdict for the plaintiff. The Court went on to hold, however, that disbelief of defendant's reason would not *require*, as a matter of law, a directed verdict for the plaintiff. As plaintiff has the ultimate burden of persuading the jury of defendant's proscribed motivation, even though the jury did not believe defendant's reason for dismissing the plaintiff, the jury could still conclude that plaintiff had not carried the burden of convincing them that defendant was motivated by plaintiff's class. Moreover, the fact finder may conclude that even though the articulated reason did not in fact exist, the decision-maker *believed* that the reason existed. This is sufficient to deny a judgment for the plaintiff. *Russell v. University of Toledo,* 537 F.3d 596 (6th Cir. 2008). However, proof that the inaccuracy of the articulated reason was obvious permits the fact finder to infer that the decision-maker did not *believe* that plaintiff committed the infractions. *Hernandez v. Spacelabs Medical, Inc.,* 343 F.3d 1107 (9th Cir. 2003).

Reeves v. Sanderson Plumbing Products, Inc., 530 U.S. 133 (2000), added a significant caveat. The reason given for plaintiff's discharge was "shoddy record keeping." Plaintiff countered with a showing that each of the alleged shortcomings either did not happen, or when there was a performance deficiency, it was the responsibility of other employees, not the plaintiff. The Court stated:

> [Such proof] is probative of intentional discrimination, and it may be quite persuasive. [However] this is not to say that such a showing * * * will *always be adequate* to sustain a jury's finding of liability. * * * If the circumstances show that the defendant gave the false explanation to conceal something other than discrimination, the inference of discrimination will be weak or nonexistent.

Thus, even if defendant's reason is totally discredited and no other legitimate reason is placed in evidence, a trial court could grant summary judgment to a perjury-committing defendant based on nothing more than judicial speculation that defendant harbored a secret, non-articulated reason.

B. INDIRECT EVIDENCE

A wide range of evidence may suggest that the actual motivation for defendant's action was other than the reason articulated. Each piece, standing alone, may not be sufficient to permit a jury verdict for plaintiff, but taken together may be adequate to carry plaintiff's burden of creating a genuine issue of fact. Some examples:

(1) Verbal

Oral or written comments by the decision-maker that indicate an animus against plaintiff's class, even if the animus expressed is not part of the decision-making process, will be admissible, and in some cases sufficiently probative to support a judgment for the plaintiff. *Reeves v. Sanderson Plumbing Products, Inc. supra;* See also Chapter 15.

(2) Dissimilar Treatment

In discipline cases evidence that the articulated reason was applied only to plaintiff and not to others who had committed "similar or even more serious violations" is strong evidence that the reason, even if it existed, was not the motivating factor. *St. Mary's Honor Center v. Hicks, supra.*

(3) Superiority

Significant disparity in performance or credentials between those of the plaintiff and favored workers of different classes can be part of a mosaic that could support a judgment for plaintiff. *Sutherland v. Mich. Dep't of Treasury,* 344 F.3d 603 (6th Cir. 2003). In *Ash v. Tyson Foods,* 546 U.S. 454 (2006), the lower court had excluded plaintiff's evidence of his superior qualifications on the grounds that to be admissible plaintiff's superiority to the favored person must be so great that it would "jump off the page and slap you in the face." The Court reversed, finding such a standard "unhelpful and imprecise," and suggested that evidence of significantly superior qualifications should be admitted, and could support a judgment for plaintiff, where plaintiff's performance or credentials were "of such weight and significance that no reasonable person in the exercise of impartial judgment could have chosen the candidate selected over the plaintiff."

Courts have held that when objective credentials of the candidates are similar and defendant makes a selection based on properly structured subjective criteria, this precludes minor objective differences in the candidates' credentials from creating an inference that the decision was improperly motivated. *Torgerson v. City of Rochester,* 643 F.3d 1031 (8th Cir. 2011) (uniformly applied standards for interviews. Each candidate awarded a numerical score. Interviewers explained scores). *Autry v. Fort Bend Indep. Sch. Dist.* 704 F.3d 344 (5th Cir. 2013), greatly expanded upon this rationale. The defendant school district created a new position of "support manager" with duties vaguely described as "a wide range of administrative oversight tasks relating to supervision, monitoring and quality control." The posted requirements for the position were a bachelor's degree or facilities management experience. Plaintiff, a black man, had been employed by the district for two years as "Operations Area Supervisor" and in this position managed the custodial staff at 16 schools, administered payroll, managed budget, and investigated accidents. For 11 years prior to that, plaintiff had been area manager for another school district. Plaintiff possessed a college degree in social work and had served 22 years in the U.S. Navy, receiving commendations for his "outstanding leadership." The white female applicant who was hired possessed only a high school diploma and had been previously employed as an "escrow coordinator" for a title insurance company. Further support for plaintiff's claim of race discrimination was a comment made to plaintiff by a member of the hiring committee that if President Obama is elected "they're going to have to take the Statute of Liberty and put a piece of fried chicken in his hand." Fifteen applicants had been interviewed by a selection committee. Four finalist were selected by the committee supposedly based on consideration of "credentials" and their unstructured impressions of the candidates' performances in their interviews. Four finalists, which included the plaintiff, were placed in rank order. The director selected the white female applicant who had received the highest committee ranking. The trial court held that no reasonable jury could find race, sex, or age discrimination, and granted summary judgment to the defendant. Notwithstanding *Ash v. Tyson Foods, supra,* directives as to the weight courts should give to superior credentials, the Fifth Circuit affirmed.

(4) "Me Too"

Suspicious discriminatory treatment against others of plaintiff's class might suggest an animus toward the class that may have influenced the adverse action against plaintiff. Such "me too" evidence of discrimination against third parties raises dangers that a trial court must confront: (1) straying from the issue to collaterally litigate whether non-parties were in fact victims of illegal discrimination, which could lead to, (2) undue complexity that could confuse the jury, and (3) the possibility that the jury would place undue weight on such evidence by concluding that defendant was a "bad person" who should be punished.

On these grounds the trial court in *Sprint/United Mgt. Co. v. Mendelsohn,* 552 U.S. 379 (2008), applied a *per se* rule that excluded from jury consideration all such "me too" evidence. The Court reversed holding that there is no absolute rule either prohibiting or requiring admission of the employer's collateral acts. Trial courts must exercise case-by-case discretion balancing the problems of jury confusion against the probative value of such evidence. *Compare: Mendelsohn v. United/Sprint Mgt. Co.,* 402 Fed. Appx. 337 (10th Cir. 2010), which on remand affirmed the trial court's exercise of discretion to exclude the proffered evidence, with *Bennett v. Nucor Corp.,* 656 F.3d 802 (8th Cir. 2011), which affirmed trial court's admission into evidence EEOC charges filed by workers other than plaintiff, letters of complaint to the EEOC regarding defendant, and affidavits by non-parties asserting discrimination that were gathered in anticipation of plaintiff's litigation.

(5) Inconsistency

Changing, inconsistent, or contradictory reasons can support a judgment for plaintiff. In *Jones v. Nat. Am. Univ.,* 608 F.3d 1039 (8th Cir.2010), defendant's response to the EEOC charge was poor "performance." At trial defendant introduced no evidence of plaintiff's performance deficiencies, but asserted plaintiff's "lack of experience." In light of plaintiff's rebuttal evidence that the person favored also lacked relevant experience, defendant's inconsistency permitted the fact finder to conclude that defendant was improperly motivated. Failure of defendant in plaintiff's case to follow procedures followed in prior cases was some evidence of proscribed motive. *Rahlf v. Mo–Tech Corp. Inc.*, 642 F.3d 633 (8th Cir. 2011). Establishing ever increasing performance goals, "moving targets" for acceptable conduct, or adopting irrationally restrictive rules suggests that the goals or rules are being manipulated and used as a pretext to get rid of certain employees. *Willnerd v. First Nat. Neb. Inc.*, 558 F.3d 770 (8th Cir. 2009).

(6) "Lost" Evidence, Lack of Candor

Defendant's inability to produce documentation that might reflect on the credibility of defendant's articulated reason, particularly if the "missing records" are in violation of EEOC rules requiring their retention or if the relevant records were destroyed in violation of normal company policy, is evidence of pretext. *Talavera v. Shah*, 638 F.3d 303 (D.C.Cir. 2011). Evasiveness in giving testimony and general lack of truthfulness and candor on collateral matters can cast doubt as to the truthfulness of the articulated reason. *Applebaum v. Milwaukee Metro. Sewerage Dist.*, 340 F.3d 573 (7th Cir. 2003).

(7) Numbers

Statistical evidence of race or sex imbalances in the employer's workforce or in its hiring or dismissal outcomes that are "significant" in that they mathematically eliminate chance as an hypothesis to explain the difference, coupled with plaintiff's prima facie showing can support, if not require, a finding of illegal motivation. *Int'l Br'hd of Teamsters v. United States,* 431 U.S. 324 (1977). *See, infra,* Chapter 17. Inconclusive, but nonetheless suspicious, statistical patterns between races, sexes, or age groups in hiring or dismissal of workers often are admitted, and, together with other evidence, can support a judgment for the plaintiff. *Jackson v. Watkins,* 619 F.3d 463 (5th Cir. 2010).

Conversely, while a statistically balanced workforce or balanced outcomes in hiring or in laying off workers cannot be a substitute for defendant articulating a reason for its disparate treatment of plaintiff, defendant's favorable statistical evidence can support its position that its articulated reason was properly motivated. *Rivera–Aponte v. Restaurant Metropol #3,* 338 F.3d 9 (1st Cir. 2003).

(8) "Alternatives?"

If plaintiff establishes that defendant should have been aware of the discriminatory effect of its articulated reason and elected to apply it notwithstanding the existence of lesser discriminatory alternatives, this evidence suggests that the device was a disguise for a proscribed animus. *Albemarle Paper Co. v. Moody,* 422 U.S. 405 (1975). For example, defendant's alleged reliance on a subjective judgment, rather than on available objective measures that would favor the plaintiff can suggest that the asserted subjective judgment was a handy pretext.

16.08: THE END: PLAINTIFF'S BURDEN OF PROOF

A. GENERALLY

If the trial court concludes that in its totality the evidence is sufficient to *support* a verdict for either party, the trial court must submit the case for resolution by the jury with the instruction that the burden is on plaintiff to establish by a preponderance of the evidence that defendant was motivated by a factor proscribed by the statutes. *U.S. Postal Serv. Bd. of Governors v. Aikens,* 460 U.S. 711 (1983). The *McDonnell Douglas* model of shifting evidentiary burdens need not be included in the instruction. Indeed, to do so could unduly confuse the jury as to plaintiff's ultimate risk of non-persuasion. The finding by the jury on the issue of defendant's motivation is one of fact, and, as such, is subjected to very limited review on appeal. *Anderson v. City of Bessemer City,* 470 U.S. 564 (1985).

B. MIXED MOTIVES: THE *PRICE WATERHOUSE* SOLUTION

While some employer decisions may be motivated by a single mental attitude (either legal or illegal), fact finders often are faced with the possibility that a decision maker may have had two motives working simultaneously, one legitimate and one illegitimate, presenting a metaphysical issue of which attitude "caused" the challenged action. *Price Waterhouse v. Hopkins,* 490 U.S. 228 (1989), directed how trial courts should address such situations. Plaintiff presented direct verbal evidence that sexual stereotyping played a role in her being denied a promotion. The employer countered with uncontested evidence that legitimate factors such as plaintiff's abusive treatment of her co-workers, also played a role in the decision. The direct evidence spoken by the decision-makers established that sex played at least *a* motivating part in the employment decision, making the employer presumptively liable. However, the Court held that "defendant may avoid this *liability* by proving by a preponderance of the evidence that it would have made the same decision had it not taken plaintiff's [protected class] into account."

C. TITLE VII AMENDMENTS AND *DESERT PALACE*

The 1991 Amendments to Title VII modified *Price Waterhouse* by providing:

> An unlawful employment practice is established when the complaining party demonstrates that race, color, religion, sex, or national origin was *a* motivating factor for any employment practice, even though other factors also motivated the practice. 42 U.S.C. 2000e–2(m).

The remedies sections of Title VII also were amended:

> On a claim in which an individual proves a violation under [42 U.S.C. 2000e–2(m) and a [defendant] demonstrates that [defendant] would have taken the same action in the

absence of the impermissible motivating factor the court—

(i) may grant declaratory * * * [and] injunctive relief * * * attorneys' fees and costs [of the plaintiff] * * * [but]

(ii) shall not award damages, or issue an order requiring any admission, reinstatement, hiring, promotion, or payment [of back wages]. 42 U.S.C. 2000e–4(g)(2)(B).

Thus, liability under section 703 of Title VII is established when plaintiff convinces the jury that "a" motive of defendant was illegitimate. If defendant, in turn, convinces the jury that it would have made the same decision on legitimate grounds, this does not negate defendant's liability, but limits the successful plaintiff's remedies to declaratory relief and an award of attorneys' fees and costs.

Desert Palace, Inc. v. Costa, 539 U.S. 90 (2003), involved a plaintiff who, unlike the plaintiff in *Price Waterhouse, supra,* presented no direct, verbal evidence of defendant's illegal motivation. Plaintiff Costa's proof followed the *McDonnell Douglas* model of inferences drawn from circumstances which indicated that defendant's proffered reason for her discharge was pretext. Defendant argued that even if one of its motives was illegitimate, it would have made the same decision based on the articulated reason. The trial court gave the jury an instruction paraphrasing the 1991 Amendments.

If you find that plaintiff's sex was a motivating factor in the defendant's treatment of the plaintiff, plaintiff is entitled to your verdict, even if you find that the defendant's conduct was also motivated by a lawful reason. If you find that defendant's treatment was motivated by both gender and lawful reasons * * * [t]he plaintiff is entitled to damages unless defendant proves by a preponderance of the evidence that the defendant would have treated plaintiff similarly even if the plaintiff's gender had played no role in the employment decision.

On appeal defendant argued that such an instruction should be given only where plaintiff established illegal motive through "direct" verbal evidence, and was not appropriate when illegal motive had to be established indirectly through circumstantial evidence. Where plaintiff's proof of motive required the jury to draw inferences, defendant argued, plaintiff should be required to carry a heavier burden and prove that the illegal considerations in fact were the cause for the disparate treatment of plaintiff. The Court rejected defendant's argument, and held that the trial court's instruction was proper. The literal language of the Title VII Amendments must be applied to all forms of evidence, circumstantial as well as direct.

D. ADEA AND *GROSS*

The 1991 Amendment noted above did not specifically amend the "because of" language in the ADEA or ADA. This congressional silence led the Court in *Gross v. FBL Financial Services, Inc.,* 557 U.S. 167 (2009), to conclude that the Amendments had no application to the ADEA. 29 U.S.C. 623(a).

Moreover, the Court rejected an interpretation of the "because of" language in the ADEA adopted in *Price Waterhouse v. Hopkins, supra,* to the effect that when plaintiff proved that a proscribed factor was "a" motivating factor, defendant would be liable unless defendant carried a burden of proving that it would have made the same decision on legitimate grounds. Adopting the rationale of the *Price Waterhouse* dissent, *Gross* held that the ADEA, 29 U.S.C. 623(a), imposed on plaintiff the full burden of convincing the jury that that age had the "determinative influence on the outcome." That is, had it not been plaintiff's age, defendant would not have discriminated against her. Proving that "but for" the discriminatory motive the employer would not have discriminated against the plaintiff does not require plaintiff to prove that plaintiff's age was defendant's sole or only motivation. *Ponce v. Billington,* 679 F.3d 840 (D.C.Cir. 2012).

E. ADA

Some pre-*Gross* courts concluded that the roots of the ADA in the Rehabilitation Act of 1973, required plaintiffs to prove that the discrimination which they suffered would not have happened had it not been for their physical or mental impairment. *Hedrick v. Western Reserve* Syst., 355 F.3d 444 (6th Cir. 2004). Others followed the shifting burden analysis of *Price Waterhouse. Parker v. Columbia Picture Indus.,* 204 F.3d 326 (2d Cir. 2000).

University of Texas, S.W. Medical Ctr. v. Nassar, ___ U.S. ___, 133 S.Ct. 2517 (2013), strongly suggests that plaintiff's burden under the ADA will be to establish that plaintiff's disability had a "determinative influence on the outcome;" that had it not been plaintiff's disability, defendant would not have discriminated against her. Both *Gross* and *Nassar* held that the 1991 causation amendment to Title VII ("a motivating factor") was limited to suits brought under section 703 of Title VII. Both cases held that the "because of" causation language found in the ADEA (*Gross*) and in the retaliation provisions in Title VII, section 704, (*Nassar*) require proof of "but for" causation, and specifically held that *Price Waterhouse* had no application to statutory schemes which require plaintiff to prove that discrimination was "because of" protected status or actions. As the ADA utilizes the "because of" language found in both the ADA and Title VII, section 704, it would seem that plaintiff's burden under the ADA would be to establish "causation in fact," the same as is required under the ADEA and section 704 of Title VII. *See also, infra,* 27.04 B.

F. RECONSTRUCTION ERA CIVIL RIGHTS ACTS

42 U.S.C. 1981, which does not use the phrase "because of," nonetheless has been construed to proscribe discrimination that is *motivated* by plaintiff's race. Prior to *Gross* a few courts had held that the 1991 Amendments addressing causation implicitly applied to 1981 actions, *Metoyer v. Chassman,* 504 F.3d 919 (9th Cir. 2007), an analysis that may have been undercut by *Gross* which limited the causation amendment to Title VII. Other courts had used the shifting burden approach of *Price Waterhouse,* which had also been applied to

claims of race discrimination under the Constitution
(42 U.S.C. 1983). *See, Mt. Healthy City Bd. of Educ.
v. Doyle,* 429 U.S. 274 (1977). *Mabra v. United Food
Workers, Local 1996,* 176 F.3d 1357 (11th Cir. 1999).
*University of Texas S.W. Medical Ctr v. Nassar,
supra,* in construing the retaliation provisions of
Title VII, distinguished these holdings construing
1981 as not being based the "because of" causation
language found in the core statutes, and by this may
have implicitly affirmed the use of the *Price
Waterhouse* shifting burden analysis where statutes
do no specifically use "because of" language.

G. USERRA

USERRA which prohibits discrimination based on
one's military service, utilizes language that differs
from Title VII and the ADEA. Courts have
interpreted this language to reach an outcome
similar to *Price Waterhouse* and *Mt. Healthy v.
Doyle, supra. Lisdahl v. Mayo Foundation,* 633 F.3d
712 (8th Cir. 2011), found that the different wording
of USERRA made the *Gross* rationale inapplicable.

H. STATE LAW

State courts interpreting "because of" language in
their respective state statutes have tended to apply
the shifting burdens analysis of *Price Waterhouse.*
Presumably, *Gross's* "but for" interpretation of the
federal ADEA will have no impact on these state
decisions. *See, Tussig v. Des Moines Ind. Comm.
Sch. Dist.,* 639 F.3d 507 (8th Cir. 2011).

CHAPTER 17

PROVING MOTIVE WITH STATISTICS SYSTEMIC "PATTERN OR PRACTICE" DISCRIMINATION

17.01: GENERAL FRAMEWORK: THE *TEAMSTERS'* MODEL

A. 703(J)

In *Int'l Br'hd of Teamsters v. United States,* 431 U.S. 324 (1977), the government alleged a "pattern or practice" of illegally motivated hiring practices. The government's proof centered upon data comparing the black and Hispanics populations nationwide and in specific geographic areas with the number of minority "line," or long haul, truck drivers currently employed by defendants. Defendants' first defense was the proviso in Title VII, 42 U.S.C. 2000e–2(j), that prohibits "preferential treatment" based solely upon comparisons between the number of persons in protected class in the available labor pool with the number of such persons in the employer's work force. The Court held that the proviso was inapplicable. The government was not "requiring" a racial balance or the grant of "preferential treatment," but relying on statistical methodology to establish liability. "[I]mbalance is often a telltale sign of purposeful discrimination." Moreover, the Court noted that plaintiff did not rely on "statistics alone" but presented other evidence of purposeful discrimination.

B. LIABILITY: *TEAMSTERS*,

The working premise of *Teamsters, supra,* was: "[A]bsent explanation, it is ordinarily expected that nondiscriminatory hiring practices will, in time, result in a work force more or less representative of the population in the community from which employees are hired." Where the employer's workforce is not "representative of the population in the community" a proper inference is that the imbalance is produced by a pattern of improper motivation.

Defendants were nation-wide employers and the union representing their employees. Plaintiff's data indisputably demonstrated that nationally, only 0.4% of defendants' "line" truck drivers were black and 0.3% Hispanic. Plaintiffs also presented evidence that defendants' work force in certain geographic areas had virtually no black "line" drivers even though in some of the surrounding communities 50% of the population was black. This demonstration of a glaring workforce imbalance, the Court held, was sufficient to establish defendants' liability unless defendants presented evidence that undermined the reliability of plaintiff's showing. The Court cautioned "that statistics are not irrefutable; they come in infinite variety and, like any other kind of evidence, they may be rebutted." In this case, however, defendants presented no effective rebuttal evidence.

The significance of *Teamsters* is the principle that when statistical data makes it "highly unlikely" that an observed imbalance in an employer's workforce occurred by chance, a court may conclude that it is likely that the result occurred by design. This assumption will result in a judgment for plaintiff unless defendant carries a burden of either demonstrating a neutral explanation for the observed disparity or by presenting a statistically sound alternative observation that shows no meaningful "imbalance." Defendants' critique that plaintiff's "snapshot" of the employer's current work force lacked precision and that plaintiff had failed to "fine tune" the demographic comparisons did not undermine the inference of improper motivation drawn from the "glaring absence of minority line drivers."

C. REMEDY

A finding that defendant engaged in a "pattern or practice" of illegal hiring requires a process to determine which individuals were actual victims of defendant's hiring practices. Defendants argued that they needed to provide a remedy only for those individuals who could establish a prima facie showing of illegal motivation along the *McDonnell–Douglas* model that required plaintiff to demonstrate each alleged victim applied for an existing vacancy they were qualified to fill and that their application was rejected. *Teamsters* held, however, that as illegal motivation had already been established by plaintiff's statistical proof, individual claimants need only demonstrate that they had either applied for a position or that they were deterred from actually applying because of defendant's known discriminatory practices.

Teamsters suggests that proof establishing that the individual was an "applicant" shifts the burden to the defendant to prove proving that each "applicant" was rejected for a legitimate reason such as lack of a vacancy or the claimant's lack of qualifications, *United States v. City of N.Y,* 717 F.3d 72 (2d Cir. 2013), indicated, however, that defendant's burden at this juncture is not one of proving a legitimate motive, but one of presenting evidence that the individual applicant was denied the position for a "legitimate, non-discriminatory reason" of sufficient strength to support a jury finding in favor of defendant. Upon such an evidentiary presentation by defendant the burden shifts to plaintiff to prove that the reason articulated by defendant was a pretext, thus resorting to the *McDonnell Douglas* model of proof. *Supra,* 16.01–16.07.

17.02: GENERAL PRINCIPLES OF STATISTICAL PROOF

Hazelwood School Dist. v. United States, 433 U.S. 299 (1977), a companion to *Teamsters,* addressed a less dramatic underrepresentation of black employees, to which the Court refined and applied the basic premise of *Teamsters*. To determine whether defendant's work force failed to be representative of the population, *Hazelwood* endorsed use of the statistical technique known as the "rule of exclusion" or "standard deviation" analysis.

The "rule of exclusion" states in mathematical terms the probability that an observed outcome (the employer's actual work force or recent hiring results) was the product of random or chance selection. It involves four steps: (1) identifying the expected outcome, (2) observing the actual outcome, (3) determining the raw difference between expected and actual outcomes, and (4) applying mathematical formulae to calculate the probabilities that the difference between expected and observed outcomes could have been produced randomly.

17.03: "EXPECTED" OUTCOMES

A. DEFINING AND REFINING GEOGRAPHIC BOUNDARIES

Determining an "expected outcome," or identifying "the community from which employees are hired," was the primary issue in *Hazelwood*. The Court considered three possibilities: (1) the school district where defendant was located, that is, the town of Hazelwood, a suburban community of the greater St. Louis, Missouri metro area, (2) St. Louis county, *excluding* the city of St. Louis, or (3) the entire metro area that *included* both the city and county of St. Louis. The parties appeared to accept that the town of Hazelwood was too narrow a boundary in that many of defendant's teachers lived outside of Hazelwood. The choice was basing an expected outcome on the racial composition of the county, which excluded the city of St. Louis, or upon the racial composition of the entire metro area, that included St. Louis. This choice was critical in that 15.4% of the teachers in the metropolitan area were black while only 5.7% of the teachers residing in the county, that *excluded* St. Louis, were black.

Plaintiff argued that because defendant hired teachers from throughout the metro area, the number of black teachers at Hazelwood should be compared to the number of black teachers in the broad St. Louis metro area. Defendant countered that St. Louis city should be excluded from any expected outcomes in Hazelwood because of an alleged lack of interest by black teachers who lived in the city to commute to the suburban area and that the city of St. Louis recruited its new teachers from predominately black colleges located in the city coupled with vigorous efforts by the city to recruit and retain minority teachers.

The Court explained the critical importance of which population should set the expected outcome focusing on the recent hiring experience of defendant Hazelwood which had been that 3.7% of all newly hired teachers were black.

> [T]he disparity between 3.7% (the percentage of Negro teachers [recently hired] by Hazelwood) and the 5.7% [Negro teachers residing in the County] may be sufficiently small to weaken the Government's proof, while the disparity between 3.7% and 15.4% [Negro teachers residing in the metro area including St. Louis] may be sufficiently large to reinforce it.

The Court remanded the case for a determination of "which of the two figures * * * provides the most accurate basis for comparison to the hiring figures at Hazelwood."

As *Hazelwood* illustrates, identifying which community most accurately reflects the "community from which employees are hired" can be as difficult as it is imprecise. For example, *EEOC v. Olson's Dairy Queens,* 989 F.2d 165 (5th Cir. 1993), involved food service jobs at defendant's ice cream shops which were located throughout the greater Houston, Texas metropolitan area. Plaintiff presented census data showing that 25% of all food service and preparation workers in the greater Houston area were black compared to defendant's total workforce which was only 8% black. Defendant countered with evidence focusing on individual shops in different neighborhoods, and demonstrated that 1/2 of the employees in its shops lived within one mile of the shop, and 80% of them lived within three miles, coupled with expert analysis that "most persons willing to accept positions are young, seeking part-time employment, and residing within a very short distance." Individual shops had a fair racial composition when compared to the neighborhood population in which each shop was located. This was sufficient to refute plaintiff's broad metro-wide basis for a comparison.

B. REFINING THE POPULATION

A comparison of the percentage of minorities or women in the employer's work force with the percentage in the area labor market or general population is appropriate in analyzing jobs that require no special expertise. * * * When a job requires special training, however, the comparison should be with those in the labor force who possess the relevant qualifications. *Johnson v. Santa Clara County,* 480 U.S. 616 (1987).

Teamsters involved line truck drivers. The Court accepted unrefined general population data because it viewed the ability to drive a large truck as "one that many persons possess or could readily acquire." Thus, the Court did not require plaintiff to present evidence of how many black and Hispanic *truck drivers* resided in the geographic areas where defendants hired its drivers. By contrast, *Hazelwood* involved school teachers. To be qualified as a teacher requires advanced education and state certification. Thus, it would not have been appropriate to rely upon general, unrefined population data as to the percentage of black *persons* residing in the geographic area. Accordingly, the parties agreed that the relevant data must focus on the percentage of black *teachers* in the relevant geographic area.

If plaintiff's data is refined to meet this threshold level, *possible* further refinement, such as requiring plaintiff also account for age, health, or interests, does not undermine the presumption flowing from plaintiff's data. *Teamsters, supra.* Defendant may, however, present *actual evidence* that additional factors going beyond basic qualifications for the position create a different expected outcome. For example, in *EEOC v. Sears, Roebuck & Co.,* 839

F.2d 302 (7th Cir. 1988), plaintiff's evidence demonstrated statistically significant underrepresentation of women in certain sales positions that required no more than a skill "already possessed or which could be readily acquired." Plaintiff's data focused on the relatively large number of women employees in departments which were compensated by a fixed salary, comparing this number to the small number of women in the departments which received higher pay based on commissions on the sales made. Defendant countered with expert testimony that women as a class lacked interest in holding uncertain, competitive, and tension-filled positions. The court affirmed a trial court conclusion that such a showing by defendant made any apparent underrepresentation of women illusory. Defendant in this case did more than point out possible flaws in plaintiff's data, but presented substantial, albeit contested, evidence that a difference in interests between males and females in such jobs rendered plaintiff's comparison based on a general population unreliable.

17.04: COMPETING OUTCOMES

Teamsters involved an observation of static "snapshots" that disclosed the number of actual minority line drivers. Recent hiring percentages of the employer, as presented in *Hazelwood,* could be another observed outcome. *Teamsters* considered defendants' recent hiring experience which disclosed some increase in hiring minorities, but this observation, the Court held, was statistically meaningless in light of the "inexorable zero" of minorities disclosed by the snapshot of the employer's total workforce.

Hazelwood, too, observed a static "snapshot" of the employer's *total current* work force, which was 1.8% black, *but also* the employer's *recent hiring experiences* which disclosed that 3.7% of the employer's new hires were black. The Court indicated that if the two outcomes presented different pictures, recent hiring data was the more probative of defendant's recent motivation.

17.05: MEASURING THE DIFFERENCE FOR "SIGNIFICANCE"

Once the expected and observed outcomes are calculated and the difference noted, it must be determined whether the difference between expected and observed outcomes is great enough to eliminate chance as an explanation for the difference. In most cases, as demonstrated by *Hazelwood,* the difference is not so great that chance intuitively can be eliminated. The "rule of exclusion," endorsed by *Hazelwood,* measures the mathematical significance of differences. It is based on an assumption known as the "null hypothesis." The "null hypothesis" is that ordinarily there will be no difference between "observed" and "actual" outcomes (the difference should be "null"). The person challenging the "null hypothesis" has the burden of disproving the hypothesis.

The "null hypothesis" and expected outcome can be visualized by using a deck of standard playing cards. Hypothetically, if one were to draw a single card from a fairly shuffled deck there would be a 50% chance of drawing a red card and a 25% chance of drawing a card of the diamond suit. If this single draw were repeated 100 times with the deck being reshuffled after each draw the expected, or most likely outcome would be 50 red cards consisting of 25 diamonds, 25 hearts, and 50 black cards consisting of 25 clubs and 25 spades.

"Observed outcome" is accomplished by actually drawing a single card from the reshuffled deck, doing it 100 times, and observing the actual result, which, for example, might be 53 black cards consisting of 25 spades and 28 clubs, and 47 red cards, consisting of 24 diamonds and 23 hearts. If this 100 card draw were repeated again the outcome could well be 49 black cards consisting of 27 spades and 22 clubs and 51 red cards consisting of 28 diamonds and 23 hearts. Repeated multiple times would produce varying outcomes. Mathematicians have concluded that when random choice is operating most outcomes will cluster near the expected outcome of equal distribution forming, if plotted, a downward bell shaped curve, becoming increasingly wider as the observed and plotted outcomes move away from the expected outcome.

While the most common or "expected" outcome is of equal distribution, less than an exact correlation between the actually observed and the expected outcomes is common and has been the product of fair and random selection. The null hypothesis of possible random selection producing the observed outcome would not be disproved by small, regularly observed differences. As the gap between observed and expected outcomes grows, the probability that the outcome was produced by chance is reduced, ultimately to where the difference becomes "highly unlikely." At this point the "null hypothesis" of random selection has been disproved.

Relatively simple formulae can be applied to the data to determine the number of "standard deviations" between the observed and expected outcome, and states the likelihood that the particular observed outcome was a product of chance in terms of a "confidence level."[1]

Mathematicians have determined that 68.2% of all randomly produced observed outcomes will come within one standard deviation on either side of the expected outcome, and over 95% of all observed randomly produced outcomes will come within 2 standard deviations of the expected outcome. While at 2 standard deviations there is only a 5% chance that the observed outcome was a product of chance, statisticians agree that chance still remains possible, albeit remote, and thus the "null hypothesis" of a random selection has not been disproved. Statisticians are "confident," however,

---

[1] The formula for calculating the standard deviation is the square root of $(P)(1 - P)n$. P= the probability of selecting a minority. (1 minus P) = probability of not selecting a minority. n = the total number of selections. The precise number of standard deviations by which a particular outcome varies from the expected outcome can be found in standard statistical tables, or can be calculated to determine a "Z" score, which takes the observed outcomes minus the number of selections, multiplied by the probability of selecting a minority, and dividing the result by the number of standard deviations.

that the "null hypothesis" of random selection has been disproved at a "confidence level" of 0.01 which is reached at 2.57 standard deviations. At this point chance could explain the outcome in only one experience out of 100. Such a disparity is deemed to have statistical "significance."

Hazelwood illustrated and explained:

If the 15.4% figure [metro area black teachers] is taken as a basis of comparison, the expected number of Negro teachers hired by Hazelwood would be 43 [rather than the 10 hired], a figure of more than five standard deviations. * * * A fluctuation of more than two or three standard deviations would undercut the hypothesis that decisions were being made randomly. * * * If, however, the 5.7% area wide figure is used, the expected number of Negro teachers hired would be roughly 16, less than two standard deviations from the observed number of 10 [thus suggesting that random choice could explain the observed outcome].

Where there are few experiences, a relatively large difference in observed and expected outcomes will be necessary to eliminate chance as an explanation for the outcome. For example, in *Ortega v. Safeway Stores,* 943 F.2d 1230 (10th Cir. 1991), a total of 21 employees were in the pool eligible for reassignment, 8 male and 13 female. Seven of the 8 male employees were reassigned. Only 2 of the 13 females were reassigned. Nonetheless, the small numbers of observed outcomes was inadequate to disprove the null hypothesis that each case was not a product of random choice or unique special circumstances. A minor shift in these raw numbers would have produced a dramatic shift in the percentages.

17.06: EMPLOYER RESPONSES

Plaintiff's disproving the null hypothesis does not itself prove illegal motivation. It only eliminates chance as a viable explanation for observed disparities, creating a presumption of improper motive. Defendant can refute this presumption by explaining in neutral terms how the significant disparity occurred. Defendant's assertion that in making each individual hiring decision, it simply hired the "best" applicant, is inadequate to refute plaintiff's showing of statistically significant work force underrepresentation. This inadequacy can be illustrated, again, by using standard playing cards.

Assume several decks of shuffled cards. Each deck represents the "population" of potential applicants. Assume a vacancy is to be filled. Hypothetically, randomly draw four cards from one deck. The drawn cards represent four applicants. The highest card of the four reflects the "best" candidate among the applicants, and the "best" candidate is "hired." Repeat the process with a new, reshuffled deck of cards. A "vacancy" occurs. Four "applicants" are randomly drawn, and the highest card drawn is hired as being the "best" of the four candidates. After repeated "hires," the expected outcome would be the same number of red and black "hires." A statistically significant difference in red or black hires indicates that something other than random

choice produced the outcome in which supposedly
the "best" applicant was selected. The extent that
the actual observed "hires" differs from the expected
equal outcome can be analyzed through a variation
on the "rule of exclusion." *See, Whitacre v. Davey,*
890 F.2d 1168 (D.C.Cir. 1989).

However, where an employer offers two or more
specific explanations for each hiring decision, such
as differences in each case in education and past
experience of the applicants, the employer has
"explained" in legitimate terms how the disparate
outcome might have been produced. In such cases
mathematically   disproving   chance   as   an
explanation   for   the   outcome   is   relatively
meaningless. *Coble v. Hot Springs School Dist. No.
6,* 682 F.2d 721 (8th Cir. 1982).

Nevertheless, these asserted multiple possible
reasons for making individual decisions can be
discounted by use of an extremely complex
calculation known as "multiple regression analysis."
Multiple regression relies on what is known as
"matching pairs." Assume two applicants with
similar education. One is male and the other is
female. The female applicant is hired. Repeat this
comparison in all of the hiring decisions. If the data
demonstrate   that   sex,   rather   than   relative
education, played a decisive role in decision-making,
education can be eliminated as a viable explanation.
This matching is applied to each of the factors that
the employer allegedly utilized. If the analyzed data
eliminates each factor as an viable explanation, it
leaves only class membership as a constant and
plausible conclusion. Plaintiff will have established

an inference of illegal motivation. *Bazemore v. Friday,* 478 U.S. 385 (1986).

If plaintiff's regression study is sufficient to allow a fact finder to conclude from the calculation that illegal motivation played a decisive role, the burden is upon the defendant to present actual evidence that it used other variables which, in fact, played significant roles in its decision-making. That plaintiff's regression study fails to include all of the *possible* variables that an employer *might have used* goes to the weight of plaintiff's evidence, not to its admissibility. *Id.*

Multiple regression requires a relatively large number of actual experiences to produce significant results and demands complex, computer-driven calculations.

17.07: FORCE REDUCTIONS

When an employer systematically reduces its workforce because of economic considerations, simple comparisons between the number of persons of one class laid off compared to the number of persons of other classes who were retained have little probative value. The interplay of many variables commonly influence each lay off decision (*e.g.,* relative salary, particular skills, ability to undertake new or different skills, nature of the job duties remaining or as realigned, and work record, which itself can include a number of factors such as attendance, performance reviews, reprimands, awards, and even the personal relationship with the decision-maker). Moreover, decisions often are made by different supervisors using varying standards or take place over a period of time that present different demands, all of which makes it very difficult, if not impossible, even for multiple regression analysis to produce significant results. *Pottenger v. Potlatch Corp.,* 329 F.3d 740 (9th Cir. 2009).

17.08: STATISTICS IN INDIVIDUAL DISPARATE TREATMENT CASES

Most cases relying on statistical disparities are brought by the government as a "pattern or practice" claim or by private parties as class actions under Rule 23, Fed. R. Civ. Proc. Some authority has indicated that even when a single plaintiff alleges individual disparate treatment, illegal motive can be established through a statistical showing. *Davis v. Califano,* 613 F.2d 957 (D.C.Cir. 1979). However, to avoid the implications of Title VII, 42 U.S.C. 2000e–2(j), *Teamsters* suggested that liability cannot be based "solely" on an employer's imbalanced work force, and indicated that plaintiff satisfied its burden by also presenting some evidence of individual discrimination. Thus, it would seem that a non-class plaintiff must establish a prima facie showing of improper motive either through direct, verbal, or circumstantial evidence using the *McDonnell Douglas* model. Defendant then articulates a reason for its disparate treatment of plaintiff. At this point plaintiff may use statistical proof to demonstrate the "pretext" of defendant's articulated reason. *Bacon v. Honda of America Mfg. Co.,* 370 F.3d 565 (6th Cir. 2004).

CHAPTER 18

DISPARATE IMPACT LIABILITY

18.01: THE MODEL

The concept of liability based on unjustified disparate impact was introduced in **Chapter 5.06(b).** The process of establishing liability based on impact involves two steps: (1) Plaintiff must prove that an identified selection device or system has an impact on plaintiff's class that is "adverse." (2) If plaintiff establishes adverse impact, the burden of proof shifts to defendant. Under Title VII and the ADA defendant must prove that the challenged device is "job related" and "consistent with business necessity." Under the ADEA defendant's burden is to prove that the challenged device is a "reasonable factor other than age." The impact theory of liability has not been extended to claims of discrimination arising under the Constitution or 42 U.S.C. 1981. *General Bld. Contractors Ass'n v. Pena,* 458 U.S. 375 (1982).

18.02: PLAINTIFF'S BURDEN: PROVING DISPARATE IMPACT

A. IDENTIFY A SELECTION DEVICE

Plaintiff first must identify with particularity the employment practice being challenged. In *Griggs v. Duke Power Co.,* 401 U.S. 424 (1971), plaintiff identified and challenged the requirement that employees must have a high school diploma and pass an employer administered objective test. *Dothard v. Rawlinson,* 433 U.S. 321 (1977), involved a focused challenge to the employer's minimum height and weight standard. In *Wards Cove Packing v. Atonio,* 490 U.S. 642 (1989), however, plaintiffs' evidence demonstrated only that a high percentage of nonwhite workers held low paying cannery jobs compared to a low percentage of minority workers in higher paying office jobs. As no identified device was being challenged, only the outcome, plaintiffs failed to establish impact-based liability. In *New York City Transit Auth. v. Beazer,* 440 U.S. 568 (1979), plaintiff challenged under Title VII an employer rule denying employment to persons enrolled in methadone-based drug rehabilitation programs. Plaintiff established that 81% of the employees referred to the employer's medical director for possible *drug abuse* were minority employees. The Court held that as defendant's *drug abuse* referral practice was not being challenged, data regarding such referrals failed to address the percentage of workers affected by the challenged *methadone-maintenance* policy.

B. DEMONSTRATE THAT THE DEVICE "CAUSED" A RESULT

Plaintiff must demonstrate that the identified device caused, or necessarily would cause, an adverse impact on a protected class. Gross statistical disparity between the percentage of males and females in a job category might demonstrate the employer's past motivation, but such data does not establish that the particular hiring practices of the employer *caused* the observed result. *EEOC v. Joe's Stone Crab, Inc.,* 222 F.3d 1263 (11th Cir. 2000). Similarly, challenging a policy of laying off higher paid workers on the grounds that the policy had an adverse impact on older workers cannot succeed by a simple showing that older workers were laid off at a higher rate than younger workers, absent proof of a causal relationship between workers' wages and their the ages. *Allen v. Highlands Hosp. Corp.,* 545 F.3d 387 (6th Cir. 2008). Similarly, use of an informal, word-of-mouth recruiting system will not be assumed to have produced an observed racial imbalance in an employer's work force. *Holder v. City of Raleigh,* 867 F.2d 823 (4th Cir. 1989).

There are two approaches to proving that the identified hiring device is causing an adverse impact on a protected class: (1) applicant pool data, and (2) applicant flow data.

(1) Applicant pool proof

Applicant pool analysis examines the relative percentages of persons, by class, in a pool of *potential* applicants (the "pool") who possess the required criteria. This data often is drawn from census or official statistical information. When the data show that a significantly higher percentage of one class lacks the qualifying criterion, courts *assume* that this employer's use of the challenged device has an adverse impact on employment opportunities of that class. Pool analysis is commonly used to measure the impact of required objective credentials, such as education levels (degrees, diplomas, etc.) and physical requirements, such as height and weight minima. In *Griggs v. Duke Power Co., supra,* census data from the state of North Carolina, where the employer was located, disclosed that 34% of white males had diplomas compared to 12% of black males. This difference was sufficient to hold, as a matter of law, that at this employer the requirement of a high school diploma as a condition of employment had an adverse impact on blacks.

Griggs also analyzed for impact the employer's requirement of a passing score on a standardized, pen-and-paper general intelligence test. EEOC data of a study involving *similar* tests disclosed that the percentage of whites who had passed such tests was 10 times higher than the passage rate of blacks. This was sufficient to support a finding that the use of a comparable test to select workers necessarily had an adverse impact on black job applicants at Duke Power.

Dothard v. Rawlinson, supra, accepted plaintiff's showing from national data that the employer's requirements of a minimum height of 5'–2" and a minimum weight of 120 lbs had an adverse impact on women. Official government data revealed that defendant's height and weight minima would exclude 41.13% of women in the U.S. but less than 1% of the male population.

Based on public records of criminal arrests and convictions, a policy of disqualifying those with criminal records has been shown to adversely affect certain minorities. *Green v. Mo. Pac. R.R. Co.,* 549

F.2d 1158 (8th Cir. 1977). Where medical data established that substantially all pregnant women would be medically advised against lifting weights in excess of 150 lbs, a rule that excluded workers who could not lift that weight would have an adverse impact on women. *Garcia v. Women's Hosp. of Texas,* 97 F.3d 810 (5th Cir. 1996).

(a) Defining the "Pool"

The appropriate geographic boundary for study (the "pool") is the defined area from which the employer draws, or would reasonably be expected to draw, its applicants. *Griggs Duke Power Co., supra,* accepted state boundaries. *Dothard v. Rawlinson, supra,* accepted *national* height and weight data even though the employer was the *state* of Alabama, based on an assumption that height and weight of males and females in Alabama were not significantly different from the height and weight of individuals in the United States. Such an assumption cannot be made when credentials may well differ between communities. For example, an inner city population may have a much higher percentage of minorities with criminal records and lower levels of education than would neighboring suburban neighborhoods. In such cases, it will be necessary for the plaintiff to establish with precision the geographical boundaries from which the employer draws its workers. *Bennett v. Roberts,* 295 F.3d 687 (7th Cir. 2002). *See also, supra,* 17.03(a).

(b) Significance of the Difference

Plaintiff's data must show, not just some difference, but a significant difference in the percentage of *classmembers* within the pool who are disqualified by the challenged device. Impact on the individual plaintiff will not suffice. In *Raytheon Co. v. Hernandez,* 540 U.S. 44 (2003), an employer had a policy of not rehiring former employees discharged for cause. Plaintiff had been discharged for failing to pass the employer's drug test. Plaintiff, who suffered from an addiction disability, completed a rehabilitation program, and had been "drug free" for a significant period of time. His application for reemployment was rejected, allegedly because of the employer's "no rehire" policy. Plaintiff challenged the policy under the ADA as necessarily having an adverse impact on persons with his disability. The Court rejected this challenge, refusing to assume, without supporting data, that the employer's "no rehire" policy necessarily produced an adverse impact on applicants who were recovering addicts.

New York City Transit Auth. v. Beazer, 440 U.S. 568 (1979), required plaintiffs to prove the necessary causation with considerable precision. Plaintiff challenged under Title VII an employer rule denying employment to persons enrolled in methadone-based drug rehabilitation programs. Plaintiff's data demonstrated that 63% of persons city-wide in *public* methadone-maintenance programs were minorities. Nevertheless, as plaintiff's data failed to include *private* programs, the data fell short of proving that defendant excluding those in rehabilitation programs adversely affected minority workers. The dissent argued, unsuccessfully, that as defendant presented no evidence that the percentage of minorities in *private* programs was significantly lower than those in *public* programs, plaintiff's data was adequate to draw an inference of an adverse impact on minority workers.

Beazer noted also that plaintiff's data on the impact of defendant's methadone maintenance "is virtually irrelevant because a substantial portion of the persons included in [methadone-maintenance programs] are either unqualified for other reasons—such as use of illicit drugs and alcohol—or have received successful assistance in finding jobs with [other] employers." Requiring plaintiffs to refine its pool data to show that those excluded by the rule are otherwise qualified and interested in employment at defendant was not required in *Griggs v. Duke Power Co., supra,* and directly conflicts with *Dothard v. Rawlinson, supra,* which found that defendant's minimum height and weight qualification had an adverse impact on women based solely on plaintiff's national height and weight data. The Court rejected the dissent's argument that plaintiff had failed to establish the impact of the policy absent proof of the percentage of women not meeting defendant's minimum height and weight standards that were "seriously interested in applying for prison guard positions."

Applying the *Beazer* standard of proof, data showing statistically higher pay and greater seniority enjoyed by male workers generally, was not sufficient, standing alone, to prove that a no-marriage rule had an adverse impact on this employer's female employees by forcing them rather than their husband to resign. Data reflecting the impact of the no-marriage rule on *this employer* was required, even though such specialized data would be unreliable because of the small sample involved. *Thomas v. Metro Flight, Inc.,* 814 F.2d 1506 (10th Cir. 1987).

Finally, even a demonstrated difference must be shown to have a "significant" effect on the employment *opportunities* of those in the protected class. A rule prohibiting men from wearing beards may be shown to affect some blacks, but virtually no whites, because some black men suffer from a skin condition unique to the race that makes shaving painful and occasionally dangerous. However, *if* the percentage of black men suffering from this condition is very small, the impact of the no-beards policy on employment opportunities of black males as a class may be insignificant. *EEOC v. Greyhound Lines, Inc.,* 635 F.2d 188 (3d Cir. 1980). Similarly, a maximum height of 6'7" would disqualify a few men, but virtually no women. However, since this height maximum would disqualify such a small percentage of the male population, the requirement did not impose a significant barrier to the employment of men. *Livingston v. Roadway Express, Inc.,* 802 F.2d 1250 (10th Cir. 1986).

(2) Applicant flow proof

Applicant flow data identifies defendant's *actual experience* using the challenged device by measuring *percentages of actual applicants* by sex, age, or ethnic class, who pass and fail the employer's selection device. For example, to prove that a no-marriage rule had an adverse impact on female employees the employer's actual experience enforcing the rule would demonstrate the percentage of male and female employees who were forced to resign because of the rule. *Thomas v. Metro Flight, Inc., supra.* Any difference in rates between classes must be "significant." A no-marriage rule that in fact disqualified four women and one man was not "significant." *Harper v. Trans World Airlines, Inc.,* 525 F.2d 409 (8th Cir. 1975). There are two formulae for determining whether different success rates are "significant."

(a) "Rule of 4/5ths"

The EEOC allows impact to be established through a simple calculation known as the "Rule of 4/5ths." 29 C.F.R. 1607.3. A device will have a presumed adverse impact if it produces a selection rate for any protected class that is less than 4/5ths—or 80%—of the selection rate for the group with the highest passage rate. To illustrate, assume an employer had 150 applicants taking a qualifying test: 100 were white and 50 were black. Seventy-five of the 100 white applicants passed giving white applicants a 75% passage rate. Of the 50 black applicants, 25 passed, giving blacks a passage rate of 50%. The passage rates of the two classes are compared applying the "Rule of 4/5ths." 80% of the passage rates of whites, which was 75%, would be a passage rate of 60% (0.8 x 75 = 60). The 50% passage rate of blacks was less than 60% (or 4/5ths) of the passage rates of whites, and thus the adverse impact of the test may be assumed.

The "Rule of 4/5ths" is unreliable when a small change in *raw numbers* would produce a dramatic change in the *percentages*. For example, an employer in an economic recession laid off 15 employees, 14 of whom were over age 40. The court held that this flow data failed to prove the impact of the device being utilized. *Clark v. Matthews Int'l Corp.,* 628 F.3d 462 (8th Cir. 2010). Thirty-seven terminations over a two year period was an insufficient experience to prove the impact. *Allen v. Highlands Hosp. Corp.,* 545 F.3d 387 (6th Cir. 2008). Forty-six persons taking the test was too few experiences given the relatively small disparities in the percentage of white and black applicants who failed the test. *LeGault v. Arusso,* 842 F.Supp. 1479 (D.N.H. 1994).

(b) "Rule of Exclusion"

A more reliable, but more complex, method of establishing the significance of an outcome is for plaintiff to eliminate mathematically through the "Rule of Exclusion" that the observed outcome was a product of chance. (*See,* Chapter 17.05) This is accomplished by first measuring the overall percentage success rate of *all test takers*. This establishes an *"expected"* outcome of a random selection. If chance were operating it would be "expected" that the passage rate of any subclass of test takers (*e.g.*, women or racial minority) would be the same as the overall passage rate of all takers. To illustrate, an employer gives an objective test to 200 *applicants* and 100 of those applicants pass the test, the success, or flow, rate is 50%. The *expected* value, that is the most common random outcome, would be that that the passage rate of any sub-class of test takers would be the same 50%.

The actual success rates of a particular class of test takers is measured to produce an *"observed"* outcome. The difference between the "observed" and "expected" 50% outcome is calculated to eliminate chance as an explanation for any observed difference. If chance cannot be eliminated as an explanation, it cannot be assumed that the selection device had an adverse impact on any class. If chance is eliminated as an explanation, the device will be assumed to be the cause of the disparate outcome.

Assume that 47% of the black test takers succeed. We know that random outcomes could still produce a pass rate of minority applicants that is somewhat more or less than the expected 50% success rate. Thus, an observed success rate of 47% of a sub-class of test takers might be the outcome produced by chance. (The "null hypothesis" of random outcome has not been disproved.)

Assume, however, that only 37% of the black test takers pass. This difference is neither so great nor so small that one can intuitively conclude that the outcome was, or was not, a product of random outcomes. Standard deviation analysis, discussed in Chapter 17.05, provides an answer. "The Rule of Exclusion" is more precise than the EEOC "Rule of 4/5ths" and its calculation accounts for the number

of experiences in determining the probabilities that
the outcome was produced by chance.

(c) Multiple Devices: Where the "Flow" Is Measured: A "Bottom Line" Defense?

Connecticut v. Teal, 457 U.S. 440 (1982),
addressed the problem of an employer which uses
more than one selection device. The employer first
gave applicants a pen-and-paper test. Those who
failed to make a minimum test score were
eliminated from further consideration. On this test,
80% of white applicants passed compared to 54% of
black applicants. Those who passed the test were
then evaluated using additional criteria that
included subjective interview scores. 22.9% of the
initial black applicants were hired, compared to
only 13.5% of the white applicants. The employer
argued that the critical point for measurement was
the "bottom line," or the ultimate percentage of
applicants actually hired. The Court held, however,
that it was appropriate to measure the impact on
black applicants of the initial screening test. A
device that disproportionately eliminated a
protected class from further consideration,
adversely affected "employment opportunities" of
that class, and was not justified by the fact that
black and white applicants were hired at similar
rates.

Connecticut v. Teal addressed a tiered system where
a single element was disqualifying. The implication
is that the impact of a multiple element selection
system where *no single device is disqualifying* is
measured at the "bottom line," comparing the

percentage, by class, of applicants ultimately hired. That performance may vary by class on *integrated* elements of this system is not a basis for challenging each element of the system. *Stout v. Potter,* 276 F.3d 1118 (9th Cir. 2002). For example, a 100 question test is a single, integrated device, and thus the final scores on the 100 questions, rather than scores on the individual questions, are analyzed for impact. *See,* 42 U.S.C. 2000e–2(k)(1)(B). (When elements of an employer's "decisionmaking process are not capable of separate analysis, the decisionmaking process itself may be analyzed as one employment practice.") Therefore, in *Connecticut v. Teal, supra,* had all candidates participated in every aspect of the selection process, with the scores on each being combined into a single final ranking, with no single element being disqualifying, the combined score would be the appropriate point to analyze the system for its impact.

(d) Flawed Flow Data

Flow data is perhaps the only measurement of the impact of a testing device and unique unannounced practices. Flow data is unreliable, however, when the requirement being challenged is self-selecting, as is often the case with announced objective qualifications. For example, if an employer has an announced policy of considering only those with a college degree, it is unlikely that those who lacked a degree would apply. Hiring flow data showing that the degree requirement had no impact on a particular class would be virtually meaningless. Similarly, an announced height minimum most certainly would have the effect of dissuading all those who did not meet the required height from applying. An affirmative action policy that encouraged application from marginally qualified minorities might have the opposite effect of exaggerating the impact of a challenged device.

18.03: DEFENDANT'S BURDEN: TITLE VII AND THE ADA

A. "BUSINESS NECESSITY" GENERALLY DEFINED

If, but only if, plaintiff demonstrates the adverse impact of the identified device on plaintiff's protected class, the burden of proof shifts to defendant to justify the use of the device. Under Title VII and the ADA, defendant's burden is to demonstrate that the device having the impact is "job related" and "consistent with business necessity." 42 U.S.C. 2000e–2(k)(1)(A) (Title VII); 42 U.S.C. 12112(b)(ADA).

Griggs v. Duke Power Co., supra, coined the term "business necessity," but went on to state that exclusionary devices would be justified if the employer proved that the challenged device was "job related." *Albemarle Paper Co. v. Moody,* 422 U.S. 405 (1975), confirmed that the employer would carry its burden if it demonstrated that a challenged test was "job related," but in doing so required strong evidence of a direct relationship between the challenged test and measured job performance outcomes. However, two years later *Dothard v. Rawlinson,* 433 U.S. 321 (1977), addressing height and weight standards for prison guards that disproportionately excluded women, stated that the requirement having a disparate impact must be shown by defendant to be "*necessary* to safe and efficient job performance." Thereafter, *Wards Cove Packing Co. v. Atonio,* 490 U.S. 642 (1989), articulated a considerably lighter burden:

> [T]he dispositive issue is whether the challenged device serves, in a significant way, the legitimate goals of the employer. * * * A mere insubstantial justification in this regard will not suffice. * * * At the same time, though, there is no requirement that the challenged practice be "essential" or "indispensable" to the employers' business to pass muster.

The holding that "business *necessity*" meant only "*substantial*" and not "essential," was expressly rejected by the 1991 Amendments to Title VII which restated the more stringent "job related" "consistent with business necessity" standard first articulated in *Griggs v. Duke Power Co., supra.* But the Amendments failed to define or clarify the ambiguous nature of, or relationship between, "job related" and "business necessity." 42 U.S.C. 2000e–2(k). To complicate matters further, legislation and history accompanying the Amendment directed that the debates on the proper definition of "business necessity" should not be considered by the courts, stating only that the "business necessity" standard would be that as defined by the courts *prior to Wards Cove Packing.*

Relying on *Dothard v. Rawlinson, supra,* some lower courts emphasize "necessity" and require the challenged device to have (1) "a manifest relationship to the employment in question," *and* (2) a demonstrated "compelling need" to maintain the practice. *Bradley v. Pizzaco of Nebraska,* 7 F.3d 795 (8th Cir. 1993). Others, looking to *Albemarle Paper Co. v. Moody, supra,* indicate that an employer carries its burden by identifying a specific business purpose that is clearly, and directly served by the device, with no obligation on the employer to prove that the device is "essential" or "indispensable" to meet the business purpose. *Lanning v. South Eastern Penn. Transp. Auth.,* 181 F.3d 478 (3d Cir. 1999). Courts appear to agree, however, that the "business necessity" standard is not "justified by routine business considerations." *Hawkins v. Anheuser–Busch, Inc.,* 697 F.2d 810 (8th Cir. 1983).

B. "LESSER DISCRIMINATORY ALTERNATIVES"

Albemarle Paper Co. v. Moody, supra, indicated that plaintiff's proof of an alternative that had less of a discriminatory impact than the challenged test would be evidence of defendant's improper *motive* in using the test, but such proof would not undercut the "business necessity" of a device established by defendant to be "job related." Nonetheless, if an alternative exists that serves the employer's business goals equally well, it would seem that the device selected was not "necessary" under the more stringent interpretation of "business necessity." *Fitzpatrick v. City of Atlanta,* 2 F.3d 1112 (11th Cir. 1993).

The 1991 Amendments addressed this issue, but left matters unclear by making it a distinct violation when the "employer *refuses to adopt such alternative.*" 42 U.S.C. 2000e–2(k)(A)(ii). This suggests that plaintiff must request the alternative and prove its viability as an alternative to the challenged device prior to filing a charge, with defendant's liability premised upon defendant's refusal to adopt the suggested lesser discriminatory alternative. *Adams v. City of Chicago,* 469 F.3d 609 (7th Cir. 2006).

18.04: ADEA: "REASONABLE FACTORS"

The ADEA specifically authorizes employers to utilize "reasonable factors other than age." 29 U.S.C. 623 (f)(1). Title VII and the ADA have no similar provision. While this is a true defense in that the employer carries the burden of proof, "reasonable factor" imposes a significantly lighter burden than that of the "business necessity" standard of Title VII and the ADA. Nevertheless, the burden is not satisfied by simple "legitimacy." "Reasonable factor" suggests, at minimum, a legitimate, business-related goal that would include factors that employers traditionally use to make business decisions, such as relative education, training, performance evaluations, and even market factors, that include relative costs or premium payments to attract applicants. *Anderson v. Baxter Health Care Corp.,* 13 F.3d 1120 (7th Cir. 1994) (individual disparate treatment case construing the "factor" defense). *Meacham v. Knolls Atomic Lab.,* 554 U.S. 84 (2008), indicated that use of seniority and the relative rank of workers to be "reasonable factors." EEOC rules list five factors to consider in determining whether the "factor" satisfies the statutory requirement: (1) The extent the factor is related to a stated *business purpose,* (2) the precision with which the factor was fairly and accurately defined, (3) limits on use of subjective discretion by supervisors, particularly if the factor may be subject to age-based stereotypes, (4) the extent the employer has assessed the degree of impact of the factor on older workers, and (5) the degree of harm to older workers and the extent the employer took steps to reduce that harm. 29 C.F.R. 1625(e)(2)(2012).

18.05: "BUSINESS NECESSITY" APPLIED TO SCORED TESTS

A. TITLE VII TESTING PROVISO

Section 703(h) reserves a right to use "professionally developed ability tests not designed, intended, or *used* to discriminate." 42 U.S.C. 2000e–2(h). In *Griggs v. Duke Power Co., supra,* the employer had used in good faith a professionally developed battery of pen and paper general intelligence tests to select employees. The Court held, however, that regardless of defendant's good faith, if defendant is unable to demonstrate that the test having an adverse impact is "manifestly related to job performance," the test is being "*used* to discriminate," thus placing the test outside the protection of the proviso. "What Congress has commanded is that any test must measure the person for the job and not the person in the abstract."

B. THE UNIFORM GUIDELINES ON EMPLOYEE SELECTION PROCEDURES

29 C.F.R. Part 1607, adopted by enforcement agencies soon after *Griggs*, requires scored tests which have an adverse impact on plaintiff's protected class to be "validated" by defendant according to professionally recognized test validation standards such as those of the American Psychological Association. *Albemarle Paper Co. v. Moody*, 422 U.S. 405 (1975), decided soon after the adoption of the Uniform Guidelines, held that scored tests do not meet the *Griggs* standard of "job relatedness" ("measuring the person for the job") unless validated according to these test validation standards. General reputation, widespread use, or casual reports of a test's job relatedness do not suffice. Even expert testimony concluding that a test reliably predicts job performance is inadequate unless the testimony is supported by professionally accepted and documented validation studies. Tests professionally validated at other employers may be used by defendant only for those jobs that replicate the job duties at employers where the tests were professionally validated. Validation studies must factually demonstrate that the challenged device is "predictive of or significantly correlated with important elements of work behavior." The Guidelines provide that tests may be validated by one of three methods: (1) content, (2) criterion, and (3) construct.

C. CONTENT VALIDITY

Content validity compares actual skills, ability, or knowledge as demonstrated by the test results to the skills, ability, or the knowledge required for the job itself. The validity of a test is established when the test itself replicates identified major or essential portions of the job. For example, a structured on-the-road test of actual driving skills would have "content validity" for selecting drivers. A welding skills test can be used to select welders. If a job requires employees to lift boxes that weigh 75 lbs, a test that measures the ability to lift that weight would be content valid.

To have content validity the test need not replicate all, or even most, skills required of the job as long as the test measures an essential or central skill, ability, or knowledge. In qualifying police officers a test that measures running speed and general stamina may have content validity even though officers perform many duties that do not require running or stamina. Firefighters will have many responsibilities that do not require lifting of weights or the ability to climb. Yet, a test that measured those basic physical skills has content validity. *Lanning v. SEPTA,* 308 F.3d 286 (3d Cir. 2002) (requirement that candidates for transit police run 1.5 miles in 12 minutes content valid even though transit officers rarely are called to run long distances). By contrast, a word processing skills test to select police officers would lack content validity because the occasional need to type a report is but a minor aspect of an officer's duties.

Griggs v. Duke Power Co., supra, teaches that general psychological, intelligence, or I.Q. tests often lack content validity as they tend to "measure the person in the abstract." However, a battery of tests that measured basic reading, writing, and mathematical proficiency to select teachers was held to have content validity, as basic literacy in these key areas was deemed essential for all certified educators. *Ass'n of Mexican–American Educators v. California,* 231 F.3d 572 (9th Cir. 2000) (en banc).

To be content valid the test must be correlated to the level of job performance that is acceptable. If an absolute standard is identified as being necessary for successful job performance, only that standard can be used as a "passing" or "cut-off" on the test. For example, testing whether employees could lift 80 lbs would not be content valid if the job only required employees to lift 75 lbs. Providing a "margin of error" not required for the job, only to protect the employee from possible injury to himself, is not "job related." *EEOC v. Dial Corp.,* 469 F.3d 735 (8th Cir. 2006).

A minimum passing score on an otherwise content valid test of knowledge is valid if set at "reasonable levels" as determined by independent professionals, even though some professionals might disagree as to the appropriate level of ability necessary. *Ass'n of Mexican–American Educators v. California, supra,* ("passing" score of 12 out of a possible 16 was upheld by fact finder as a "reasonable" minimum passing grade).

Selection according to *relative rank* on the test is valid only if the score correlates to *relative job performance*. Thus, a person who can operate a word processor at 50 words per minute is presumably a more efficient word processor than one who can type only 40 words per minute. A person who makes fewer errors on a driving test is presumably a better, safer driver than one who makes significantly more errors.

D. CRITERION RELATED (OR "PREDICTIVE") VALIDITY

Criterion related, or predictive, validity establishes that a test with no content relationship to job duties nonetheless *predicts* with some accuracy future job performance. This is accomplished by demonstrating a statistically significant correlation between test performance and identified measurements of actual job performance. To illustrate, a music identification test to select music teachers may have *content* validity in that it replicates a necessary job skill in teaching music. However, *if* defendant can demonstrate that persons who perform well on a music test also perform well as truck drivers, the music test can be used to select future truck drivers. A significantly positive correlation between performance on the music test and truck driving performance establishes the criterion, or predictive, validity of the music test.

Evaluating job performance usually requires that an independent expert analyze a particular job for its major or key components ("criteria") and then develop an objective method to evaluate, measure, and score worker performance on those criteria. Vague criteria that rely on subjective, generalized conclusions or comparisons of workers by supervisors will not suffice. *Albemarle Paper Co. v. Moody, supra.*

Based on these identified job criteria, job performance of individual workers is scored by evaluators unaware of the worker's test scores (to avoid test results influencing job performance scores). The job performance being evaluated must be that which a test taker would undertake upon being employed or soon after a brief orientation. A test may not be used to select entry level employees for future jobs that will be gained only after promotion from the entry level position. However, performance in a formalized training program, as opposed to actual job performance, may be used as the criterion measure if the training program has a strong content relationship to the future job. Thus, a test for selecting candidates for police academy can be validated by comparing admission test scores with performance in the academy, rather than their job performance as police officers. *Washington v. Davis,* 426 U.S. 229 (1976).

Validation studies are conducted in two contexts. The preferred method, and the one requiring the fewest number of participants to produce reliable results, is a "predictive study." All, or a representative sample, of the employer's applicants are given the test before they begin work. Test takers are hired without regard to their test scores. Their job performance is measured soon after they begin work. The test scores are compared to the scores given to their job performance.

A second, and more difficult method, that was addressed in *Albemarle Paper Co. v. Moody, supra,* is "concurrent validation." The performance of recently hired employees who had previously taken the test are evaluated on their job performance. Or, alternatively, a representative sample of current employees whose job performances were evaluated are given the test, and these test scores are compared to their previous job performance evaluations.

Concurrent validation has significant problems. Applicants who were rejected based on their low scores on the non-validated test will not be included in the study, and job performance of current workers may have been evaluated after a significant length of time doing the job. Or where current employees are given the test, their employment prior to taking the test may influence test outcomes. If accounted for by the expert conducting the study such difficulties are not necessarily fatal, but complicate the analysis and usually require much larger samples to produce reliable results. 29 C.F.R. 1607.14C.

Validation requires a detailed correlation analysis of all test scores and actual job performance ratings. Test scores and job performance ratings are plotted. A positive "practical correlation" exists when the plotting demonstrates that those who do well on the test statistically tend to do well in performing job duties, and conversely those who do poorly on the test tend to perform less well on the identified job criteria. Envision lines forming a 90 degree right angle axis, with job performance rating on one axis and test performance rating on the other. The test and job performance score of each employee in the study represent a single dot plotted in the axis. A positive correlation exist when a pattern of all the results demonstrate a rough 45 degree upward angle. A predictive correlation does not require, and rarely will ever attain, a perfect 100%, or 1.0 correlation. Outliers (*i.e.*, a few who do well on the test, but poorly on the job, and conversely, or do poorly on the test but do well on the job) are inevitable, even on tests having high predictive value. Expert analysis can identify a professionally acceptable level of correlation sufficient for the test to have "practical predictive validity."

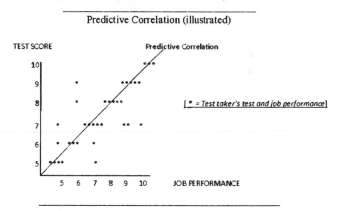

Predictive Correlation (illustrated)

If the study demonstrates "practical predictive validity" the employer then must demonstrate the "statistical significance," meaning a mathematical demonstration that the "practical predictive validity" was not a product of a chance or random outcome. This, too, will require expert statistical analysis. *Supra,* Chapter 17.05.

The employer's study in *Albemarle Paper Co. v. Moody, supra,* failed on a number of grounds including that it did not establish meaningful job performance "criteria," and employee job performances were evaluated after extensive periods on the job or on jobs high on the line of progression rather than on the entry level jobs for which the tests were used. Even if some studies were otherwise reliable, "[the] odd patchwork of results" made them statistically unreliable.

E. TEST "FAIRNESS"

Validation studies ideally include an investigation into possible "unfairness" of the test itself. The failure to evaluate "fairness" was one of the many flaws *Albemarle Paper* found in defendant's study. "Unfairness" is an hypothesis, not uniformly accepted by experts, that a test predicting job performance of white male employees may not predict job performance of persons from different cultural backgrounds. "Fairness" can best be assured by "differential validation," or distinct validation studies of the test for each class. This presents practical difficulties, and often it is impossible to have sufficient numbers in each group to produce outcomes with statistical reliability. Current Guidelines, while requiring an investigation into "fairness," do not require differential validation. "Fairness" may be satisfied by a showing that the sample being tested included a cross-section of classes or that the testing materials themselves were closely evaluated for "cultural bias" in wording or content.

F. CONSTRUCT VALIDATION

Validation through identification of a "construct" is a largely theoretical, and thus rarely encountered, methodology that attempts to identify a necessary psychological trait or characteristic, such as patience, initiative, or cooperativeness, which experts can determine to be critical for a particular job (*e.g.*, "patience" for a teacher, "self-restraint" for a police officer, "cooperativeness" for team research project). The study measures the degree that applicants possess the required trait and compares actual performance, a process that is similar to criterion-related validation.

18.06: AVOIDING TEST VALIDATION— ADJUST IMPACT

Validation, even when plausible, is difficult, unpredictable, and expensive. As validation is required only if the test produces an adverse impact on a protected class, practical alternatives might be to adjust the scoring on the test to eliminate its impact or abandon the results of the test in favor of other selection devices. Either approach has barriers.

A. ADJUST (OR "NORM") RAW SCORES?

Adverse impact of a test often could be avoided by using "within group" scoring that adjusts ("norms") raw scores within classes. For example, on physical tests of strength or speed the average difference between men and women has been documented. If the raw test performance is adjusted to account for statistical percentage difference between average performances of men and women, the use of the test would produce little adverse impact on women. Alternatively, needing ten new employees, the employer might separately rank test performance of minority and non-minority test takers and select the five top scoring minority test-takers and the top five non-minority test-takers regardless of their respective scores.

Such post-test adjustments rely on proscribed classifications and thus facially violate Title VII. Moreover, as amended in 1991, Title VII specifically provides:

It shall be an unlawful employment practice for [a covered entity] * * * to adjust scores of, use different cut-off scores, or otherwise alter the results of employment related tests on the basis of [protected classifications]. 42 U.S.C. 2000e–2(l).

B. REJECT RESULTS?

Ricci v. DeStafano, 557 U.S. 557 (2009), placed severe limitations on an employer's right to disregard test results and utilize an alternative method of selection or add an additional layer of selection devices to fill existing vacancies. The defendant city had 8 vacant positions for lieutenant in the firefighter force. Of the 77 candidates taking the qualification examination, 18 had passing scores (17 whites and 1 Hispanic), with the top 10 performers all being white. This result meant that if the test results were certified, none of the vacant lieutenant positions would be filled by black applicants. After much debate, the city's civil service board deadlocked on whether to certify the test results, which left the lieutenant positions vacant. The 18 test-eligible firefighters sued alleging disparate treatment racial discrimination.

The employer defended on the grounds that even if motive can be ascribed to a political body that was deadlocked on a decision, the motive of those who voted to reject the test had been to avoid potential Title VII liability on a suit brought by minority test takers based on the disparate impact of the test on minority applicants. The Court rejected this argument holding that the white plaintiffs were victims of racially motivated disparate treatment by the evenly divided commission vote, even though only 8 of the 18 plaintiffs would have received the appointment had the test results been accepted.

The Court then held that rejecting the results of a test based solely on the *disparate racial impact* of the test was no defense to plaintiff's *disparate treatment* claims. "Fear of litigation cannot alone justify an employer's reliance on race to the detriment of individuals who passed the examinations." The Court based its reasoning on the statutory prohibition against test result adjustments (42 U.S.C. 200e–2(j)), *supra*, stating:

> If an employer cannot rescore a test based on the candidates' race, then it follows a fortiori that it may not take the greater step of discarding the test altogether to achieve a more desirable racial distribution of promotion-eligible candidates * * *.

In attempting to strike a balance between disparate impact and disparate treatment liability, the Court instructed that a defendant could avoid disparate treatment liability if there was "a strong basis in the evidence" that the "test was deficient" and "remedial actions were necessary." The Court went on to conclude that:

> [T]here is no genuine dispute that the City lacked a strong basis in evidence to believe that it would face disparate-impact liability if it certified the examination results. * * * There is no evidence—let alone the strong basis in evidence—that the tests were flawed because they were not job related or because other, equally valid and less discriminatory tests were available to the City. * * * [Indeed, defendant] turned a blind eye to evidence that supported the exam's validity.

That the employer had no "strong basis in the evidence" to disregard the test does not preclude non-party minority test-takers from establishing the employer's liability for implementing the very test which *Ricci* required the employer to follow. *Briscoe v. City of New Haven,* 654 F.3d 200 (2d Cir. 2011).

The employer is thus caught in a "catch–22" dilemma by being forced to follow un-validated test results that have a clear adverse impact on black applicants that could well result in the employer's liability to the minority test takers who failed the test. Moreover, an employer observing the adverse impact of a test may not safely disregard the results of the test before it professionally determines through validation studies that the test is not "job related."

The disparate treatment found in *Ricci* was premised on the disappointed expectations of those who were made immediately eligible to fill existing vacancies. Its holding would not necessarily affect rejection of a test that was found to have an adverse impact prior to implementing the test, perhaps even allowing the rejection of test results prior to announcing outcomes and thus creating "expectations" in identified persons.

The employer may also elect *in advance* to make the test an inconclusive factor, to be combined with other scored evaluations such as interviews, past efficiency ratings, or race-neutral adjustments based on vague factors such as "overcoming economic adversity."

Ricci does not directly appear to undermine affirmative action steps permitted under standards sanctioned in *Steelworkers v. Weber,* 443 U.S. 193 (1979), and *Johnson v. Transp. Agency, Santa Clara County,* 480 U.S. 107 (1987). *See also,* section 116 of the 1991 Civil Rights Act which provides, "Nothing in the amendments shall affect * * * affirmative

action * * * that [is] in accordance with the law."
Thus, using differential test scores or ignoring test
outcomes in order to meet a hiring ratio sanctioned
by *Weber may* still be permissible. *See, Officers for
Justice v. Civil Serv. Comm.,* 979 F.2d 721 (9th Cir.
1991); 29 C.F.R. 1608.

18.07: TESTS AND THE ADA

Similar to Title VII, the ADA imposes a burden on
employers to establish "job relatedness" and
"business necessity" of screening devices having an
adverse impact on those with plaintiff's disability.
In addition the ADA makes it illegal for employers
to fail:

> to select and administer tests * * * in the most
> efficient manner to insure that a job applicant
> or employee who has a disability that impairs
> sensory, manual or speaking skills that such
> test accurately reflect * * * whatever factor that
> such test purports to measure, rather than
> reflecting the impaired sensory, manual, or
> speaking skills of such employee or applicant
> (except where such skills are the factors that
> the test purports to measure). 42 U.S.C.
> 12112(b)(7).

The ADA thus requires employers to insure the
"fairness" of the test to persons with disabilities.

A requirement that adversely affects *some* disabled
persons, such as a lifting requirement, cannot be
challenged by a plaintiff that does not suffer from
the disqualifying disability. A person whose medical
condition limited his lifting, but did not

"substantially limit a major life activity," could not challenge a lifting requirement. *Fuzy v. S & B Engineers & Constructors*, 332 F.3d 301 (5th Cir. 2003).

As testing for current illegal drug use is authorized by the ADA, persons suffering from the disability of addiction may not challenge the test based on the adverse impact such tests have on addicts. *Buckley v. Consol. Edison*, 127 F.3d 270 (2d Cir. 1997).

18.08: BUSINESS NECESSITY OF OBJECTIVE, NON–SCORED DEVICES

A. GENERAL PRINCIPLES

Selection devices that do not involve scored testing—educational credentials, experience, or background requirements (*e.g.*, criminal or credit records)—need not be professionally "validated." *Hawkins v. Anheuser–Busch, Inc.*, 697 F.2d 810 (8th Cir. 1983). "Business necessity" is similar to the terms in the statutory defense that allow exclusions of the protected class where the exclusion is a "bona fide occupational qualification *reasonably necessary* to the normal operation of that particular business." (BFOQ) (42 U.S.C. 2000e–2(e)(1). While broadly referring to the BFOQ defense in defining "business necessity" courts appear to impose a lighter burden than the BFOQ. *Compare, UAW v. Johnson Controls, Inc.*, 499 U.S. 187 (1991) (BFOQ), *with Washington v. Davis*, 426 U.S. 229 (1976) (business necessity). Nevertheless, employer convenience or increased costs will not be sufficient to establish that the device or practice is either "job related" or "consistent with business necessity." *DeClue v. Central Ill. Light Co.*, 223 F.3d 434 (7th Cir. 2000). Providing unsanitary toilet or changing facilities that subjected female employees to greater health risks was not justified by the employer showing that providing separate or sanitary facilities would be inconvenient and involve increased costs. *Lynch v. Freeman*, 817 F.2d 380 (6th Cir. 1987). Nor can "business necessity" be based on simple customer or co-worker preference. *Bradley v. Pizzaco of Nebraska*, 7 F.3d 795 (8th Cir. 1993).

Business necessity often is based on a non-scientific assessment of the content relationship represented by the challenged credential and duties of the job (e.g., library science degree for a professional librarian, law degree for an attorney). "Business necessity" invokes a sliding scale. In sustaining a college degree and prior experience requirements for commercial airline pilots, *Spurlock v. United Airlines, Inc.*, 475 F.2d 216 (10th Cir. 1972), explained:

> When a job requires a small amount of skill and training and the consequences of hiring an unqualified applicant are insignificant, the courts should examine closely any pre-employment standard or criteria which disproportionately discriminates against minorities. * * * On the other hand, when the job clearly requires a high degree of skill and the economic and human risks involved in hiring an unqualified applicant are great, the employer bears a correspondingly lighter

burden to show that his employment criteria are job related.

B. "BUSINESS NECESSITY:" SPECIFIC APPLICATIONS

(1) Paper Credentials

Griggs v. Duke Power Co., supra, indicated that general credentials, such as high school diplomas or college degrees, are not "necessary" for lower level or semi-skilled positions. *Walls v. Miss. Dep't of Pub. Welfare,* 730 F.2d 305 (5th Cir. 1984). But such credentials have been sustained as being "job related" for higher level positions such as managers (*Hawkins v. Anheuser–Busch, Inc., supra*), or where inadequate performance would place the public at risk (*e.g.,* police officers, firefighters, and pilots). *Davis v. Dallas,* 777 F.2d 205 (5th Cir. 1985) (2 years of college with "C" or better grades "necessary" for police officers).

(2) Experience

Similar to education, experience rarely is "necessary" for lower level, manual or semi-skilled jobs, such as truck driver, when the skills can be easily acquired over a short period of time. *Kilgo v. Bowman Transp. Inc.,* 789 F.2d 859 (11th Cir. 1986). General supervisory experience was not a "business necessity" for a supervisory position in a nursing home. *Walker v. Jefferson County Home,* 726 F.2d 1554 (11th Cir. 1984). Relevant past experience or training will be "necessary" when the job requires a significant skill that normally is acquired, or would be significantly enhanced, through acquired experience, or if serious economic or human risks flow from poor job performance. *Spurlock v. United Airlines, Inc., supra,* (500 hours of prior flight experience required for commercial airline pilot).

(3) Physical Requirements

Minimum height and weight requirements rarely are a "business necessity." The alternative of actually measuring applicants' physical ability to perform specific job duties makes it unnecessary to use an applicant's height or weight as a proxy for job requirements that demand strength, endurance, or agility. *Dothard v. Rawlinson,* 433 U.S. 321 (1977). Moreover, tests measuring a physical ability, such as stamina, if shown to produce an adverse impact, must have a "content validity" established by applying professionally developed test validation guidelines. *Lanning v. Southeastern Penn. Transp. Auth.,* 181 F.3d 478 (3d Cir. 1999).

(4) Criminal Convictions, Credit Ratings

The "business necessity" of past anti-social behavior or financial problems depends upon the nature of the behavior, temporal proximity of the behavior, and the nature of the job. If the job requires a high level of trust and integrity, access to valuable property, or is in law enforcement, the lack of serious criminal convictions or indications of serious financial instability may be a "job related." Where the employee will come into close contact with co-workers or customers the aggressive nature of past behavior may be sufficiently "job related" to disqualify those with a record of such behavior. *El v. Southeastern Penn. Trans. Auth.*, 479 F.3d 232 (3d Cir. 2007). However, disqualifying those with past, but relatively serious, criminal convictions may not be "necessary" for low level, manual labor jobs. *Green v. Mo.Pac.R. Co.*, 549 F.2d 1158 (8th Cir. 1972).

The absence of arrests, as opposed to convictions, has little probative value, except perhaps for jobs requiring a very high level of trust and where the arrests were for offenses indicative of questionable turpitude. Disqualification based on relatively minor criminal behavior that was remote in time (*e.g.*, "youthful indiscretions") may not be "necessary" for most jobs.

Establishing the adverse impact of the use of credit ratings may prove difficult. *EEOC v. Kaplan Higher Learning Educ. Corp.*, 96 EPD 44,739 (N.D. Ohio 2013) (defendant had failed to keep records of the race of applicants, and the court rejected as unreliable "guesswork" an EEOC study that compared driver's license photographs with the names of applicants). If impact is proved credit ratings or financial stability rarely would be "job related." *Johnson v. Pike Corp.*, 332 F.Supp. 490 (N.D. Cal. 1971). Moreover, when credit information is used to make job decisions federal law requires notification to the individual of its use with reasons and the source of the information. 15 U.S.C. 1681. In addition, discriminating because of a garnishment based on a single indebtedness or

because of an individual's bankruptcy may violate
15 U.S.C. 1674 and 11 U.S.C. 1525.

(5) Security Clearance

A criminal record, poor credit standing, or other
behaviors may result in an individual being denied
a national security clearance. Title VII specifically
allows employers to refuse employment or to
discharge an employee from a position that requires
a security clearance under any statute or executive
order and the individual is unable to obtain the
necessary clearance. 42 U.S.C. 2000e–2(g). This
proviso clearly precludes liability based on the
impact of a federally required security clearance.
Moreover, *Toy v. Holder,* 714 F.3d 881 (5th Cir.
2013), held that the proviso also protects improperly
motivated denial of a security clearance. *Cf.
Rattigan v. Holder,* 643 F.3d 975 (D.C.Cir. 2011),
which held that an individual may have a claim
against an employer who provided false or
misleading information for the purpose of having
the employee denied a necessary clearance. *Supra,*
14.02 E.

(6) Veterans

Title VII provides that "Nothing contained in [the
Act] shall be construed to repeal or modify any
Federal, state, territorial or local law creating
special rights or preferences for veterans" (42 U.S.C.
2000e–11), thus permitting *public employers* to give
statutorily mandated preferences for veterans.
Moreover, the USERA, 38 U.S.C. 4301, prohibits

discrimination *against* individuals because of their past military service or present military obligations.

(7) Grooming Standards

When neutral grooming standards are shown to have an adverse impact upon protected classes, establishing the "business necessity" of the standard may be difficult. In *Bradley v. Pizzaco of Nebraska,* 7 F.3d 795 (8th Cir. 1993), defendant, a retail pizza establishment ("Dominos Pizza"), required its delivery personnel to be clean shaven, a requirement shown to adversely affect black males because of a skin condition that affects only blacks. The court reasoned that neither customer preference nor "conclusory" testimony of company personnel concerning a neat personal appearance, without exploring alternatives, were sufficient to establish "necessity."

"Manifest danger" to third parties that prompt employers to require employees to wear certain protective clothing or limit certain hair styles, may on this basis, constitute a "business necessity." *Fitzpatrick v. City of Atlanta,* 2 F.3d 1112 (11th Cir. 1993) (prohibiting facial hair for firefighters was "necessary" to allow tight seals on breathing apparatus).

(8) Friends and Relatives

Giving *preference* to the employer's friends and relatives may be a facial form of racial discrimination. If so, the practice could be justified only as being a bona fide occupational qualification under the stringent standards of 42 U.S.C. 2000e–2(k)(2). Even if not facial discrimination, such preferences often can be shown to perpetrate the racial composition of the work force, thus having an adverse impact on a particular race. Establishing the "business necessity" of nepotism will be difficult. *Thomas v. Washington County School Bd.*, 915 F.2d 922 (4th Cir. 1990).

A policy of *excluding* immediate relatives, spouses, or close friends of current employees if shown to have an adverse impact, has been held to be "job related" based the possibility of conscious, unconscious, or apparent favoritism, potential conflicts of interests in matters of discipline or reward, and the danger of bringing personal disputes into the workplace. *EEOC v. Rath Packing Co.*, 787 F.2d 318 (8th Cir. 1986).

(9) Residency

A "resident only" requirement for firefighters imposed by a municipal employer was shown to have an adverse impact on black applicants based on the largely white population of the defendant community. It is difficult for an employer to show a "business necessity" for employees to live in the community of the employer. An *assumption* that employees living outside a community will have higher tardiness and absenteeism rates is not the proof required for the defense. Even if the job requires emergency responses necessitating short response times, (*e.g.*, police officers or firefighters), not requiring employees to maintain their in-town residency undercuts any assertion that residency is necessary. *North Hudson Reg. Fire & Rescue v. NAACP,* 665 F.3d 464 (3d Cir 2012).

(10) Recruiting Methods

It is difficult to marshal the necessary data showing that informal or word-of-mouth recruiting has a disparate impact. *Chicago Miniature Lamp Works,* 947 F.2d 292 (7th Cir.1991). When disparate impact has been proved, it is difficult for the employer to demonstrate the "business necessity" of such a practice. Convenience of casual hiring and expense associated with advertising vacancies and active recruiting are insufficient. Moreover, recruiting practices have no relationship to *"job performance."* *Barnett v. W.T. Grant Co.,* 518 F.2d 543 (4th Cir. 1975).

18.09: BUSINESS NECESSITY OF SUBJECTIVE SYSTEMS

In *Watson v. Fort Worth Bank & Trust,* 487 U.S. 977 (1988), defendant argued that the impact analysis of *Griggs v. Duke Power Co., supra,* should be limited to objective screening devices, and could not, as a matter of law, be applied to subjective screening systems, such as interviews, where results necessarily include judgments of the interviewers. The Court held, however, that *if* plaintiff could isolate the particular subjective practice and demonstrate the disparate effect of the practice on a protected class, the impact analysis of *Griggs* could be applied.

Often there is difficulty in having a sufficient number of experiences with the system to produce significant impact. *EEOC v. Joe's Stone Crab,* 220 F.3d 1263 (11th Cir. 2000). Where impact is proved for jobs involving manual labor or rote work that do not involve subjective constructs (*e.g.,* "personality," "leadership," "initiative"), and objective measurements such as tests, can predict job performance, it is difficult for a defendant to prove the "necessity" of selections based on subjectivity. *Rowe v. Cleveland Pneumatic Co.,* 690 F.2d 88 (6th Cir. 1982).

Watson v. Fort Worth Bank & Trust, supra, cautioned that where the job inherently involves performances that can best be evaluated subjectively, a subjective system that evaluates the constructs necessary for successful job performance should be sustained as "necessary." The Court listed as examples of acceptable subjectivity: common sense, good judgment, originality, loyalty, and tact. Thus, for example, where a supervisory position requires working closely with subordinates and co-workers, an interview system that evaluates the applicants' "cooperation" and "leadership potential" would seem to be "job related." For sales jobs or positions requiring personal contact with the public a subjective evaluation of the candidates' demeanor, grooming, patience, and personality would seem to be "job related." Artisans could be selected on a subjective evaluation of the quality of their work. *See, e.g., Verniero v. Air Force Academy,* 705 F.2d 388 (10th Cir. 1983).

Even if subjective evaluation is unavoidable, unduly vague and unchecked subjectivity may not be "necessary." The failure to adopt a structured process that checks possible conscious or unconscious bias could be seen as a failure of the employer to adopt a less discriminatory alternative, itself a failure to prove "business necessity," or such a failure to structure subjectivity would be strong evidence of illegal *motive. Torgerson v. City of Rochester,* 605 F.3d 584 (8th Cir. 2010).

CHAPTER 19

SENIORITY: IMPACT AND MOTIVE

19.01: THE SENIORITY PROVISO

Title VII and the ADEA have provisos purporting to preserve the right to apply different terms or conditions "pursuant to a bona fide seniority system * * * provided that such differences are not the result of an intention to discriminate because of [protected class]." 42 U.S.C. 2000e–2(h) and 29 U.S.C. 623(f)(2)(A). The ADEA includes an additional precaution: "No such seniority system shall require or permit the involuntary retirement of an individual * * * because of age." The ADA has no expressed provisions regarding seniority. Nevertheless, making an accommodation to an individual's disability that would undermine expectations granted by an employer's seniority system, in most cases, will be an "undue hardship" and thus need not be granted to the individual with the disability. *US Airways v. Barnett,* 535 U.S. 391 (2002).

"Seniority" is defined as a "scheme that, alone or in tandem with non-'seniority' criteria allots ever improving employment rights or benefits as the [employees'] relative lengths of pertinent employment increases. * * * The principal feature of any and every 'seniority system' is that preferential treatment is dispensed on the basis of some measure of time." *California Brewers Ass'n v. Bryant,* 444 U.S. 598 (1980).

19.02: *TEAMSTERS* CONSTRUES THE PROVISO

A collective bargaining agreement in *Int'l Br'hd of Teamsters v. United States,* 431 U.S. 324 (1977), provided for two categories ("units") of truck drivers: "line" (inter-city) and "local." By virtue of pre-Act discrimination whites had been assigned to the more desirable, higher paid "line" positions, and minority drivers to the lower paid "local" routes. Defendants established a system that set seniority within each unit to determine priority for a promotion *within that unit.* Consequently, drivers with substantial seniority in the "local" (largely minority) unit could not use their seniority to bid into vacancies in the more desirable and largely white "line" driver unit. The Court recognized that this "unit" method of calculating seniority had an adverse impact on minority applicants, and presumably could not be justified as a "business necessity" as defined by *Griggs v. Duke Power Co., supra. See,* Chapter 18. The Court held, however, that, "[T]he unmistakable purpose of [the seniority proviso] was to make it clear that the routine application of a bona fide seniority system would not be unlawful under Title VII." Unlike the testing proviso found in the same section of the Act, the seniority proviso does not include the word "used," which omission led the Court to conclude that challenges to seniority systems must be premised on proof of "an intention to discriminate." Use of seniority is proscribed only if plaintiff proves that distinctions were not made pursuant to a good faith application of a "bona fide system."

On its face the proviso only permits defendants "to apply" different standards pursuant to a bona fide system. *American Tobacco Co. v. Patterson,* 456 U.S. 63 (1982), held, however, that the proviso also protected good faith *adoption,* as well as the *application,* of seniority systems.

19.03: *TEAMSTERS* APPLIED: "SYSTEMS"

To be preserved against impact challenges, the seniority being adopted or applied must be part of a "system." A "system" need not be in a binding contractual commitment, but it must be regularized and predictable to the extent that it creates legitimate expectations of ever improving employment opportunities measured in defined and increasing lengths of time. Seniority is not part of a "system" if it is little more than *ad hoc* decisions that take into account in some imprecise way length of service, relies on weak, non-binding guidelines frequently ignored, or contains numerous exceptions regularly invoked. *Williams v. New Orleans S.S. Ass'n.,* 673 F.2d 742 (5th Cir. 1982). *See also, U.S. Airways Inc. v. Barnett,* 535 U.S. 391 (2002) (ADA).

The proviso preserves not just the passage of time elements of a "system," but also those "ancillary rules that accomplish necessary functions, but which may not themselves be directly related to length of employment." *California Brewers Ass'n v. Bryant,* 444 U.S. 598 (1980). The Court explained:

> [E]ach seniority system must also have rules that delineate how and when the seniority time clock begins ticking, as well as rules that

specify how and when a particular person's seniority may be forfeited. Each seniority system must also have rules that define which passages of time will 'count' toward the accrual of seniority and which will not. * * * Rules that serve those necessary purposes do not fall outside the [seniority proviso] simply because they do not, in and of themselves, operate on the basis of some factor involving the passage of time.

The Court applied this principle to a system that classified employees as "permanent" only after they had worked a minimum of 45 weeks in any year, and "temporary" if they worked fewer than 45 weeks per year. "Temporary" employees were laid off before "permanent" employees, regardless of their respective total lengths of employment. Most of the "permanent" employees were white males. The industry had suffered an economic decline resulting in recently hired women and minorities remaining "temporary" even though many "temporary" employees had longer overall periods of employment than some "permanent" employees. Layoffs were primarily among "temporary" employees, producing an adverse impact on women and minorities. The Court held that the "permanent"/"temporary" distinction was ancillary to the time-based system and thus protected against impact-based liability.

Teamster, supra, previously had held that seniority calculated within defined "units" which would be lost if the employee transferred to another unit, was a protected aspect of the "system." Granting a preference to current employees over outside applicants, hiring an outsider only if no qualified employee applied, or adding subjective factors that modify strict length of service, such as allowing time in service to be controlling unless the junior employee is "more qualified" than a more senior employee do not "depart fundamentally" from common notions of what constitutes "seniority." *Allen v. Prince George's County,* 737 F.2d 1299 (4th Cir. 1984). However, a rule that *prevents* an employee from transferring out of the unit, effectively disqualifying the employee from filling vacancies in other units, may not be "seniority." *Chambers v. Parco Foods, Inc.,* 935 F.2d 902 (7th Cir. 1991). It is uncertain whether giving new applicants a *priority* over current workers in other units is part of a "seniority system." *Compare, United States v. Lee Way Motor Freight,* 625 F.2d 918 (10th Cir. 1979), *with Herbert v. Monsanto Co.,* 625 F.2d 1111 (5th Cir. 1982).

California Brewers, supra, noted that rules which provide when the seniority clock begins running, such as initial periods of probation or training, will be protected elements of a seniority system. Systems also may have rules which provide conditions when seniority may not be accumulated or lost entirely through breaks in service, such as by lay-offs, discharges, and resignations. Provisions that set terms under which an employee may later regain any lost seniority are protected. *United Airlines v. Evans,* 431 U.S. 553 (1977). *California Brewers, supra,* cautioned, however, that non-time triggering rules may not "depart fundamentally from commonly accepted notions concerning acceptable contours of a seniority system, simply because those rules were dubbed 'seniority.'" Thus, educational requirements or passing an objective test could not be superimposed as a condition before earning seniority and thus be insulated by the seniority proviso from impact analysis.

19.04: PREVIOUS ILLEGALITY

Teamsters v. United States, supra, upheld a seniority system even though it perpetuated *pre-Act* racial discrimination in the employer's job assignments. *Franks v. Bowman Transp. Co.,* 424 U.S. 747 (1976), which pre-dated *Teamsters,* involved the power of trial courts to order employers to rehire victims of discrimination and to grant full *remedial* seniority credits which they would have earned had it not been for the illegal discrimination. The employer argued that the earned seniority of incumbent employees was preserved by the 703(h) seniority proviso, and that a court order of artificial, remedial seniority undermining such seniority expectations was prohibited. The Court disagreed, holding that the remedial obligations imposed on the courts by 42 U.S.C. 2000e–5(g), required courts to "make whole" victims of illegal discrimination, which, in all but extraordinary cases, included ordering seniority credits running from the date of the illegal refusal to hire or discharge.

United Airlines, Inc. v. Evans, 431 U.S. 553 (1977), involved *post-Act,* presumably illegal, sex discrimination against an employee who was rehired after the defendant had revoked its discriminatory policy. The collective bargaining agreement provided that an employee's seniority would be lost by any significant break of service, and that the seniority of rehired employees would be measured only from the date of their re-employment. Economic conditions resulted in lay-offs, and plaintiff was laid off based on her lack of seniority as measured by the system. Plaintiff argued that the provision in the seniority system that resulted in her loss of seniority for a break in service could not be bona fide, because it perpetuated the effects of the employer's *illegal* discrimination. The Court, however, saw no meaningful distinction from *Teamsters* stating:

> [A] challenge to a neutral system may not be predicated on the mere fact that a past event which has no present legal significance has affected the calculation of seniority credit, even if the past event might at one time have justified a valid claim against the employer.

Thus, had plaintiff filed a timely challenge to her initial discharge and prevailed, she would have been entitled to full remedial seniority that would include retaining her past seniority and seniority credits lost between the date of her dismissal and her reinstatement. *Franks v. Bowman Transp. Co., supra. Infra,* 28.04. However, plaintiff's failure to file a timely challenge to her original discharge rendered the remedial demands directed by *Franks v. Bowman Transp. Co.* inapplicable.

19.05: BONA FIDES OF THE SYSTEM

A system that has separate lines of seniority for men and women or provides that women and men earn or lose seniority at different rates would not be bona fide as such provisions are based on a sex classification. A system that did not calculate pre-Act pregnancy leave in the same manner as other medical leaves could be bona fide as the distinction was legal at the time. However, calculating seniority earned or lost because of pregnancy leave taken *after* the 1978 Pregnancy Discriminatory Act, if calculated differently from seniority gained or lost because of similar medical leaves, is discriminatory on its face, and thus lacks bona fides. *See, AT & T Corp. v. Hulteen,* 557 U.S. 701 (2009). Moreover, a system that imposes the loss of accumulated seniority when a woman takes leave required by her pregnancy may be sex discrimination even if breaks in service for conditions other than for pregnancy result in a similar loss of seniority. As the system makes a pregnancy distinction that uniquely burdens women, this was held to be the equivalent of sex, and will not be saved by the seniority proviso. *Nashville Gas Co. v. Satty,* 434 U.S. 136 (1977).

If the employer articulates that the disparate treatment of plaintiff was the result of an application of a facially legitimate seniority system, the burden is upon the plaintiff to prove defendant's illegal motive for its adoption or in its application. *Pullman–Standard v. Swint,* 456 U.S. 273 (1982). In finding that plaintiff had failed to prove defendant's lack of good faith in adopting or applying the seniority system, *Teamsters v. United States, supra,* noted some objective markers of defendants' subjective good faith. The seniority units there were rational, widely utilized in the industry, and certified as appropriate bargaining units by the National Labor Relations Board. White and black drivers within respective units were treated the same. By implication, proof that defendant's system was idiosyncratic, irrational, or erratically applied would be strong evidence that the system was not "bona fide." *Williams v. New Orleans S.S. Ass'n,* 673 F.2d 742 (5th Cir. 1982). Moreover, the discriminatory effect of elements in a system, while not itself conclusive proof that the system is not bona fide, can be some evidence of a discriminatory motive for making a precipitous change that disadvantages a protected class. *See, Lorance v. AT & T Technologies,* 490 U.S. 900 (1989) (addressing the timeliness of filing the charge). An otherwise rational unit system is unprotected by the proviso if the system is amended to provide greater seniority for units that were predominately male, for the purpose of providing greater job security for male employees, to the disadvantage of female workers. *Id.*

PART 4

DISCRIMINATION IN THE WORK PLACE: COMPENSATION AND OTHER "TERMS AND CONDITIONS OF EMPLOYMENT"

The prohibitions found in the core statutes include discrimination in "compensation." "Compensation" is not limited to salary, but includes bonuses, commissions, stock options, insurance coverage, expense allowances, vacation and sick leave, and similar fringe benefits, as well as current allocation of benefits to be received upon retirement. *Arizona Governing Committee v. Norris,* 463 U.S. 1073 (1983). The statues sweep even more broadly to encompass other "terms and conditions of employment" and thus "strike[ ] at the entire spectrum of disparate treatment." *Meritor Savings Bank, FSB v. Vinson,* 477 U.S. 49 (1986). Proving illegal work place discrimination presents issues different from those when the alleged discrimination is in the selection of the work force. The Equal Pay Act presents a distinct and alternative vehicle for establishing illegal sex discrimination in pay.

CHAPTER 20
THE EQUAL PAY ACT

20.01: GENERALLY

The EPA was enacted as an amendment to the Fair Labor Standards Act (FLSA) that regulates minimum wage, overtime pay obligations, and child labor. 29 U.S.C. 206(d). The EPA thus adopts the coverage and remedial provisions of the FLSA. While originally enforced by the Department of Labor, it is now enforced by the EEOC.

A. COVERAGE

Coverage of the FLSA, and thus the EPA, is based on individual employee contact with interstate commerce ("engaged in" or "production of goods for") or the gross annual amount of "sales made or business done" by the "enterprise" (currently set at $500,000). 29 U.S.C. 201. The number of employees is not relevant for EPA coverage.

B. BASIC PRINCIPLES

The EPA sets an objective standard for determining an employer's obligation. Plaintiff must prove that the work of male and female employees was "equal" in three aspects—"skill, effort, and responsibility." The equal work must be performed under working conditions that are *"similar,"* paid at different "rates," and performed within the same "establishment."

If plaintiff establishes these objective elements, the burden shifts to the employer to prove that the pay rate difference between the male and female employees was based on (i) a seniority system, (ii) a merit system, (iii) a system that measures the quantity or quality of production, *or* (iv) "any other factor other than sex."

Men are protected under the same standards as are women. In contrast to Title VII, the EPA does not require plaintiff to prove that the difference in pay rates was motivated by sex. Good faith violations of the EPA are possible.

If a violation is established, compliance cannot be accomplished by lowering the wage rate of the higher paid employee (29 U.S.C. 206(d)(1)) or by transferring employees to a different job. *Hodgson v. Miller Brewing Co.,* 457 F.2d 221 (7th Cir. 1972). The wage rate of the lower paid employee must be raised to be equal to that of the higher paid employee. The past pay difference is considered unpaid wages which plaintiff may recover for up to two years prior to the date suit was filed, or three years if the violation was "willful." The successful plaintiff may recover an additional amount equal to the back pay liability as liquidated damages. However, the trial court may reduce or deny the liquidated amount if the employer establishes that the pay provided was based on a reasonable and good faith belief that it was in compliance with the Act.

The EPA may be enforced by law suits filed either by the EEOC or the underpaid worker, with no requirement that they first utilize or exhaust the pre-suit administrative processes required under Title VII, the ADEA, and the ADA.

20.02: "EQUAL WORK" ELEMENTS

A. GENERALLY

Equal work is established by comparing three elements of the jobs themselves: (1) skill, (2) effort, and (3) responsibility. Equality is determined by actual job duties, not written job descriptions or hypothetical assignments. The focus is upon duties not upon the relative potential, skills, or performance of the *workers* performing the jobs. For example, work that is the same is not made unequal because one of the employees performing it has a college degree or has had specialized training. *Waters v. Turner Wood & Smith Ins. Agency,* 874 F.2d 797 (11th Cir. 1989). Bona fide performance or educational differences may justify different pay rates, but such factors must be established by the employer pursuant to one of the four statutory defenses. The elements of equal work may not be offset against each other. That is, a job that requires greater skill is not "equal" to a similar job that requires less skill but greater effort.

Where work is in fact not "equal" because different duties have been assigned to male and female employees, there can be no EPA violation. Discriminatory job assignments or work load discrimination, if based on the sex of the employee, will violate Title VII, but not the EPA. *Berry v. Bd.*

of Supervisors of L.S.U., 715 F.2d 971 (5th Cir. 1983).

"Equal work" does not require the work to be "identical." *Corning Glass Works v. Brennan,* 417 U.S. 188 (1974). Work is "equal" when job duties are "substantially equal." *Hein v. Oregon College of Educ.,* 718 F.2d 910 (9th Cir. 1983). Mere "comparability" or "similarity" does not suffice. *Sprague v. Thorn Americas, Inc.,* 129 F.3d 1355 (10th Cir. 1997).

If plaintiff proves that two jobs share a "common core of tasks" rendering them largely identical, secondary duties assigned to one employee will render the two jobs "unequal" only if four conditions are met. (1) The additional chores must be significant. Inconsequential, *de minimis* assignments such as requiring one worker to turn off lights, make coffee, or answer an occasional telephone call are insufficient. *Hodgson v. Fairmont Supply Co.,* 454 F.2d 490 (4th Cir. 1972). (2) The extra duties must actually be performed in *each pay period.* The extra duties must be a regular and recurring part of the job, not an *ad hoc* duty occasioned by a unique situation or infrequent event. *Brennan v. Prince William Hosp. Corp.,* 503 F.2d 282 (4th Cir. 1974) (occasional inserting catheters and lifting heavy patients). (3) Additional duties of a comparable nature must not be assigned to the lower paid employee. For example, the extra secondary duty of the higher paid employee stocking a drink machine is offset by the lower paid employee being required to carry out the rubbish. *Brennan v. South Davis Comm. Hosp.,* 538 F.2d 859 (10th Cir.

1976). (4) The extra duties must be rationally related to the pay difference. If the extra duties usually are performed by other employees who earn less than the higher paid employee now performing them, such secondary duties may not make otherwise equal jobs unequal. *Shultz v. Wheaton Glass Co.*, 421 F.2d 259 (3d Cir. 1970).

B. SKILL

"Skill" is defined to be the ability or dexterity used to perform the actual job duties. Skills that are fundamentally different are not "equal" simply because they involve equal *skillfulness*. The work of a carpenter and plumber are not "equal." However, employees performing work that is fundamentally the same, but requires somewhat different types of skill, as where male and female assembly line workers perform different manual tasks in the assembling process, may have substantially equal skills. *Hodgson v. Daisy Mfg. Co.,* 317 F. Supp. 538 (W.D. Ark. 1970), *aff'd* 445 F.2d 823 (8th Cir. 1971). Operation of different machines that are a part of an integrated print binding process may require equal skill. *Thompson v. Sawyer,* 687 F.2d 257 (D.C. Cir. 1982). *Cf. Fosberg v. Pac. N.W. Bell Tel. Co.,* 840 F.2d 1409 (9th Cir. 1998), which held that manually diagnosing mechanical malfunctions required a fundamentally different skill than diagnosing the same malfunctions using a computer.

C. EFFORT

"Effort" is the physical or mental exertion actually expended performing the work. Greater *physical* effort of one job is not balanced against greater *mental* effort required in another. Work of a qualitatively different nature is not equal even if the two jobs require the same level of exertion. For example, a janitorial job that required dusting and light mopping of a large area is not equal to a janitorial job that required heavy wet mopping of smaller areas simply because the two jobs were outwardly similar and may have been equal in terms of calories expended at the end of each day. *Usery v. Columbia Univ.,* 558 F.2d 953 (2d Cir. 1977). A male academic administrator's primary duty was to save a flagging academic program and create a graduate program. A female administrator's primary duty was to improve the institution's outside fundraising. Because the nature of their effort and responsibilities were fundamentally different, their jobs were not "equal." *Cullen v. Indiana Univ. Bd. of Trustees,* 338 F.3d 693 (7th Cir. 2003).

D. RESPONSIBILITY

"Responsibility" is the degree of accountability required. It can involve different supervisory obligations, decision-making authority, levels of accountability for consequences, or the degree of independence and trust. A bank teller who handles small deposits, and another teller who handles large inter-bank transactions, have unequal levels of responsibility. *Victoria Bank & Trust Co.,* 493 F.2d

896 (5th Cir. 1974). A clerk who handles narcotic drugs has more responsibility than a clerk who handles over-the-counter medicines. *Hodgson v. Behrens Drug Co.*, 475 F.2d 1041 (5th Cir. 1973). A female coach of a university's female basketball team had less responsibility than the male coach of the male team in that the male team was of higher public visibility and produced more revenue than did the female team. *Stanley v. Univ. So. Cal.*, 13 F.3d 1313 (9th Cir. 1994).

To be "equal," "responsibility" must be of the same quality. Supervisors of different departments or divisions often have different, and thus not "equal," responsibilities. *Wheatley v. Wicmico County*, 390 F.3d. 328 (4th Cir. 2004). College teaching in different academic disciplines often requires different skills and responsibilities. Teaching law is different than teaching physics. *Spaulding v. Univ. of Wash.*, 740 F.2d 686 (9th Cir. 1984). Supervising more employees, dealing with more clients, or managing a larger payroll involves greater "responsibility." *Cullen v. Indiana Univ. Bd. of Trustees, supra.*

20.03: "WORKING CONDITIONS"

Unlike skill, effort, and responsibility, which must be "equal," the working conditions where the work is performed need only be "similar." *Corning Glass Works v. Brennan*, 417 U.S. 188 (1974), defined "working conditions" to encompass the physical surroundings and hazards of the job, such as exposure to unpleasant temperatures, wetness, noise, fumes, dust, vibrations, threats to health or safety, exposure to toxic materials, and outdoor vs. indoor work. In *Corning Glass, supra,* males and females performed identical jobs of "inspector." The higher paid male employees worked on the night shift. The lower paid female employees worked the day shift. The employer argued that the time of day in which work is performed is a "working condition," and thus the work performed in the less desirable night shift was being performed under dissimilar working conditions. The Court disagreed. "Working conditions" is a term of art used by labor relations experts to evaluate *job content*, which does not include shifts or the hours of the day the jobs are performed. Plaintiff, thus, had established a prima facie case of an EPA violation, requiring the employer to prove that the "shift differential" in pay rates was a "factor other than sex." *Infra,* 20.07.

20.04: SAME "ESTABLISHMENT"

The equal work of the two employees must be performed in the same "establishment." "Establishment" is more narrow than "employer" and generally refers to a distinct physical location of a covered "employer." A single employer may have many "establishments." For example, a retail enterprise may have five stores selling identical products, each in a different neighborhood. Presumably, each store of this employer would be a different "establishment," and thus different pay rates of the distinct stores cannot be compared. Separate physical locations of an employer may constitute a single "establishment" if: (1) there is central authority for hiring and maintaining employee relations, (2) records are centrally maintained and administered, and (3) there is movement of employees between the physical locations. 29 C.F.R. 1620.9. Thus, if the five stores of a retail enterprise were centrally managed and employees moved freely between stores, the five stores would constitute the same "establishment." All schools in a district may be in a single "establishment" when they are centrally managed by a governing board. But because different departments or a different campus in a university system often have some autonomy in selection, pay and assignments of professors, and because professors rarely move between departments, it could be the department or campus, and not the university, that constitutes the "establishment." *Compare, Brennan v. Goose Creek School Dist.,* 519 F.2d 53 (5th Cir. 1975), *with Alexander v. Univ. of Mich., Flint,* 509 F.Supp. 627 (E.D.Mich. 1980).

Units or departments within a single physical location presumptively are the same "establishment." Men's and women's clothing departments within the store will be within the same establishment even though each department sells a different product. Occasionally, distinct "establishments" can exist in the same physical location, but only if they involve significantly different activities and the different activities are kept operationally distinct. For example, an airline's international and domestic flight operations in the same building may be considered separate "establishments." *Maguire v. Trans World Airlines,*

Inc., 535 F.Supp. 1238 (S.D.N.Y. 1982), *rev'd w/o opinion* 722 F.2d 728 (2d Cir. 1983).

20.05: UNEQUAL "RATES" OF PAY

"Pay rates" includes not just salary but all compensatory benefits such as bonuses, insurance, vacation pay, expense allowances, etc. The EPA requires that the *"rates"* of pay, not gross pay received, be unequal. A female manager of the female section of a health club was paid a commission *rate* of 5% of the dues of female club members, and the male manager was paid a commission *rate* of 7.5% of the dues of male club members. Because there were fewer male club members, the *gross* salary paid to the male and female managers was equal. However, as the "rates" of pay were unequal, the EPA was violated. *Bence v. Detroit Health Corp.,* 712 F.2d 1024 (6th Cir. 1983).

Where employees are paid a fixed sum based on relatively short periods of time, such as a week or month, the gross wages are translated into an hourly rate of pay. Thus, when male and female employees receive the same weekly pay, but female employees are required to work 48 hours, while male employees work only 40, the hourly *rate* of pay for male employees is higher than the rate paid to female employees. *Hein v. Oregon College of Educ.,* 718 F.2d 910 (9th Cir. 1983).

However, when compensation is set in reference to longer periods, such as one year, as is common for professionals and executives not subject to the overtime provisions of the Fair Labor Standards

Act, gross salary would not be broken down into an hourly rate. The "rate" would be the annual wage. Thus, if male and female attorneys are both paid $100,000 per year they are being paid at the same "rate" regardless of the number of hours in the year each may have worked. *Berry v. Bd. of Supervisors of L.S.U.*, 715 F.2d 971 (5th Cir. 1983).

20.06: BETWEEN MALE AND FEMALE

The EPA requires a comparison between two or more employees of the opposite sex. Comparisons are not limited to employees working simultaneously. A former female employee's previous pay rate may be compared to the male employee who succeeded her. *Lawrence v. CNF Transp. Inc.*, 340 F.3d 486 (8th Cir. 2003). Or her current pay rate may be compared to that of her immediate or even remote male predecessors. *Clymore v. Far–Mar–Co.*, 709 F.2d 499 (8th Cir. 1983).

Literally, the Act is violated when *any employee* of the opposite sex is performing work equal to the plaintiff and receiving a higher rate of pay. One Court has suggested, however, that when a substantial numbers of men and women are performing equal work and employees of the opposite sex are paid at rates both more and less than the plaintiff, there is no EPA violation. *Yant v. United States,* 85 Fed. Cl. 264 (2009). Other courts have required plaintiff to identify a "comparator;" that is *the* employee of the opposite sex performing equal work who has a background and credentials similar to those of the plaintiff. *Houck v. VPI,* 10

F.3d 204 (4th Cir. 1993). Pay rates between plaintiff and this similarly situated employee are compared. Finally, some authority provides that pay comparisons should be based on the *average* pay rate of those of the opposite sex doing equal work. If the average rate of the opposite sex is the same or less than the pay rate of plaintiff there is no EPA violation. If the average is higher, the EPA is violated with the higher average serving as the measure of defendant's liability. *Heymann v. Tetra Plastics Corp.,* 640 F.2d 115 (8th Cir. 1981).

20.07: DEFENDANT'S BURDEN: EPA DEFENSES

A. GENERALLY

If plaintiff carries the burden of establishing unequal pay rates between sexes for equal work performed within the same establishment, the employer avoids liability only by establishing that the difference in pay rates was based on bona fide *systems* that measured (i) seniority, (ii) merit, (iii) quantity or quality of work, or (iv) "any other factor other than sex."

B. SENIORITY SYSTEMS

The "seniority systems" defense in the EPA will be satisfied if the "system" meets the standards required by Title VII. (*Supra,* Chapter 19) in that it systematically allocates ever increasing benefits based on ever increasing time of employment. A system is not "bona fide" if it is facially based on sex, had its genesis in sex discrimination (such as sex segregated units), or was adopted for the purpose of disadvantaging women. However, the fact that a facially neutral system disadvantages one sex does not deprive the system of its bona fides. Thus, an employer may use relative seniority as a wage setting factor even though the more senior, and thus higher paid, workers are men.

To be a "system" seniority must be articulated, objective, predictable, and regularly followed. While a "system" need not be a product of contract, haphazard or idiosyncratic pay patterns cannot be justified by *ad hoc* or *post facto* conclusions that the higher paid employee had more "seniority." *Brock v. Georgia Southeastern College,* 765 F.2d 1026 (11th Cir. 1985).

C. MERIT SYSTEMS

The "merit systems" defense, similar to seniority, must be shown by the employer to be established as a system that routinely uses objective measurements of relative job performance. Pay differences based on regularized annual performance evaluations of all workers would constitute a "merit system." But mere *ad hoc,* subjective conclusions that one employee had more "merit" is not a "system."

D. QUALITY OR QUANTITY OF WORK

The "quality or quantity of work" defense appears to be a cautionary proviso that protects employer use of pay systems based solely on measured output (or "piecework"). If males and females are paid at the same "rate" for their output, their "rate of pay" will be the same, even if the employee of one sex who has greater output earns more gross pay than and the plaintiff. However, if different rates for similar quality or quantity of work performed are based on the sex of the employee performing the work, the system would lack the necessary sex-neutral bona fides. "Quality of work" would seem to encompass, as would "merit systems," systematic sex-neutral performance evaluations.

E. "FACTOR OTHER THAN SEX"

"The factor other than sex" defense is an omnibus, catch-all defense that encompasses a wide range of objective elements. The defense requires the employer to establish the sex-neutrality of the "factor" and that the "factor" is an objective and rational method for setting pay differences.

(1) Sex Neutrality

Facial sex distinctions cannot be a "factor *other than sex.*" Sex distinctions in actuarial tables upon which different pension deductions were based, was not based on "any other factor other than sex." "Sex is exactly what the [actuarial table] is based on." *Los Angeles Dep't of Water & Power v. Manhart,* 435 U.S. 702 (1978). An employer conducted training program that excluded women, recruited only men, or systematically discouraged women from participating could not qualify as a "factor other than sex." *Shultz v. First Victoria Nat. Bank,* 420 F.2d 648 (5th Cir. 1969).

Even a factor neutral on its face is not "other than sex" if the factor perpetuates *this employer's* past illegal sex discrimination or segregation. An employer that granted a "shift differential" in pay for night work when women were excluded from night work, and then "red circled" a higher rate of pay for male employees previously holding a higher paying night position cannot be a "factor other than sex." *Corning Glass Works v. Brennan,* 417 U.S. (1974). Where the employer previously set salaries based on sex, and then bases current salary on the employee's "past pay" *at this employer*, "past pay" is not a "factor other than sex" because it perpetuates this employer's past discriminatory practices. *See, Bazemore v. Friday,* 478 U.S. 375 (1974) (Title VII, race discrimination). However, simply because a factor *results* in lower pay for one sex does not deprive the factor of its necessary bona fides. For example, basing a starting salary for new employees on the salary earned at *other employers* can be a bona fide factor. *Kouba v. All State Ins. Co.,* 691 F.2d 873 (9th Cir. 1982). That socio-economic factors often result in women generally being paid less than men does not preclude the employer from using prior salary, or other factors such as experience, simply because the employer is aware of this result and continues to use the "factor" in spite of its effect of producing lower pay for women. *AFSCME v. State of Washington,* 770 F.2d 1401 (9th Cir. 1985) (sex discrimination under Title VII).

(2) "Factor"

"Factor" is ambiguous, but presupposes a level of business rationality weightier than "legitimate, non-discriminatory reason," but less burdensome than "business necessity." *County of Washington v. Gunther,* 452 U.S. 161 (1981). *See also, Meacham v. Knolls Atomic Power Lab.,* 554 U.S. 84 (2008) ("factor other than age" defense in ADEA). While some informality and subjectivity are not fatal (*Taylor v. White,* 321 F.3d 710 (8th Cir. 2003)), a reason will not be a "factor" if it is so subjective, unpredictable, or irrational that it reflects little more than the employer's day-to-day personnel needs. *Shultz v. First Victoria Nat. Bank, supra,* rejected as a factor a vague "training program" not shown by defendant to be rationally related to actual "training." There were no materials, no regularized rotation among tasks, no program of instruction, and no clear goals or performance measurements.

The EEOC and some courts hold that a "factor" must derive from either the personal characteristics of the workers (such as education, training, or experience) or from special needs connected to the employer's business. *Glenn v. General Motors Corp.,* 841 F.2d 1567 (11th Cir. 1988). Legitimate special employer needs would include: (1) temporary vs. permanent employment; (2) full-time v. part-time employment; (3) participation in bona fide, structured training programs; (4) probationary period; (5) salary matching that reflects market requirements to attract or retain employees (*Kouba v. All State Ins. Co.,* 691 F.2d 873 (9th Cir. 1982));

(6) maintenance of the pay of a higher paid worker while temporarily performing normally lower paying job duties in response to an emergency or other exigencies ("red circling"). "Red circling" that maintains a rate originally established on sex-based job cannot be a "factor other than sex." *Corning Glass Works v. Brennan, supra);* and (7) shift premiums to attract or reward employees working at undesirable times (*e.g.,* nights, week-ends, holidays, etc.). The night shift premiums involved in *Corning Glass Works v. Brennan, supra,* failed as a defense because they were based on the employer's past discrimination that prohibited women from working the higher paid night shift. Paying a premium to "heads of household" would not be a "factor other than sex" because such a factor did not relate to any employment related qualities of the worker and lacked a relationship to *employer* needs.

Some courts consider any rational sex-neutral basis for making pay differences to be a "factor" regardless of whether it has a relationship to employer needs or special qualities of the worker. In addition to those business related factors listed above, this authority would accept as a "factor" sex-neutral premium payments to "heads of household" or higher pay to employees having a family or social relationship with the employer. *EEOC v. J.C. Penney Co., Inc.,* 843 F.2d 249 (6th Cir. 1988).

CHAPTER 21

DIRECT COMPENSATION UNDER TITLE VII, ADA, AND ADEA

21.01: TITLE VII AND THE EPA: THE "BENNETT AMENDMENT"

As Title VII requires discrimination "because of sex," the motive behind differences in compensation between sexes is key. Title VII attempts a reconciliation with the EPA in a provision known as the "Bennett Amendment," which allows employers to make pay distinctions "if such differentiation is *authorized* [by the EPA]." 42 U.S.C. 2000e–2(h).

County of Washington v. Gunther, 452 U.S. 161 (1981), construed this amendment in a case involving male and female prison guards who were *not* performing "equal work" within the meaning of the EPA. Defendant contended that since the pay differential for male and female guards did not violate the EPA, the "Bennett Amendment" required a finding that Title VII was not violated. The Court disagreed, holding that a pay difference is *"authorized"* by the EPA only when the difference is based on one of the four statutory defenses in the EPA. *Supra,* **20.07.** Thus, a finding that the work of male and female guards was not "equal" did not preclude plaintiff from proving that the pay difference was motivated by sex in violation of Title VII.

This interpretation results only in the EPA defenses being incorporated into Title VII. The *Gunther* dissent argued that such a holding renders the Amendment meaningless, as any factor illegally motivated could not possibly be a "factor other than sex." The majority pointed out, however, that the Amendment has viability in that it would affect liability based on impact. The Bennett Amendment would allow employers to avoid liability if the challenged criteria was a "factor other than sex," a burden which the Court assumed to be lighter than proving that the factor is "job related" and consistent with "business necessity" as is required by Title VII.

21.02: PROVING MOTIVE UNDER THE CORE STATUTES

A. FACIAL DISTINCTIONS

Salary scales drawn along class lines carry their own indicia of illegal motive. Basing raises on prior illegal discrimination perpetrates the motivation originally held by the defendant. *Bazemore v. Friday,* 478 U.S. 385 (1986). Verbal (or "direct") evidence, such as "women do not deserve the same pay as men" or "old deadwood shouldn't be paid as much as young bucks," would tend to prove that any difference was influenced by improper motive. Ostensibly neutral distinctions, such as those resulting from the application of a seniority system will violate Title VII only if plaintiff proves that defendant adopted the system to disadvantage a protected class.

B. CIRCUMSTANTIAL EVIDENCE

Courts have applied to pay differences the general *McDonnell Douglas v. Green* model of proof used in hiring, promotion, and discharge cases. *Supra,* Chapter 16. Plaintiff must first demonstrate that the jobs of employees from different classes have "significant similarity," and that these *"similarly situated"* employees are compensated at different rates. Work need not be "equal" under the stringent EPA standard. *Miranda v. B & B Cash Store, Inc.,* 975 F.2d 1518 (11th Cir. 1992). However, plaintiff's initial prima face burden is not satisfied by a showing that two wholly different jobs receiving different pay simply have an abstract "comparable worth" to society or to this employer. *AFSCME v. Washington,* 770 F.2d 1401(9th Cir. 1985).

Some courts, ignoring the implications of *County of Washington v. Gunther, supra,* require plaintiff to prove that a higher paid comparator in a class different from plaintiff performs work that is "equal" under the objective standards of the EPA. Absent a facially discriminatory classification or "direct" evidence of sex motivation, a failure to establish a prima facie violation of the EPA is seen as a failure to establish a prima facie inference of illegal motive. *Tademe v. St. Cloud State Univ.,* 328 F.3d 982 (8th Cir. 2003).

After plaintiff establishes a prima facie case, defendant's burden is to "articulate a legitimate, non-discriminatory reason" for the pay difference, which may include any "reason," even if the reason articulated is subjective or lacks a relationship to

the job or to the employee's performance. *Miranda
v. B & B Cash Grocery, Inc., supra.* Others have
adopted the more stringent EPA standard as
defendant's burden, by requiring the employer to
"articulate" (but not necessarily prove) a "factor
other than sex" as defined under the EPA, which
requires some degree of business relatedness that
exceeds being merely *"a"* reason that is abstractly
"legitimate." *Korte v. Diemer,* 909 F.2d 954 (6th Cir.
1990).

If defendant "articulates" a reason for the pay
difference, the burden re-shifts to plaintiff to
present additional evidence that the articulated
reason for the pay difference was a pretext, and to
carry the burden of proving defendant's illegal
motive for compensating its workers of different
classes at different rates. Chapters 16.08 and 16.09,
supra, outline pretext evidence and discuss
plaintiff's ultimate burden of proof.

C. STATISTICAL EVIDENCE

It is difficult to establish illegal motive for pay
differences with statistics. Mere elimination of
chance as a hypothesis for differences is largely
meaningless in that there are a large number of
legitimate variables used to determine individual
salaries, such as education, past experience, former
salary, length of service, work history, and past
performance evaluations. That one class of workers
earns less than workers of another class, even in the
same or similar job categories, does little to
demonstrate that the difference was improperly
motivated. *Coble v. Hot Springs School Dist. No. 6,*

682 F.2d 721 (8th Cir. 1982). Nevertheless, sophisticated statistical techniques, such as "multiple regression analysis" can account for the numerous variables used to set salaries and statistically conclude that the only reason that consistently accounts for the observed pay difference is membership in a protected class. *Bazemore v Friday,* 478 U.S. 385 (1986). *Supra,* Chapter 17.

21.03: IMPACT–BASED LIABILITY

A. TITLE VII AND ADA

Impact-based liability depends on isolating with precision a device that is causing an adverse impact on a protected class. Thus, where a single factor, or even a subjective process, is producing an adverse salary structure, the adverse impact of that factor can be used to establish liability. Chapter 18. Again, because salaries are often the product of diverse legitimate elements such as education, experience, prior salary, past performance, etc., it may be impossible to isolate a single element and prove with the necessary precision that any given device is causing an observed pay difference between classes.

B. ADEA

Occasionally it is possible to isolate a single factor that produces differences in compensation for older workers, such as "market forces," or education levels. However, the ADEA allows employers to justify the use of such elements if they are "factors other than age" (borrowing language from the EPA). "Factors other than age" need not meet the stringent standard of being "job related" or a "business necessity," but need be only a rational system regularly applied. Relative salary, education levels, etc. can be "factors other than age" even though they are not a business necessity. Chapters 18.04 and 20.06.

CHAPTER 22

INSURANCE

22.01: TITLE VII AND THE PREGNANCY DISCRIMINATION ACT (PDA)

While Title VII does not require employers to provide employees with health benefit programs, distinctions in employer sponsored programs that are drawn along class lines violate the Act. The Pregnancy Discrimination Act (PDA) amendments to Title VII state specifically: "Women affected by pregnancy, childbirth, or related conditions shall be treated the same for all employment related purposes, including receipt of benefits under fringe benefit programs, as other persons not so affected but similar in their ability or inability to work." 42 U.S.C. 2000e(k).

Even if an employer demonstrates that women (or any other protected class) have higher health care costs than other classes, higher costs cannot justify an employer passing on these costs to members of a protected class or reducing benefits to that class in order to equalize cost differences. *Arizona Governing Committee v. Norris,* 463 U.S. 1073 (1983).

The employer that provides access to the insurance as part of its employee benefit package does not avoid liability because a participating independent underwriter created the discriminatory policy. The employer offering the insurance to its employees coupled with the employer's contractual relationship with the underwriter is sufficient to attribute discrimination in the insurance policies to the "employer." *Arizona Governing Committee v. Norris, supra.*

If an employer provides no health benefits to its employees, and the employee procures an insurance policy that includes discriminatory distinctions, no Title VII claim would lie against either the employer or the insurance company. However, the Affordable Health Care Act of 2011 will require insurers in 2014 to offer non-discriminatory policies that make no pregnancy or childbirth distinctions, and will prohibit denial of coverage for pre-existing conditions, including pregnancy, childbirth, and related medical complications.

Even if the employer provides health care benefits to its employees, it has no obligation to provide benefits to *dependents* of employees. If it does provide dependent coverage, that coverage cannot discriminate along class lines. Thus, the benefit package provided dependents may not exclude or provide lesser benefits for pregnancy and childbirth. The level of pregnancy and childbirth protection provided dependents must be equal to that provided to *employees* who suffer from conditions similarly affecting their ability to work. *Newport News Shipbuilding & Dry Dock Co. v. EEOC,* 462 U.S. 669 (1983).

Procedures to get pregnant are considered protected "pregnancy and childbirth," *Hall v. Nalco, Co.,* 534 F.3d 644 (7th Cir. 2008), and must be covered in an employer-provided health benefit plan. The EEOC also has concluded that contraception to prevent pregnancy falls within "pregnancy and childbirth," and thus contraception coverage must be included in any such policies. *Accord: Catholic Charities of Sacramento v. Superior Court,* 109 Cal.Rptr.2d 176 (2001), *aff'd* 85 P.3d 67 (2004); *Erickson v. Bartell Drug Co.,* 141 F.Supp.2d 1266 (Wash.2001). *Contra, Standridge v. Union Pac. R.R. Co.,* 479 F.3d 936 (8th Cir. 2007) (contraceptives are neither childbirth nor pregnancy, and if coverage is denied both men and women, there is no sex discrimination).

Even for employers with health care plans Title VII provides that nothing shall require an employer to pay for benefits covering abortion except where the life of the mother would be endangered if the fetus were carried to term or where medical complications have arisen from an abortion. 42 U.S.C. 2000e–(k).

Employer sponsored life insurance may not utilize actuarial tables to determine either the amount of premium that an employee must pay or the amount of benefit coverage an employee receives that are based on the race, national origin, sex, or religion of the employee. *Arizona Governing Committee v. Norris,* 463 U.S. 1073 (1983).

22.02: ADEA

Certain distinctions in the benefits paid by insurance plans based on actuarial costs associated with *aging,* that would violate Title VII if made on the basis of race or sex, are authorized by the ADEA. Health plans may reduce benefits paid to workers based on their age where the amount of payment or costs incurred by the employer on behalf of the older worker is no less than the costs incurred on behalf of younger workers. Employers may not, however, require older workers to pay greater amounts in order to *maintain* the benefits enjoyed by younger workers. Employers may offer *voluntary* participation in a plan that permits older workers to receive benefits equal to that of younger workers by increasing the contribution from older workers to the extent the increased contribution reflects actual increased cost to the employer of providing the equal coverage. 29 U.S.C. 623(i). Maintaining equal benefits for older workers even though costs for them are increasing does not constitute age discrimination against younger workers. *Supra,* 10.02.

"No such employee benefit plan * * * shall excuse the failure to hire any individual, and no such * * * plan shall permit the involuntary retirement of any individual * * * [because of age]." 29 U.S.C. 623(f)(2)(B).

22.03: ADA

Employers may not refuse to hire an individual with a disability, one who is regarded as having a disability, or one who has a record of a disability because of a perceived economic impact on the employer's benefit program. 29 C.F.R. 1630.16(f) App. Employers may not exclude employees from the general coverage of the benefit program because of the individual's impairment or his record of impairments. *Carparts Dist. Ctr., Inc. v. Automotive*

Wholesaler's Ass'n, 37 F.3d 12 (1st Cir. 1994). Moreover, an employer may not discriminate against any person or deny them access to the health benefits provided others because of the individual's *relationship* to or association with an individual with an impairment. *Trujillo v. Pacifcorp.,* 524 F.3d 1149 (10th Cir. 2008).

Similar to the ADEA, the ADA specifically allows health care plans to make generally applicable risk distinctions that utilize bona fide industry accepted standards that limit risks to categories that contain both disabled and non-disabled persons. 42 U.S.C. 12201(c). For example, a plan may exclude from coverage dental care while including eye care in that persons needing eye and dental care each contain individuals who do and do not suffer from a disability. A plan may have different payment caps between different classes of medical service, such as limiting payment for physical therapy, as both disabled and non-disabled persons are being limited in their use of this benefit. Co-pay obligations may vary, for example, by imposing on patients greater obligations to pay for prescriptions than for office visits. The Mental Health Parity Act, 42 U.S.C. 300gg–5, however, generally requires health insurance to provide mental health benefits at the same level as provided for physical conditions.

A health care plan that excludes from coverage, or provides reduced benefits to, conditions that include *only* persons with an identified disability or a discrete group of disabilities is suspect and may violate the ADA. For example, a plan that places lower caps for the treatment of HIV positive than it

places on other viral conditions would lack bona
fides in that the distinction is a facial discrimination
against a defined disability. The EEOC has
indicated that to justify discriminatory treatment of
a particular disability employers must demonstrate
the "business necessity" of such discrimination. A
mere reasonable, cost-based justification for the
discrimination will not suffice. Courts, however,
have permitted employers to use otherwise bona
fide plans even if the plan limits the amount of
benefits to some disabilities if the limitation is
based on industry accepted actuarial data. *Weyer v.
Twentieth Century Fox Film Corp,* 198 F.3d 1104
(9th Cir. 2000).

CHAPTER 23

PENSIONS AND RETIREMENT

23.01: TITLE VII

Los Angeles Dep't of Light & Power v. Manhart, 435 U.S. 702 (1978), held that it was sex discrimination to require individual women to pay more into an employer's defined benefit pension plan than was required of men. The actuarial fact that women *as a class* live longer than men, and thus statistically women eventually would draw from their pensions an amount similar to that of men was no defense to individual, sex-based distinctions. *Manhart's* reasoning was extended to defined *contribution* plans offered by employers but managed by independent underwriters. *Arizona Governing Committee v. Norris,* 463 U.S. 1073 (1978). The program made no distinction as to payments by employees into the retirement fund. However, the underwriter offered differing benefit options upon retirement, one of which provided for larger monthly payments to male retirees than was provided for similarly situated females based on the shorter life expectancies of men. Like discriminatory *contributions,* a sex-based difference in retirement *benefits* was proscribed. Similarly, providing higher severance pay or other benefits to males than to similarly situated females is actionable sex discrimination. *Gerner v. County of Chesterfield,* 674 F.3d 264 (4th Cir. 2012).

23.02: ADEA

A. BENEFIT ALLOCATIONS

No pension or retirement plan "shall excuse the failure to hire any individual and no such * * * plan shall permit the involuntary retirement of any individual * * * because of his age." 29 U.S.C. 623(f)(2)(B). While generally prohibiting age discrimination in pension programs, the ADEA specifically authorizes plans to set a minimum age as a condition for eligibility to receive retirement benefits, to calculate benefits based on the number of years of participation in the plan, and impose a maximum amount of retirement benefits an employee may accrue. 29 U.S.C. 623(*l*)(1)(a) and 29 U.S.C. 623(f)(2)(B).

When a plan makes an age distinction that disadvantages older workers, the employer has the burden of proving the bona fides of the plan and its application to plaintiff. To be a qualifying "plan" using such an age distinction it must be accurately described in writing and provide benefits in accordance with the written terms. The Act includes complex and detailed provisions as what is required in those terms to be considered bona fide.

Kentucky Retirement Sys. v. EEOC, 554 U.S. 135 (2008), involved a plan that permitted retirement after 5 years of service and the employee reaching age 55. The ADEA permits employers to place both conditions on pension eligibility. 29 U.S.C. 623 (*l*)(1)(a). But the plan also made an age distinction between "pension-eligible" workers who were forced to retire because of a job related disability. Younger workers facing disability retirement who, because of their age, would receive a smaller pension benefit, were provided an enhancement bonus to their pensions that was not provided older workers who were disabled. The Court held that this distinction was not "because of age," but was a good faith attempt to equitably address the disparate economic consequences faced by younger workers who are forced through disability to retire on a small retirement benefit, compared to the "full" retirement benefit that older, disabled workers would receive.

B. RETIREMENT: FORCED AND "VOLUNTARY"

Except for certain bona fide executives over age 65, employees may not be forced to retire because of their age, and retirement plans cannot be used to force retirement. The ADEA does, however, permit "voluntary early retirement incentive programs" as long as the plan does not disadvantage older workers. 29 U.S.C. 623(f)(2)(B)(ii). It violates the ADEA to offer early retirement benefits to younger workers greater than those offered older workers if the difference is based on age. However, incentives based solely on an employee's years of service or salary are analytically distinct from proscribed age discrimination (*Hazen Paper Co. v. Biggins,* 507 U.S. 604 (1993)), and may be used to allocate incentives. *Jankovitz v. Des Moines Ind. Comm. School Dist.,* 421 F.3d 649 (8th Cir 2005).

In all cases retirement based on age, even if induced by incentives, must be "voluntary." A retirement is not voluntary if rejection of the employer's offer of a "voluntary" retirement package is coupled with the threat of lay-off or of a reassignment to a different job at reduced pay if the employee refuses to accept retirement. *Vega v. Kodak Caribbean, Ltd.,* 3 F.3d 476 (1st Cir. 1993). A "one time only" offer with a "take it leave it" time window for acceptance, unaccompanied by any threats of job loss or demotion, can be "voluntary." *Henn v. National Geographic Soc.,* 819 F.2d 824 (7th Cir. 1987).

C. WAIVER OF CLAIMS

"Voluntary" retirement programs often are conditioned upon the eligible employee executing a waiver of any age discrimination claims. Such waivers will be enforced against the employee if, but only if, they meet seven specific statutory standards. 29 U.S.C. 626 (f). (*Infra,* 31.01 outlines the standards). A waiver not meeting these requirements cannot be enforced against the employee, even if the employee failed to return the consideration paid by the employer to secure the waiver. *Oubre v. Entergy Operations,* 522 U.S. 422 (1998). An employer's failure to satisfy the statutory standards required for an enforceable waiver does not establish that the employee's retirement was involuntary.

CHAPTER 24

LEAVES AND REASSIGNMENTS

24.01: GENERALLY

Normal assignment of daily duties and true "lateral" transfers to similar jobs with the same benefits and similar working conditions generally are not deemed to adversely affect a "term or condition of employment." *Harlston v. McDonnell Douglas Corp.*, 37 F.3d 379 (8th Cir. 1994). However, transfers to jobs that entail more onerous duties, have less prestige, and limit future job opportunities will affect "conditions of employment," even though the transfer involved no loss in salary or other tangible benefit. *Burlington Northern & Santa Fe R.R. v. White*, 548 U.S. 53 (2006) (Alito concurring). Even if job duties are no more onerous, permanent reassignment to a job with significantly less responsibility, to work under the supervision of persons holding lower grade levels may adversely affect "terms and conditions of employment." *Youssef v. FBI*, 687 F.3d 397 (D.C. Cir. 2012). Allowing or denying vacation, setting annual leave, or allocating medical leave along proscribed lines is a facial violation of the core statues.

24.02: TITLE VII: PREGNANCY, CHILDBIRTH, AND CHILDCARE LEAVES

Denying leave for childbirth or pregnancy that is granted to other medical conditions similarly affecting the ability to work is pregnancy (and thus "sex") discrimination. 42 U.S.C. 2000e–(k). Even if leaves are not normally granted for illness or injury, Title VII makes it proscribed sex discrimination to deny a woman leave that is necessitated by the birth of her child. It is not sex discrimination, however, to deny a father leave to participate in the birth of his child, simply because the statutory right is granted to mothers. *California Fed. Sav. & Loan Ass'n,* 479 U.S. 272 (1987).

Title VII does not require the employer to grant leave to the mother to *care* for her newborn child beyond the period of time required by the medical needs occasioned by the pregnancy or the child's birth. *Piatanida v. Wyman Ctr.,* 116 F.3d 340 (8th Cir. 1997). If the employer grants mothers leave for *childcare,* it is sex discrimination to deny similar *childcare* leave to fathers. *Shafer v. Bd. of Pub. Educ.,* 903 F.2d 243 (3d Cir. 1990).

Where an employer has provided leave or duty assignment accommodations for employees who suffer from non-pregnancy related medical conditions (*e.g.,* back problems, nausea, strained muscles, influenza, etc.), the denial of similar leave or duty reassignment to women who are in medical need of such accommodation due to their pregnancy is sex discrimination. *Ensley–Gaines v. Runyon,* 100 F.3d 1220 (6th Cir. 1996).

In *Hall v. Nalco Co.,* 534 F.3d 644 (7th Cir. 2008), the employer argued that the discharge of a woman for taking time off to undergo fertility treatments could not be discriminatory because denial of leave to secure fertility treatments applied equally to men. The court disagreed, holding the dismissal for seeking methods to become pregnant was sex discrimination in that such a policy would fall almost exclusively on women because it was based on their unique child bearing capacity. Imposing a requirement that *all employees* be able to lift 150 lbs, a weight that medical evidence indicated that most pregnant women could not safely lift, was held to have an adverse impact on women requiring the employer to demonstrate the "business necessity" of the policy. *Garcia v. Women's Hosp. of Texas,* 97 F.3d 810 (5th Cir. 1996). *Chapter 7 Tr. v. Gate Gourmet, Inc.,* 687 F.3d 1249 (11th Cir. 2012), held that the employer violated Title VII when it denied a light duty assignment to a pregnant employee and summarily discharged the employee when she could no longer perform her current duties because of her pregnancy. The court expressly held that liability could be established without plaintiff presenting any "comparator" evidence that light duty assignments had been granted to males. *Supra,* Chapter 5.03.

Many courts, however, have demanded a showing of "discrimination" and refuse to apply an analysis of "undue burden" on women whose pregnancy inhibits their ability to comply with an employer's uniformly applied attendance or leave rules. *Troup v. May Dep't Stores, Co.,* 20 F.3d 737 (7th Cir. 1994) ("Employers may treat pregnant women as badly as they treat similarly affected but nonpregnant employees"). *Stout v. Baxter Healthcare Corp.,* 282 F.3d 856 (5th Cir. 2002), held that a draconian application of an attendance policy resulting in the discharge of a woman whose absences were necessitated by her early labor and miscarriage was not sex discrimination. When workers generally are required to stand, as would be the case for "greeters" or check-out clerks, the employer need not allow the pregnant worker to sit or be allowed occasional rest breaks. *Walsh v. National Computer Sys.*, 332 F.3d 1150 (8th Cir. 2003).

These courts also have shown a reluctance to find any "discrimination" in the application of employers' leave or job assignment policies. For example, *Serendynj v. Beverly Healthcare, LLC,* 656 F.2d 540 (7th Cir. 2011), held that granting an accommodation to employees suffering from a physical "disability" as defined by the ADA, while denying an accommodation to women whose pregnancy necessitated a similar accommodation, was not discriminatory because normal pregnancy is not a disability under the ADA. *Young v. UPS, Inc.,* 707 F.3d 437 (4th Cir. 2013), found that denying an accommodation to physical manifestations of pregnancy was not discriminatory even when employees who suffered from non-disabling impairments were accommodated when the impairment was "job related." As pregnancy impairments were not "job related," there was no "discrimination" against pregnancy.

Such cases seem inconsistent with Supreme Court and statutory directives. Ungenerous leave and work assignment policies applied to pregnancy necessarily place a significant burden on women not suffered by men. Even prior to the PDA the Court held that burdensome application of neutral rules to pregnancy constitutes "sex" discrimination. *Nashville Gas Co v. Satty,* 434 U.S. 347 (1977) (the loss of seniority caused by absences when absences caused by pregnancy imposes a unique "burden" on women and thus constitutes "sex" discrimination). Moreover, Title VII specifically directs that it is unlawful discrimination when:

> the complaining party demonstrates that a respondent uses a particular employment practice that causes a disparate impact on the basis of race, color, religion, sex or national origin and the [employer] fails to demonstrate that the challenged practice is job related for the position in question and consistent with business necessity. 42 U.S.C. 2000e–2(k)(1)(A).

Draconian leave policies or the cost of providing minimal work assignment adjustments rarely, if ever, would constitute a "business necessity."

Proposed federal legislation, the Pregnant Workers Fairness Act (H.R. 5647), would amend Title VII to make clear that employers would be required to make reasonable accommodation for medical conditions occasioned by pregnancy. The proposal has stalled in Congress.

24.03: FAMILY AND MEDICAL LEAVE ACT, 29 U.S.C. 2601, (FMLA)

A. GENERALLY

An "eligible employee" of a covered "employer" is entitled to a total of 12 workweeks of unpaid leave during any 12 month period for one or more of the following: (1) Birth, adoption, or grant of foster custody of child in order to care for the child; (2) To care for a spouse, parent, or child of the employee with a "serious health condition;" or (3) Because a "serious health condition" makes the employee unable to perform the functions of the job.

If an employer provides leave benefits longer than the twelve weeks required by the FMLA, the employer may consider the leave cumulative rather than consecutive, allowing only leave in excess of that required by the FMLA. *Ragsdale v. Wolverine World Wide, Inc.*, 535 U.S. 81 (2002).

Leave authorized by the FMLA confers on employers no right to require employees to take unpaid leave. Indeed to require an employee to take leave because she is pregnant, has given birth, or suffers from a medical condition associated with pregnancy or childbirth violates Title VII. Requiring an employee to take leave because he is "regarded as having" a disability can violate the ADA.

B. COVERAGE AND ELIGIBILITY

Employers are covered only if they have 50 or more employees. Employees are "eligible" for authorized leave only if they have been employed by the covered employer for the previous 12 month period and worked during that period at least 1,250 hours. Leave rights extends to males and fathers as well as to females and mothers.

C. CHILDBIRTH AND CHILDCARE

The father as well as the mother may claim leave for the birth, adoption, or receipt of a foster child. Childcare leave after the child's birth also may be taken by the mother and father, but the cumulative amount may not exceed 12 weeks during that calendar year, and must be taken within 12 months following the birth of the child. 29 U.S.C. 2612(f).

D. "SERIOUS HEALTH CONDITION"

The right of an eligible employee to take leave to care for himself, a child, spouse, or parent requires that the person cared for suffer from a "serious health condition." If both eligible employees in one family are employed by the same employer each is independently entitled to separate 12 weeks of unpaid leave to care for their own serious health conditions, and the leave may be taken simultaneously or consecutively with each other. Leave taken to care for serious health conditions may be taken intermittently or on a reduced work week schedule when "medically necessary." Thus, an employee whose serious condition medically precludes work for more than six hours of a normal eight hour day may claim two hours of leave per day. *Whitaker v. Bosch Braking Sys. Div.,* 180 F.Supp.2d 922 (W.D. Mich. 2001). If an employee needs one day a week to care for a parent who needs dialysis, the employee could claim that leave day per week as unpaid medical care leave. 29 U.S.C. 2612(b).

"Serious health condition" that requires the grant of leave need not reach the level of being a "disability" under the ADA, nor need the condition be life threatening, incapacitating, or chronic. *Navarro v. Pfizer Corp.*, 261 F.3d 90 (1st Cir. 2001). However, "serious" excludes routine medical care, such as physical examinations, dental work, elective minor out-patient procedures, and non-incapacitating conditions like headache, stomach upset, or common colds. The inability to perform essential job functions is a key factor in determining the condition's "seriousness." The duration of the incapacity must also be considered. The statute specifically provides that to be entitled to leave to care for a sick or injured child, the condition must result in the child being absent from school for at least three days. Thus, incapacitations for less than three days would rarely, if ever, be considered "serious." A short term head cold is not "serious." Sinus infections, migraine headaches, and influenza would be "serious."

"Normal" pregnancy, to be distinguished from childbirth, is not per se a "serious health condition." 29 C.F.R. 825.114(a)(a)(2)(i). However, at the point in her pregnancy when the eligible employee is unable to perform essential functions of her job because of her condition, she will be considered as having a "serious health problem," at which time leave must be granted.

E. NOTICE

Even if leave is authorized, employees who simply absent themselves without giving proper notice may be terminated for an unauthorized absence. *Brown v. Automotive Comp. Holding, LLC,* 622 F.3d 685 (7th Cir. 2010). When "practicable" the employee must provide the employer 30 days' notice prior to taking leave. Regulations allow lesser notice of one or two working days upon learning of the need, except in "extraordinary circumstances" or when otherwise "not feasible." 29 C.F.R. 825.303(a). "Extraordinary circumstances" would seem to include serious injuries suffered in an accident or the sudden onset of an incapacitating illness.

Notice does not demand formality or invoking the statute. Indicating the nature of the reason and intent to take leave will suffice. *Tate v. Farmland Indus., Inc.,* 268 F.3d 989 (10th Cir. 2001). However, a telephone call merely informing the employer that the employee was not "feeling well," was not notice requesting leave. *Scobey v. Nucor Steel–Ark.,* 580 F.3d 781 (8th Cir. 2009).

F. MEDICAL CERTIFICATION

Upon receiving the employee's notice and request for medical leave the employer may require the employee to provide a certificate of incapacity issued by a health care provider. 29 U.S.C. 2613(a). This request must be in writing, detail the obligations under the Act, and consequences flowing from the employee's non-compliance. 29 C.F.R. 825.301(b)(1)(ii). The employee has 15 days from receipt of the employer's request to supply the requested medical certificate. The employer may not terminate the employee during this 15 day period. Unless the employer makes an appropriate and timely demand for a certificate of incapacity, the employee may not be dismissed for failing to provide documentation. *Branham v. Gannett Satellite Inf. Network,* 619 F.3d 563 (6th Cir. 2010).

G. BENEFITS AND REINSTATEMENT

While leave need not be paid and no new benefits need accrue, if the employer has a group health plan, the employer is required to maintain the employee's coverage while on FMLA authorized leave. 29 U.S.C. 2416(c). At the end of the leave employees are entitled to full reinstatement without loss of pre-leave *accrued* rights or benefits, such as seniority or pension. Only "reasonable cause" will justify denial of full reinstatement. *Sanders v. City of Newport,* 657 F.3d 722 (9th Cir. 2011).

H. NON–DISCRIMINATION

The FMLA prohibits discrimination because of the request for FMLA leave or for taking leaves authorized by the Act. This prohibition against discrimination extends to leave requests made *prior* to the time the employee becomes eligible. In *Pereda v. Brookline Senior Living Communities, Inc.,* 666 F.3d 1269 (11th Cir. 2012), plaintiff notified her employer that she was pregnant and that she would be seeking birth and childcare leave in the coming months. At the time plaintiff gave notice she had worked for an insufficient period of time to be eligible for leave. *Supra,* 24.03(b). However, plaintiff would have become eligible for childbirth and care leave before the expected birth date. Soon after plaintiff gave notice she was subjected to harassment and eventually discharged. Plaintiff stated a claim under FMLA.

I. DAMAGES

Plaintiffs may recover damages for injuries caused by illegal denial of authorized leave or the refusal to reinstate the employee after taking authorized leave. 29 U.S.C. 2617(a)(2). While damages can be secured against state government employers for violations of the *family care* leave provisions of the FMLA, as such provisions address sex discrimination pursuant to Congressional powers created by the 14th Amendment, 11th Amendment concepts of sovereign immunity preclude recovery of damages for state violations of the *self-care* provisions of the Act. *Coleman v. Maryland Court of Appeals,* ___ U.S. ___, 132 S.Ct. 1327 (2012).

24.04: LEAVES FOR MILITARY SERVICE: THE UNIFORMED SERVICES EMPLOYMENT AND REEMPLOYMENT ACT, 38 U S. C. 4301 (USERA)

In addition to prohibiting discrimination because of military service obligations, USERA requires prompt reemployment of "any person whose absence from a position of employment is necessitated by reason of service in the uniformed services." 38 U.S.C. 4312(a). Thus, an employee whose military obligations in the reserve require that he attend drill one week-end per month and train full time for three weeks per year must be allowed to fulfill those obligations, and the employer may not retaliate against the employee because of his current, past, or future military commitments. *Staub v. Proctor Hospital,* ___ U.S. ___, 132 S.Ct. 1327 (2011).

Upon reemployment the veteran will be "entitled to the seniority and other benefits determined by seniority that the person had at the date of the commencement of the [military] service * * * plus the additional rights and benefits that such employee would have attained if that person had remained continuously employed." 38 U.S.C. 4316(a). Re-employed veterans who had worked for the employer for 180 days may not be discharged within one year except for cause.

24.05: LEAVES, DUTY ASSIGNMENTS, AND RELIGIOUS BELIEFS: THE DUTY TO MAKE "REASONABLE ACCOMMODATION"

A. GENERALLY

Title VII imposes on employers an affirmative duty to "reasonably accommodate" an employee's bona fide religious observances or practices if to do so does not impose on the employer an "undue hardship." 42 U.S.C. 2000e–(j). This requires *reasonable* grants of leave or other duty assignments for religious observances or practices in order to avoid conflicts with the employee's religious beliefs or practices. *See, supra,* Chapter 8.

The relationship between "reasonable accommodation" and "undue hardship" was defined in *Ansonia Bd. of Educ. v. Philbrook,* 479 U.S. 60 (1986). Plaintiff was a teacher. His faith required refraining from work during certain holy days, which conflicted with scheduled school days six days a year. A collective bargain agreement provided that teachers would be allowed paid leave for three days per year to observe religious holidays. The contract also provided for up to 18 days of paid sick leave, and 3 days paid leave for "necessary personal business." Paid leave could only be used for the purposes specified in the contract, and thus could not be transferred for use in another category. This policy required plaintiff to take three days of *unpaid* leave in order to observe the holy days. As an accommodation plaintiff requested that the three days *paid* leave the contract allowed for "necessary personal business" be used by him for observance of the holy days. As an alternative plaintiff requested that his pay be reduced only by the amount necessary to hire a substitute teacher for the three days of his absence. The employer rejected both proposals.

The lower court held that even if the accommodation provided (3 days paid and 3 days unpaid) was on its face "reasonable," the employer must accept the accommodation suggested by the employee unless to do so would cause "undue hardship." The Supreme Court reversed:

> [W]here the employer has already reasonably accommodated the employee's religious needs, the statutory inquiry is at an end. The employer need not show that each of the employee's alternative accommodations would result in undue hardship. * * * [T]he extent of undue hardship on the employer's business is

at issue only where the employer claims that it is unable to offer any reasonable accommodation without such hardship."

On remand, the court of appeals affirmed a trial court finding that the employer's leave policy of 3 days paid and 3 days unpaid leave reasonably accommodated plaintiff's religious observances. *Philbrook v. Ansonia Bd. of Educ.*, 925 F.2d 47 (2d Cir. 1991).

B. "REASONABLE" DEFINED

Trans World Airlines, Inc. v. Hardison, 432 U.S. 63 (1977), which preceded *Ansonia*, defined more precisely the extent of an employer's accommodation obligations. *Hardison* involved an employee whose religious faith prevented him from working on Saturday, his Sabbath, to which he had been assigned pursuant to seniority provisions in a collective bargaining agreement. Plaintiff lacked the seniority under that contract to secure relief from the Saturday assignments and there were no volunteers who had greater seniority than plaintiff willing to accept Saturday work.

In terms of accommodation, the employer had reduced Saturday work to that necessary to maintain operations and had permitted voluntary trading of shifts between qualified employees. However, the employer and the union refused to modify the contractual seniority provisions to *require* shift changes that would result in workers senior to plaintiff being assigned Saturday work.

The employer also refused to offer premium pay to induce workers to volunteer for Saturday work.

The Court held that the employer's attempt to reduce the impact of Saturday work and facilitate voluntary shift exchanges was "reasonable," and in any event, both accommodations proposed by plaintiff were unreasonable, and/ or constituted an "undue hardship" on the employer. Disregarding seniority practices specifically preserved in 42 U.S.C. 2000e–(2)(j) could not be reasonable, and asking an employer to bear more than the *de minimis* cost of providing premium pay for Saturday work would be an "undue hardship."

De minimis thus is the talisman for "reasonable" under Title VII. Minor adjustments, such as allowing workers to leave a few minutes early, that impose minimal burdens on employers and impinge little on the work load of co-workers often are "reasonable." *EEOC v. Ilona of Hungary, Inc.*, 105 F.3d 1679 (7th Cir. 1997). But it is "unreasonable" to disregard neutral ways of allocating undesirable, but necessary, work that would shift undesirable work to those who had no religious objection. *Harrell v. Donahue,* 638 F.3d 975 (8th Cir. 2011). *See also, U.S. Airways v. Barnett,* 535 U.S. 391 (2002) ("reasonable accommodation" under the ADA does not require disregarding regularly followed systems of seniority even when seniority is not contractually imposed). It was an "undue hardship" on a retail employer whose busiest day was Saturday to allow a sales employee leave on Saturday to attend religious services. Under the circumstances, offering the employee a transfer to a different job and allowing shift swapping were reasonable accommodations. *Sanchez–Rodriguez v. AT & T Mobility Puerto Rico, Inc.,* 673 F.3d 1 (1st Cir. 2012).

Permitting employees not to be assigned some particular duty that interferes with their religious beliefs (*e.g.,* a pharmacist filling prescriptions for contraceptives) may be reasonable if the adjustment does not go to a critical aspect of the employee's normal job duties, does not place "customers" at risk, or shift to co-workers more than minimal burdens. However, allowing an employee to refuse to perform important duties of the job, essentially re-writing the job description, is unreasonable. Reasonable accommodation does not extend to a police officer who objects to assigned enforcement duties because of his religious objections to the law. *See, Rodriguez v. City of Chicago,* 156 F.3d 771 (7th Cir. 1998).

24.06: LEAVES, DUTY ASSIGNMENTS AND THE AMERICANS WITH DISABILITIES ACT, 42 U.S.C. 12101, (ADA)

A. GENERALLY

In addition to prohibiting discrimination against persons because of their "impairments" the ADA imposes on employers an affirmative obligation to make "reasonable accommodations" to the mental or physical *disabilities* of applicants or employees unless the accommodation would impose on this employer an "undue hardship." Notwithstanding language similarity to Title VII, the employer's duty to make accommodations under the ADA is significantly greater than the *de minimis* requirement imposed on employers by Title VII to accommodate religious observances and practices. *Supra,* 24.05.

Amendments in 2008 changed dramatically the definition of "disability," making many cases interpreting that term that arose prior to January 1, 2009 no longer reliable.

B. "ESSENTIAL" VS. NON–ESSENTIAL DUTIES

It is critical to distinguish between duties which are "essential," or core, to the job and those which are merely incidental or secondary. If the particular duty plaintiff cannot perform because of an impairment is not "essential" to that job, the employer may not discriminate against the person based on the "impairment." For example, if an individual had an impairment that precluded him from climbing a pole, and climbing was deemed a non-essential, secondary element to the job of a T.V. cable installer, an otherwise qualified plaintiff would have to be retained in the position in spite of his inability to climb. *Skerski v. Time Warner Cable Co.,* 257 F.3d 273 (3d Cir. 2001). This means that all medically defined physical or mental "impairments," regardless of whether the impairment is a "disability," must be accommodated to the extent that any *non-essential* duties that plaintiff cannot perform must be assigned to others. *See,* Chapter 12.04.

To secure an accommodation for an inability to perform job duties that are "essential" plaintiff must prove that his/her medically recognized physically or mental impairment is a "disability." This requires proof that a mental or physical impairment "substantially limits one or more major life activities." Thus, if the ability to climb is found to be "essential" for a cable installer, only *if* plaintiff's impairment that limits his ability to climb was found to "substantially limit a major life activity" would the employer be required to explore possible accommodations. If such an accommodation was found to be unreasonable, or imposed on the employer an "undue hardship," plaintiff would remain unqualified and need not be hired or retained. *Skerki v. Time Warner Cable Co., supra.*

C. "DISABLED" DEFINED

Toyota Motor Mfg. Kentucky, Inc. v. Williams, 534 U.S. 184 (2002), stated that the ADA should be "interpreted strictly to create a demanding standard for qualifying as disabled." ADA Amendments expressly rejected *Toyota's* "strict, demanding" standard: "To achieve the remedial purposes of the Act, the definition of 'disability' should be *broadly construed.*"

(1) Impairment

To be "disabled" the individual must suffer from a medically recognized physical or mental condition recognized as an "impairment." Traits or characteristics such as height, left handedness, baldness, and physical attractiveness are not "impairments." *See,* 11.03 *supra,* for the definition of, and exclusions from, "impairment."

The medical condition of *addiction* to alcohol and drugs is a disability. 42 U.S.C. 12114 (b). However, the inability of the employee to meet the employer's normal performance and attendance standards are not protected. The inability to secure necessary licenses or perform essential job tasks because of the addiction need not be accommodated. *Maddox v. Univ. of Tenn.,* 62 F.3d 843 (6th Cir. 1995). Adjusting a work schedule to permit an addict to secure medical treatment for addiction or participate in a rehabilitation program would be one of the few instances where a reasonable accommodation might be required. *See,* 42 U.S.C. 12114(b). *Supra,* 11.05.

Age is not, as such, an "impairment." Medical conditions often the result of, or exacerbated by, aging such as osteoporosis, arthritis, emphysema, failing eyesight, and heart disease can be "disabilities" that must be reasonably accommodated. *Appel v. Inspire Pharmaceuticals, Inc.,* 428 F.App'x 279 (5th Cir. 2011).

Normal pregnancy is not an impairment. 29 C.F.R. 1630.2(h)(1). Medical complications arising from pregnancy and childbirth that substantially limit a mother's major life activity will constitute a disability requiring accommodation. *Gorman v. Wells Mfg. Co.,* 209 F.Supp.2d 870 (S.D. Iowa 2002).

(2) "Major Life Activity"

Physical or mental "impairments" are "disabilities" only if the impairment limits *a* "major life activity." The Amendments provide a *non-exclusive* list of "major life activities:" "caring for oneself, performing manual tasks, seeing, hearing, eating, sleeping, walking, standing, lifting, bending, speaking, breathing, learning, reading, concentrating, thinking, communicating, and working." The inability to have sex or to reproduce is a major life activity. *Bragdon v. Abbott,* 524 U.S. 624 (1998). The impairment need limit only one "major life activity" to be a "disability."

The 2008 Amendments also list examples of bodily functions that are in themselves "major life activities:" defective immune systems; abnormal cell growth; digestive disorders; bladder, neurological, brain, respiratory, circular, endocrine, and reproductive malfunctions. Thus, any serious disease such as cancer, epilepsy, HIV infection, tuberculosis, diabetes, and cardio-vascular conditions, are disabilities without regard to whether the disease manifests current symptoms. As cancer inhibits normal cell growth, it affects a "major life activity." *Katz v. Adecco, USA,* 845 F.Supp. 539 (S.D.N.Y. 2012). An individual with any of such condition will be impaired in a "major life activity" regardless of the lack of symptoms or the effect of the disease on the individual's ability to perform activities, care for himself, or work.

(3) "Substantially Limited"

Toyota Motor Mfg., Kentucky, Inc. v. Williams, 534 U.S. 184 (2002), applying a "strict and demanding" standard, defined the statutory requirement of "substantially limit" to require that the impairment "prevents or *severely restricts*" the performance of the "major life activity." The Amendments expressly rejected this "severely restricts" standard, and redefined "substantially limits" to mean *"materially* limits." EEOC implementing guidelines indicate that one is "materially limited" if the individual has significant difficulty in performing a "major life activity" "that the average person in the general public can perform with little or no difficulty." 29 C.F.R. 1630.2. In making this determination courts will examine: (i) the severity of the condition, (ii) duration of the condition, and (iii) the manner in which it was contracted. 29 C.F.R. 1630(j)(2). For example, high cholesterol levels and painful varicose veins may be impairments, but unless they are currently impairing either bodily functions or one's ability to secure work or care for one's self, they may not be "disabilities." *See, Murphy v. United Parcel Serv.,* 527 U.S. 516 (1999).

Where "working" is the *only* major life activity impaired by plaintiff's condition, plaintiff must establish a broad of range of work that her impairment renders her unable to perform. *Duncan v. Washington Met. Area Transit Auth.,* 240 F.3d 1110 (D.C. Cir 2001). One is not materially limited in major life activity of working merely because he is precluded from "one type of job, or specialized job, or job of choice." *Sutton v. United Air Lines, Inc.,* 527 U.S. 471 (1999).

Pre–Amendment interpretation of the Act held that in addition to being "severe," "the impairment must *also* be permanent or *long term." Toyota Motor Mfg. v. Williams, supra.* As construed by the EEOC the Amendments direct that the duration of the impairment is but *one factor*—along with the severity and manner of the condition—to be weighed in determining when an impairment is "substantial." Major trauma or surgery that totally disables the individual, but only for a few weeks, *can* be a "disability" that must be accorded reasonable accommodation. 29 C.F.R. 1630.2(j)(4) App. There is no precise formula for determining when the combination of severity, duration, and manner will result in a conclusion that the impairment "substantially limits a major life activity."

For guidance one can look to other statutory provisions. Discrimination based on an individual "being regarded as" having a disability, may be defended by proof that plaintiff's impairment is both "transitory *and* minor." In this context EEOC defines "transitory" to mean an impairment "lasting or expected to last for six months or less." *Supra,* 11.03(c). This 6 month duration guideline that defines "transitory" has *no direct application* in determining the severity of the impairment that defines "disabled," but it may place an outer limit. An impairment lasting over 6 months would be "long term." The Family and Medical Leave Act, 29 U.S.C. 2601 *et seq.,* requires the grant of leave to parents to care for a child if the illness is "serious." "Serious" is defined in that statute to exclude illnesses that require the child to be absent from school less than 3 days. It would seem, then, an impairment lasting less than 3 days would not be "long term." With these outer limits providing the parameter, as the impairment approaches a duration of six months, the less severe need be the condition for it to be considered "substantially limiting." Relatively minor, but chronic, long lasting limitations, such as migraine headaches, hypertension, or shingles can be disabilities. Conversely, the closer the impairment comes to being measured in days, the greater must be its severity to be considered "*substantially* limiting." Serious injury; system malfunction, such as a heart attack or stroke; or infection, such as influenza, that largely incapacitates an individual for a period measured in weeks, if not days, could be "disabilities."

(4) Conditions Ameliorated, Episodic, or in Remission

The Amendments specify that: "An impairment that is episodic or in remission is a disability if it would substantially limit a major life activity when active." That the limit on a major life activity is brief or occurs infrequently is no longer relevant. Examples of protected episodic disorders are epilepsy, diabetes, asthma, and depressive and bi-polar disorders. "[A] person with post-traumatic stress disorder who experiences intermittent flashbacks to traumatic events is substantially limited in brain function and thinking." 29 C.F.R. 1630.2(j)(1)(vii).

The amended ADA and implementing regulations also provide that except for ordinary eye glasses or contact lenses: "The determination of whether an impairment substantially impairs a major life activity shall be made without regard to the ameliorative effects of mitigating measures." *Id.* A person who suffers from health impairing hypertension but whose blood pressure has been reduced to normal levels by medication is "disabled." An amputee is an individual with a disability notwithstanding that with a prosthesis he is not substantially limited in any major life activities. A person with a substantial hearing impairment will be disabled notwithstanding the fact that a hearing aid does, or could, produce near normal hearing. A person with diabetes has a disability even if the condition is being successfully managed by diet and exercise.

The Act specifically provides, however, that uncorrected poor eyesight will not be a substantial limitation if *ordinary* eyeglasses or contact lenses can correct the individual's sight to come within "normal" ranges. Nonetheless, if a qualification standard requires a level of uncorrected vision, and the individual cannot meet the standard, the employer must demonstrate that the uncorrected vision standard is "job related and consistent with business necessity."

D. "REASONABLE ACCOMMODATION"

(1) Generally

The ADA requires employers to make "reasonable accommodations" for a person's disability unless to do so imposes on this employer an "undue hardship." The disabled individual must disclose to the employer the nature of the disability, describe the inability to perform according to the employer's policies, and suggest with some specificity an accommodation that would allow her to perform. *Enica v. Principi,* 544 F.3d 328 (1st Cir. 2008). Plaintiff must establish that in the ordinary run of cases, on its face, the proposed accommodation is feasible and plausible. "The simple fact that an accommodation would provide a 'preference'—in the sense that it would permit the worker with a disability to violate a rule that others must obey—cannot in and of itself—automatically show that the accommodation is not 'reasonable.'" *U.S. Airways Inc. v. Barnett,* 535 U.S. 391 (2002).

The ADA contains a non-mandatory list of accommodations that should be considered and *may* be reasonable: "job restructuring, part-time or modified work schedules, reassignments to vacant positions, modification of equipment or devices, appropriate adjustment or modification of examinations, training materials or other policies, the provision of qualified readers or interpreters." 42 U.S.C. 12111(9)(B). "Reasonableness" under the ADA may require the employer to undertake significant costs to modify equipment, provide access to the work place, suffer some lost efficiency because of required leaves, breaks or re-scheduling, and may impose burdens on co-workers through restructured duty assignments that are more than *de minimis*. Accommodation is not reasonable if it would alter fundamentally the nature of the duties the disabled individual will perform or change the nature of the employer's business operations. Nor does accommodation require employers to provide workers with "private benefits" used away from the work place such as wheelchairs, medications, hearing aids, prosthetic limbs, etc. 29 C.F.R. 1630.9 App.

"Reasonableness" "is a relational term; it evaluates the desirability of a particular accommodation according to the consequences that the accommodation will produce." *Borkowski v. Valley Central School Dist.*, 63 F.3d 131 (2d Cir. 1995). In establishing that in the ordinary run of cases, on its face, the proposed accommodation is feasible and plausible, "plaintiff bears only the burden of identifying an accommodation, the costs of which, facially, do not clearly exceed its benefits." Summary judgment may be granted for a defendant only "in cases in which the plaintiff's proposal is either *clearly ineffective* or *outlandishly costly*." *Walton v. Mental Health Ass'n of Southeastern Pa.*, 168 F.3d 661 (3d Cir. 1999).

If plaintiff carries this burden, the burden then shifts to defendant to demonstrate that the proposed accommodation imposes on this particular employer a hardship deemed to be "undue." "If defendant responds by providing an accommodation that is reasonable, it does not lose its reasonableness merely because it was not the accommodation preferred or suggested by the employee, nor does it shift a burden to the employer to demonstrate that the accommodation preferred by the employee would impose on the employer an undue hardship. *Ansonia Bd. of Educ., v. Philbrook,* 479 U.S. 60 (1986) (Title VII accommodation of religious observance); *Steffes v. Stepan Co.,* 144 F.3d 1070 (7th Cir 1998). That an accommodation was provided in the past does not establish its reasonableness. Employers are free to discontinue unreasonable accommodations or those imposing undue hardships. *Watson v. Lithonia Lighting,* 304 F.3d 749 (7th Cir. 2002).

(2) Reasonableness Applied

(a) Duty Adjustments and Transfers

When lifting, climbing, or stooping are "essential" aspects of the particular job (*i.e.,* nurse or cable T.V. installer) assigning occasional lifting, climbing, or stooping to other workers and reassigning lighter duties to the disabled person may be reasonable. *Skerski v. Time Warner Cable Co.,* 257 F.3d 273 (3d Cir. 2001). Reasonable accommodation may require reassignment of a qualified disabled person to a vacant, similar position. *Smith v. Midland Brake, Inc.,* 180 F.3d 1154 (10th Cir. 1999). Merely giving disabled workers a "tie breaking preference" over *equally qualified* non-disabled applicants is not *per se* a reasonable accommodation. *EEOC v. United Airlines, Inc.,* 693 F.3d 760 (7th Cir. 2012). Transfer to vacancies that involve similar job duties, but at a different establishment located where the disabled employee could receive better medical care for his disability would be a reasonable accommodation even if the disabled person does not need an accommodation to be able to perform current job duties. *Sanchez v. Vilsack,* 695 F.3d 1174 (10th Cir. 2012).

Reasonableness does not require transfer to a position that requires significant training or promotion to a higher paying or supervisory position. *Lucas v. W.W. Grainger, Inc.,* 257 F.3d 1249 (11th Cir. 2001). Transfers that would require redefining core job duties or require assigning significant, burdensome duties to other employees is not reasonable. *Alexander v. The Northland Inn,* 321 F.3d 723 (8th Cir. 2003). Transfer is not reasonable if it entails the displacement of an incumbent employee. Nor is it reasonable for an employer to disregard an existing and regularly applied seniority system to fill vacancies, even if the seniority system creates no legally enforceable contract rights. *U.S. Airways v. Barnett,* 535 U.S. 391 (2002).

(b) Attendance and Leaves

When an individual's disability makes him regularly unable to report to work, rarely would it be reasonable to allow the employee to work at home or to tolerate repeated extended leaves taken with little or no notice. *Tyndall v. Nat. Educ. Cnt'r,* 31 F.3d 209 (4th Cir. 1994). "It is a rather common sense idea that if one is unable to come to work, one cannot be a qualified individual." *Sampler v.*

Providence St. Vincent Medical Cntr. 675 F.3d 1233
(9th Cir. 2012). *Cf. Core v. Champaign Cnty Bd. of
Comm'rs,* (S.D.Ohio, 2012), 2012 WL 4959444,
which recognized that in some circumstances
telecommuting, at least as an interim measure, may
be reasonable.

Allowing short leaves needed to recover from illness
or injury usually is reasonable and must be granted.
Ward v. Mass. Health Research Inst., 209 F.3d 29
(1st Cir. 2000). Unpaid leaves of a significant, but
finite period, to permit the employee to undergo
medical treatment or rehabilitation have been seen
as reasonable accommodations. *Humphrey v.
Memorial Hospitals Ass'n,* 239 F.3d 1128 (9th Cir.
2001). Even relatively long-term leaves to secure
medical attention for serious chronic illness, like
cancer, may be a reasonable accommodation.
Garcia–Ayala v. Lederle Parenterals, Inc., 212 F.3d
638 (1st Cir. 2000) (one year leave reasonable).

(c) Breaks and Work Schedules

Allowing short, regular, and recurring work
breaks for necessary rest or medication often is
reasonable. *Johnson v. Sullivan,* 824 F.Supp. 1146
(D.Md. 1991). But adjusting an individual's
schedule could be unreasonable when the nature of
the job requires uninterrupted performance or a
break taken by one employee would necessitate
ceasing operations or awkwardly inserting a
substitute worker (e.g., assembly line). *Grubb v.
Southwest Airlines,* 296 Fed.Appx. 383 (5th Cir.
2008). Unless an employer generally has part time
positions, granting indefinite part time work to

accommodate a disability may not be reasonable. *Terrell v U.S. Air,* 133 F.3d 621 (11th Cir. 1998). Even if facially reasonable, granting such leaves may impose on this employer an "undue hardship." *Walsh v. United Parcel Serv.,* 201 F.3d 718 (6th Cir. 2000).

(d) Rules

The employer may have miscellaneous rules that an individual with a disability cannot honor such as limiting access to the premises to employees only or prohibiting animals. Reasonable accommodation may require the accommodation that permits access by necessary service animals and assistants. *Johnson v. Gambrinus Co.,* 116 F.3d 1052 (5th Cir. 1997). An employer may require employees, such as greeters or check-out persons, to stand. Disabilities such as arthritis often make extended standing extremely painful. A reasonable accommodation to the employer's rule might be to provide either rest breaks and/or stools on which the disabled employee may sit. A rule restricting workers from wearing perfumes or scents may be a necessary reasonable accommodation to an employee with asthma who has severe reactions to certain scents. *Core v. Champaign Bd. of Cnty Comm'rs,* (S.D.Ohio, 2012). 2012 WL 495,944.

(e) Physical and equipment modifications

Modifications to the physical workplace often are seen as reasonable accommodations, even when the modifications impose significant economic costs, particularly when the device or structural change is necessary to assure that the disabled individual has access to the job. Examples of reasonable physical accommodations: providing access ramps or lifts, altering the height of work stations, widening access doors, and insuring accessibility of sanitary facilities. 29 C.F.R. 1630.2(o)(1)(ii). Equipment necessary for the individual to perform, such as ergonomic furniture, sound enhancers, visual or verbal enhancement on communications equipment may be reasonable, albeit often costly, accommodations. *Fink & Marett v. N.Y. City Dep't of Personnel,* 53 F.3d 565 (2d Cir. 1995). If climbing is an essential aspect of the job, reasonable accommodation of a climbing disability might include providing a mechanical "cherry picker" lift. *Skerski v Time Warner Cable Co.,* 257 F.3d 273 (3d Cir 2001).

(f) Personal assistants

Assistants to aid the disabled worker are listed by the ADA as an accommodation to be considered. It is not reasonable, however, to require hiring a full time assistant who only occasionally assists a single disabled person or for the assistant to perform essential job duties *for* the disabled person. In such cases the economic or efficiency costs outweigh the needs of the disabled employee. However, it can be reasonable to provide an assistant that permits or enables the disabled individual to perform the essential functions. For example, a school teacher's sight disability made it difficult for her to maintain discipline in the classroom. It may be facially reasonable for the school system to provide an assistant to assist the teacher in maintaining classroom decorum. The assistant is not performing the essential duty of teaching, but allows the disabled person to perform the essential teaching duty. *Borkowski v. Valley Cent. School Dist.*, 631 F.3d 131 (2d Cir. 1995). Reasonable accommodation of a deaf employee might require the employer to provide an ASL interpreter at weekly staff meetings. Merely providing the deaf employee with pre- and post-meeting notes was not a reasonable accommodation. *EEOC v. UPS Supply Chain Solutions,* 620 F.3d 1103 (9th Cir. 2010).

E. "UNDUE HARDSHIP"

It is common for courts to make no clear distinction between the "reasonableness" of the accommodation and whether an accommodation would impose an "undue hardship." The relationship of the dual terms can be viewed in terms of their focus and which party bears the burden of proof. Plaintiff carries an initial burden of proving that in the general, ordinary, or usual case the accommodation, on its face, appears reasonable. *Walton v. Mental Health Ass'n of Southeastern Pa.*, 168 F.3d 661 (3d Cir. 1999). "Reasonableness" focuses on the general as viewed from the perspective of the plaintiff. If plaintiff carries this burden the employer must make the accommodation unless *in this particular instance,* the accommodation would impose on this employer a hardship that is "undue." *U.S. Airways v. Barnett,* 535 U.S. 391 (2002). The focus of "undue hardship is on the specific employer and the extent that the accommodation would burden *this* employer.

"Undue hardship" is defined as "an action requiring significant difficulty and expense" * * * weighing in each case: "the effect on expenses and resources and upon the operation of the facility" in light of specific factors including: the size of the particular facility and of the employer, the financial resources of the employer, impact on overall efficiency, and extent of burdens shifted to other employees. 42 U.S.C. 12111(10).

In *Van Zande v. Wisconsin Dep't of Admin.*, 44 F.3d 538 (7th Cir. 1995), an employee whose disability confined her to a wheel chair sought the accommodation of lowering a counter and sink in an employee *break room*. The sink and counters in the employee *rest room* had been lowered to accommodate the plaintiff. The court held that the marginal benefit and "convenience" of a lower break room counter did not outweigh the significant expense of making the modification, and thus was an "undue hardship," even though the cost of the modification was small relative to the resources of the employer (the State of Wisconsin). By contrast, building a private work space for an employee with a disorder involving the ability to concentrate did not impose on the employer an undue hardship. The work space was necessary for the employee to perform his work, not just a convenience. *Areneson v. Sullivan,* 946 F.2d 90 (9th Cir. 1991). The cost of providing necessary equipment such as phone amplifiers, large screen monitors, and ergonomic furniture rarely is considered an undue hardship, even for smaller employers, because such accommodations are necessary to assure performance of the job. *Crane v. Lewis,* 551 F.Supp. 27 (D.D.C. 1982).

F. "INTERACTIVE PROCESS"

The ADA, as implemented by EEOC regulations, requires that when an apparently reasonable accommodation is suggested by a disabled individual, the employer should not ignore or reject the suggestion out of hand, but should engage in an informal "interactive process" that explores with the disabled person the reasonableness of the request and offer alternatives that might meet the individual's needs with less hardship on the employer. 29 C.F.R. 1630.2(o)(3). The employee has a reciprocal obligation to respond to the employer's suggestions, an obligation that is not satisfied by the employee insisting on the proposed accommodation and refusing to consider employer suggested, facially rational alternatives.

Neither the ADA nor EEOC regulations suggest liability for a failure to engage in the process. Nonetheless, an employer's rejection of suggested accommodation without re-engaging the disabled individual in a problem solving dialogue may preclude a summary judgment for the employer (*Taylor v. Phoenixville School Dist.*, 184 F.3d 296 (3d Cir. 1999)), or create a presumption that the employee's suggested accommodation is reasonable, thus requiring the employer to demonstrate that the accommodation would impose an undue hardship. *Shapiro v. Twn'sp of Lakewood,* 292 F.3d 356 (3d

Cir. 2002). The benefit to the employer of engaging in the interactive process is that to do so in good faith allows the employer to avoid damages in the event the employer is ultimately held liable for failure to make a reasonable accommodation. 42 U.S.C. 1981A(a)(3). The employee's failure to engage in the interactive process also may make the employer's offered accommodation presumptively reasonable, and thus increase the chance of a summary judgment for the employer. *Steffes v. Stepan Co.,* 144 F.3d 1070 (7th Cir 1998).

CHAPTER 25

INTANGIBLE "TERMS AND CONDITIONS"

25.01: GENERALLY

The core statues broadly prohibits discrimination that affects adversely "the individual's status as an employee" as to his/her "terms, conditions, and privileges of employment" (42 U.S.C. 2000e–(a)(1) and (2)). The prohibition is not limited to tangible job benefits. Discrimination need not cause physical or psychological injury nor affect adversely the employee's job performance. *Harris v. Forklift Systems,* 510 U.S. 17 (1993). However, regardless of the bigoted motivation for the treatment, the statutes "do not reach genuine but innocuous differences." *Oncale v. Sundowner Offshore Services, Inc.,* 523 U.S. 75 (1998). *Supra,* 5.02. Distinguishing between unprotected "innocuous differences" and discrimination rising to the level of adversely affecting "terms and conditions of employment" is a primary issue.

In addition to the disparate treatment rising to the level of adversely affecting terms and conditions of the individual's employment, the adverse treatment of the plaintiff must be shown to be "because of" her protected class. A man badgering a woman because of personal animosity is not proscribed sex discrimination.. *Medina-Rivera v. MUN, Inc.,* 713 F.3d 132 (1st Cir. 2013).

25.02: BURDENSOME RULES

A. GENERALLY

An otherwise legitimate rule imposed on one class but not on others that significantly limits access of that class to employment opportunities is proscribed. For example, a no-marriage policy applied only to women is sex discrimination. *Sprogis v. United Air Lines, Inc.,* 444 F.2d 1194 (7th Cir. 1971).

B. GROOMING CODES

A grooming code that requires men to have short hair and women to have long hair and requires women, but not men, to wear facial make up and high heeled shoes does not violate Title VII because the rule is not so burdensome that it undermines either a basic right (such as marriage) or employment opportunities of classes when with relative ease the employee can comply with the employer's rule. However, when a grooming code drawn along sex lines is not an "innocuous difference," but places a significant burden on one sex, it constitutes proscribed discrimination. *Jesperson v. Harrah's Operating Co.,* 444 F.3d 1104 (9th Cir. 2006). Thus, a draconian grooming code, requiring employees to be svelte, not wear eyeglasses, and dress according to a strict standard, if imposed because of the class of employees, is sex discrimination even if all members of the workforce are women. *Gerdom v. Continental Airlines, Inc.,* 692 F.2d 602 (9th Cir. 1982).

When grooming and work place rules conflict with dress, grooming, or similar practices directed by an employee's religious beliefs, Title VII requires employers to make "reasonable accommodation" to such religious beliefs when to do so does not constitute an "undue hardship. *Supra,* 24.05. In most situations allowing head coverings, facial hair, or display of modest religious symbols would be a reasonable modification of an employer's general dress or grooming standards. However, if the modification required by the religious belief presents a risk to the employee or to others (*e.g.,* facial hair that impedes safe use of gas mask for firefighters, *Bhatia v. Chevron, U.S.A.,* 734 F.2d 1382 (9th Cir. 1984)), or significantly interferes with identification of employees to customers (*e.g.,* uniform required of retail "associates") significant modifications will be unreasonable. *Cloutier v. Costco Wholesale Corp.,* 390 F.3d 126 (1st Cir. 2004).

Public employers, under a constitutional duty of religious neutrality, have greater leeway to prohibit wearing clearly religious clothing or symbols while meeting the public (*United States v. Bd. of Educ.,* 911 F.2d 882 (3d Cir. 1990)), or the discussion of religion with customers or co-workers. *Grossman v. S. Shore Public School Dist.,* 507 F.3d 1097 (7th Cir. 2007).

Allowing employees to have religious texts or post traditional religious symbols at semi-private work stations usually is reasonable even if some workers might be offended. *Dixon v. Hallmark Companies,* 627 F.3d 849 (11th Cir. 2010). However, if the display amounts to unwanted proselytizing or advocates intolerance toward other workers, the accommodation would be unreasonable. *Peterson v. Hewlett–Packard Co.*, 358 F.3d 599 (9th Cir. 2004) (religious passages condemning homosexuality need not be accommodated).

C. "ENGLISH ONLY"

While a facially neutral and uniformly applied rule may be seen as lawful under Title VII because it is not "discriminatory" (*Troup v. May Dep't Stores*, 20 F.3d 734 (7th Cir. 1994), many courts recognize, in differing contexts, that even neutral policies or practices uniformly imposed may be "discriminatory." For example, a rule requiring *all employees* to speak English at the workplace is not facially discriminatory, but if imposed for the purpose of discouraging individuals of certain national origins from seeking or remaining at work, the improper motivation for the rule will constitute national origin discrimination. Alternatively, an "English only rule" may be considered a facial form of national origin discrimination in that such a rule affects primarily those whose national origins are from outside the United States. *Maldonado v. City of Altus*, 433 F.3d 1294 (10th Cir. 2006). At the very least the burdensome impact of such a rule on those of immediate foreign ancestry requires the employer to demonstrate the "business necessity" for its application. *Garcia v. Spun Steak Co.*, 998 F.2d 1480 (9th Cir. 1993).

25.03: TANGIBLE BENEFITS ALLOCATED "BECAUSE OF SEX:" QUID PRO QUO DISCRIMINATION

Unwelcomed advances toward an individual because of a desire to have a sexual relationship can be actionable sex discrimination. It makes no difference that the harasser is the same sex as the victim. Both homosexual and heterosexual advances are sex discrimination. *Oncale v. Sundowner Offshore Services*, 523 U.S. 75 (1998). This is because the sex of the employee played a critical role in motivating the offensive action. *Meritor Savings Bank, FSB v. Vinson*, 477 U.S. 57 (1986). When the employer denies a tangible job benefit, such as a pay increase or promotion, because the employee rejects the sexual advances of an employer this is *per se* sex discrimination, which is called "quid pro quo" sex discrimination. *Id.* However, an employee who is granted a tangible job benefit because she entered into a sexual relationship has no claim of sex discrimination when she is demoted upon the *employer* terminating the relationship. *Mosher v. Dollar Tree Stores*, 240 F.3d 662 (7th Cir. 2001). It is proscribed sex discrimination, however, when the employee is terminated because the *employee* refuses to continue or resume what had begun as a consensual relationship. *Holly D. v. Cal. Ins. Tech.*, 339 F.3d 1158 (9th Cir. 2003).

25.04: INTANGIBLE "HOSTILE ENVIRONMENT"—HARASSMENT

A. THE BASIC ELEMENTS

Even if no tangible job benefits are denied, creating or permitting a hostile working environment is actionable discrimination. Establishing hostile environment liability has three elements. The environment must be: (1) that which a reasonable person in plaintiff's class would find hostile or abusive; (2) be perceived by the plaintiff to be so (*Faragher v. City of Boca Raton,* 524 U.S. 775 (1998)); and (3) the hostility must be "because of" plaintiff's protected class. *Oncale v. Sundowner Offshore Services,* 523 U.S. 75 (1998).

A "hostile work environment" is not created by casual comments or "ordinary socializing," "flirtation," or "horseplay" simply because sensitive persons may be offended. "Minor annoyances that all employees experience, * * * and personality conflicts," * * * [such as] snubbing by supervisors and co-workers are not actionable * * *." *Burlington Northern & Santa Fe R. Co.,* 548 U.S. 53 (2006). On the other hand, to be actionable the conduct need not reach the level of being unendurable, intolerable, or so severe that the conduct drives the victim from the workplace or affects the victim's mental or physical health. *Harris v. Forklift Sys., Inc.* 510 U.S. 17 (1993).

As USERA prohibits only the "denial of any *benefit* of employment" based on an individual's military service (38 U.S.C. 4311(a)), harassment of an employee because of his military service that does not adversely affect a *tangible* job benefit may not be actionable. *Carder v. Continental Airlines,* 636 F.3d 172 (5th Cir.2011).

B. OBJECTIVELY OFFENSIVE: UNREASONABLE

(1) Generally

There is no mathematically precise test to determine the point at which offensive, unprofessional, or boorish incidents cross the line of "ordinary socializing in the workplace" to create an objectively hostile environment. Analysis requires:

> a careful consideration of the social context in which the particular behavior occurs and is experienced by its target. A professional football player's working environment is not severely or pervasively abusive * * * if the coach smacks him on the buttocks as he heads onto the field—even if the same behavior would reasonably be experienced as abusive by the coach's secretary (male or female) back in the office. The real social impact of workplace behavior often depends on a constellation of surrounding circumstances, expectations, and relationships that cannot be captured by a simple recitation of words used or the physical acts performed. *Oncale v. Sundowner Offshore Services, Inc.,* 523 U.S. 75 (1998).

Defendant's conduct must be viewed from the perspective of individuals within plaintiff's class.

Ellison v. Brady, 924 F.2d 872 (9th Cir. 1991). For example, an employer's regular use of the term "boy" to refer to adult black males or placing a hangman's noose over the workstation of a black worker might go largely unnoticed by many white employees, but could be so offensive or threatening to reasonable black employees to be actionable. *Rogers v. Western–Southern Life Ins. Co.,* 12 F. 3d 668 (7th Cir. 1993). Because women are disproportionately victims of sexual assaults, behavior that men might find relatively inoffensive could be viewed by reasonable women to be threatening and hostile. *EEOC v. NEA, Alaska,* 422 F.3d 840 (9th Cir.2005) (screaming threats and obscenities while making threatening gestures to all employees could create a hostile environment for women). As views of humor often differ by sex, jokes, displays of scantily clad women, graffiti, graphic depictions of sexual activity, or comments ladened with sexual innuendo that men might find humorous, or at worst, in "bad taste," could strike reasonable women as sexually demeaning and particularly embarrassing, thus creating a hostile environment. *Hoyle v. Freightliner, LLC,* 650 F.3d 321 (4th Cir. 2011). Excessive comments on a woman's clothing or her attractive appearance that men might find gallant could create unreasonable working conditions for a reasonable woman. *Burlington Industries, Inc. v. Ellerth,* 524 U.S. 742 (1998).

(2) Factors

The courts weigh and balance a number of factors to determine whether a jury could find that a reasonable person in plaintiff's class was a victim of a hostile working environment.

(a) Location

Behavior by co-workers away from the work place is less likely to create a hostile *working* environment than would similar behavior directed at the plaintiff in the workplace. However, a hostile working environment can be created by a supervisor who engages in repeated sexual propositions, badgers, or assaults a subordinate employee at her home or in her hotel room. Such "private" behavior undermines the working relationship that in turn infects the work environment of the victim. *Moring v. Arkansas Dept. of Corrections,* 243 F.3d 452 (8th Cir. 2001). Objectionable behavior need not be in person but can be displayed over the telephone, e-mail, or through social media.

(b) Intensity or Quality

Behavior that involves physical contact or is physically threatening is more likely to create a hostile environment than mere words. The harassing behavior need not be explicitly racist or sexist. Sabotage of an employee's work station, damaging his working tools, giving him demeaning assignments, such as cleaning the toilets, or petty belittling of plaintiff's work can constitute unlawful harassment. *Patton v. Keystone RV Co.,* 455 F.3d

812 (7th Cir. 2006). Words and gestures that are particularly hurtful, such as obscene racial epithets, mocking parodies, humiliating ridicule, or implicit threats have more of an impact on working conditions than does general bawdiness. *Rodgers v. Western Southern Life Ins. Co.,* 12 F.3d 668 (7th Cir. 1993). For example, repeatedly calling a female plaintiff a "bitch" and a "dumb bitch" created for her a sexually hostile working environment. *Passananti v. Cook County,* 689 F.3d 655 (7th Cir. 2012). Regular referring to Hispanic employees as "spics" is likely to create a hostile environment. *Rivera v. Rochester Genessee Regional Trans. Auth.,* 702 F.3d 685 (2d Cir. 2012). By contrast, an off-color comment at which male workers laughed could not, standing alone, create a hostile working environment. *Clark County School Dist. v. Breeden,* 532 U.S. 268 (2001).

Ambiguity is important. For example, calling a black plaintiff "buffalo butt" did not create a hostile environment. *Hicks v. Gates Rubber Co.,* 833 F.2d 1406 (10th Cir. 1987). A co-worker placing a bumper sticker on the car of a black female employee stating: "When All Else Fails, Blame the White Male" was held to be more of a sarcastic jab at modern trends than an expression of hostility toward plaintiff. *Lockwood v. Donahoe,* (D. Alaska, 2012), 2012 WL 1906555.

(c) Frequency

Unless it involves a humiliating transfer or sexual assault by a supervisor, single incidents rarely infect the total working environment sufficiently to make it "hostile." *Mathirampuzha v. Potter, Postmaster General,* 548 F.3d 70 (2d Cir. 2008) (single physical male on male assault insufficient). However, *Rivera v. Rochester Genesee Reg'l Transp. Auth. supra,* involved a plaintiff complaining to his supervisor of racial harassment by co-workers. In the presence of these co-workers the supervisor responded, "Suck it up and get over it nigger." The insulting nature of the curse by one's supervisor in the presence of allegedly harassing co-workers can be sufficient to permit a finding that the curse created a hostile environment.

Often it is a coalescence of relatively minor actions or incidents, which in their totality and over time, create the hostile environment. Thus, an occasional flirtatious glance, a single request for a date, or an isolated slur will not create a hostile environment. However, a male supervisor regularly staring at a female worker's breasts can make the environment hostile to her. *Billings v. Town of Grafton,* 515 F.3d 39 (1st Cir. 2008). All relevant incidents may be used in the evaluation, even those that fall outside of the period for filing a charge of discrimination. *National R.R. Passenger Corp. v. Morgan,* 536 U.S. 101 (2002).

Rampant sexual favoritism and pervasive, welcomed as well as unwelcomed, sexual advances can create a hostile atmosphere that negatively infects the terms and conditions of employment even for employees not directly subjected to the advances. *Miller v. Dep't of Corrections,* 115 P.3d 77 (Cal. 2005); 29 C.F.R. 1604.11(a)(2) & (3).

(d) Relationship Status

A hostile environment is most likely to be created where words or conduct are directed at the plaintiff. Broad general statements or insults directed at others have less of an immediate effect on bystanders. *Ladd v. Grand Trunk Western R.R.*, 552 F.3d 495 (6th Cir. 2009). Hearsay reports of sexual advances against others rarely can create a hostile environment. *Liebovitz v. N.Y.C. Transit Auth.*, 252 F.3d 179 (2d Cir. 2001).

Insults or actions by supervisors, particularly when directed at the plaintiff, have a greater impact on a reasonable person than would similar boorish behavior by co-workers. An employee usually can walk away from a co-worker's insult, firmly insist that it be stopped, or seek relief by complaining to superiors, defensive tactics not readily available against harassing supervisors.

Outsiders, such as customers or independent contractors, rarely create a hostile working environment. However, the failure of the employer to take reasonable remedial steps to protect the employee from an ongoing pattern of abuse from non-employees can be actionable. *Aguiar v. Bartlesville Care Ctr.* (10th Cir. 1/28/11) (unreported), 2011 WL 1461541 (employee of nursing home repeatedly harassed by a patient).

(e) Race or Sex of the Parties

While actionable harassment can take place when the victim is of the same class as the perpetrator (*e.g.*, male-on-male or black-on-black), the race or sex of the harasser may alter its impact. A pat on the buttocks of an employee may have a different impact on the victim when the parties are of the same sex. *Oncale v. Sundowner Offshore Serv. Inc.,* 523 U.S. 75 (1998). A racial slur normally insulting to blacks may lose much of its sting—may even be a compliment—when uttered casually by one black employee to another.

(f) Good Faith

While a hostile environment may be created without an apparent malicious intent (*Ellison v. Brady,* 924 F.2d 872 (9th Cir. 1981)), an expressed animus intensifies the poisonous effect of offensive actions more than does banal insensitivity. *Clarke County School Dist. v. Breeden,* 532 U.S. 268 (2001).

The courts have not reached consistent conclusions regarding when the conduct of defendant was sufficiently offensive to permit a jury verdict that a hostile environment had been created. *Redd v. N.Y. State Div. of Parole,* 687 F.3d 166 (2d Cir. 2012), for example, held that a female supervisor touching the female plaintiff's breasts three times over a five month period was sufficiently severe or pervasive to create a hostile or abusive environment. By contrast, *Alvarez v Des Moines Bolt Supply, Inc.,* 626 F.3d 410 (8th Cir. 2010), affirmed a summary judgment for defendant despite a male supervisor commenting on the female plaintiff's breast size, slapping her on the buttocks, regularly "brushing" her body, squeezing her neck, grabbing her hair, soliciting her for sex, suggesting on one occasion that she perform a strip dance, and questioning plaintiff's ability to lift her harasser's genitals.

C. SUBJECTIVELY OFFENSIVE—UNWELCOME

In addition to the behavior being hostile and offensive, plaintiff must demonstrate that personally, or subjectively, defendant's behavior created for her an abusive or hostile environment. It is not necessary for the victim to verbally protest or register a formal complaint. A court may assume that plaintiff was a reasonable person, and infer that conduct which a reasonable person would find abusive or hostile would be similarly offensive to the plaintiff. Defendant may refute this inference.

"The correct inquiry is whether [plaintiff] by her conduct indicated that alleged sexual advances were *unwelcome,* not whether her participation * * * was *voluntary." Meritor Savings Bank, FSB v. Vinson,* 477 U.S. 57 (1986).

While 'voluntariness' in the sense of consent is not a defense * * * it does not follow that a complainant's sexually provocative speech or dress is irrelevant as a matter of law in determining whether she found particular sexual advances unwelcome. * * * Such evidence is obviously relevant." *Meritor Savings Bank, FSB v. Vinson, supra.*

Thus, defendant may refute the inference that the offensive behavior was unwelcomed by plaintiff with evidence that plaintiff willingly joined in the ribald atmosphere, "giving as good as she got." *Holly D. v.*

California Inst. of Tech., 339 F.3d 1158 (9th Cir. 2003).

Trial courts will face evidentiary issues as to whether evidence of plaintiff's past behavior, even if relevant, is admissible, which requires weighing the probative value of the evidence of plaintiff's past behavior against possible prejudicial misuse by the jury. Fed. R. Evid. 412. *Meritor Savings Bank, FSB v. Vinson, supra,* indicated not only could plaintiff's "provocative speech and dress" be admitted, but also a jury may be allowed to consider evidence of plaintiff's acknowledged "sexual fantasies" about the harasser. Sexually explicit conversations with plaintiff's alleged harasser are admissible because they directly relate to the issue of whether plaintiff invited or "welcomed" *this particular* supervisor's advances. *Sheffield v. Hilltop Sand & Gravel Co.,* 895 F.Supp. 105 (E.D. Va. 1995). Nevertheless, courts have excluded evidence of plaintiff's occasional use of swear words and general sexual banter as lacking sufficient probative value to establish that a particular supervisor's advances were welcomed. *Hocevar v. Purdue Frederick Co.,* 223 F.3d 721 (8th Cir. 2000). Plaintiff being photographed nude for a magazine has little, if any, probative value on the issue of whether she welcomed work place sexual advances, and could unduly inflame the jury. *Burns v. McGregor Electronic Indus.,* 989 F.2d 959 (8th Cir. 1983). While discrete consensual sexual activity of plaintiff with one co-worker does not implicitly invite sexual advances from other workers, and may not be admissible, openly promiscuous behavior of the plaintiff can suggest that sexual advances are welcomed from all. *Holly D. v. California Inst. of Tech.*, 339 F.3d 1158 (9th Cir. 2003).

That an employee at an earlier time had a consensual affair with a supervisor does not require a holding that current solicitations by the supervisor are welcomed. After the employee indicates a desire to end the relationship, badgering her to continue or resume the relationship is actionable. *Llampallas v. Mini–Circuits Lab. Inc.*, 163 F.3d 1236 (11th Cir. 1998).

D. "DISCRIMINATION BECAUSE OF"

Treatment must be shown to be "discrimination because of" a protected class. *Medina-Rivera v. MUN, Inc.*, 713 F.3d 132 (1st Cir. 2013). The statutes do not protect workers against indiscriminate "jerks, bullies, and persecutors." Illegal harassment of an employee can be based either on sexual desire or a hostility towards plaintiff's class. *Wasek v. Arrow Energy Serv.*, 682 F.3d 463 (6th Cir. 2012). The sexual or racial nature of the treatment itself can establish the necessary motivation. Thus, grabbing plaintiff's genitals, using sexual language, or threatening rape can establish sex motivation even though only a single employee was subjected to the offensive behavior. *Oncale v. Sundowner Offshore Services, Inc., supra; Rene v. MGM Grand Hotels, Inc.*, 305 F.3d 1061 (9th Cir. 2002). Hostility to a class, and thus improper motivation, is established through the display of racist or sexist symbols and graffiti. *Suders v. Easton*, 325 F.3d 3d 432 (3d Cir. 2003).

Treating plaintiff differently than others in terms of job assignments or harshness of criticisms is sufficient to establish motivation. *Wasek v. Arrow Energy Serv., supra.* For example, placing banana peels at a black employee's work place and co-workers wearing Confederate apparel can create a hostile environment for the black worker. Motive can be inferred from the incident of disparate treatment and the racial connotations of the harasser's behavior. *Jones v. UPS Ground Freight,* 683 F.3d 1283 (11th Cir. 2012).

Actionable "discrimination" is not dependent solely on improperly motivated disparate treatment, but exists, without regard to motivation, where a practice has an unjustified disparate impact on a protected class. *Griggs v. Duke Power Co.,* 401 U.S. 424 (1971). Thus, "it is error to conclude that the conduct is not because of sex merely because the abuser consistently abused men and women alike." *EEOC v. National Education Assn, Alaska,* 422 F.3d 840 (9th Cir. 2005). A supervisor who engaged in often unprovoked, but frequent profane, shouting at all workers and made threatening gestures while in the "personal space" of both men and women created a discriminatory workplace for women based on the greater *effect* such abusive behavior would have on women. *Id.* Similarly, creating or tolerating a working environment replete with sexual activity, propositions, discussion, and innuendo can be discriminatory against women because women will be more negatively affected by such behavior than will men. *Miller v. Dept. of Corrections,* 36 Cal. 4th 446, 115 P.3d 77 (2005). *Cf., Smith v. Hy–Vee,* 622

F.3d 904 (8th Cir. 2010), which indicated that regular lewd, sexually provocative behavior by a female employee toward a fellow female worker that included regularly rubbing plaintiff's buttocks, discussing genitalia, and graphically depicting sexual intercourse was not discriminatory in large part because the harasser subjected all her co-workers, both male and female, to similar vulgar and inappropriate sexually charged behavior.

25.05: CONSTRUCTIVE DISCHARGE

A plaintiff who resigned in the face of actionable harassment, but who failed to establish that the environment was sufficiently intolerable to warrant her resignation, will not be entitled to reinstatement and back pay. Her remedies for actionable harassment will be limited to the recovery of damages, plus her attorneys' fees and costs. However, if the employee establishes that her resignation was a reasonable response to working conditions made "intolerable," the "voluntary" resignation is deemed to be a "constructive discharge." A "constructive discharge" entitles plaintiff to the remedies available to employees who are subjected to an actual, discriminatorily motivated discharge that include reinstatement with seniority and back wages running from the time of plaintiff's resignation. *See, infra,* Chapter 28.

A "constructive discharge" occurs when the employee resigns because her abusive working environment has become "so intolerable that a reasonable person in the employee's position would have felt compelled to resign." *Pennsylvania State Police v. Suders,* 542 U.S. 129 (2004). In determining whether plaintiff's working conditions have become "intolerable" courts consider: (1) the extent or degree of harassment (*e.g.,* racial insults or sexual assaults); (2) whether the action involved a demotion to significantly reduced duties or salary or humiliating assignments that might include subjecting a senior employee to the supervision of a much younger, less experienced employee; (3) an abrupt assignment to more dangerous or significantly more onerous duties; (4) an ongoing pattern of belittling or badgering that, in spite of objections, has continued unabated; (5) relocation to clearly inferior surroundings, such as a small windowless cubicle with sparse furnishings, reductions in fringe benefits (such as travel and expense accounts), and deprivation of support staff; and (6) repeated encouragements or demands for the employee to resign, particularly if coupled with threats that not resigning could result in a reassignment on significantly less favorable terms. *Dediol v. Best Chevrolet, Inc.,* 655 F.3d 435 (5th Cir. 2011). Most courts reject an additional requirement that plaintiff prove that the employer engaged in the harassment for the purpose of forcing the employee to resign. *Goldmeier v. Allstate Ins., Co.,* 337 F.3d 629 (6th Cir. 2003).

25.06: ATTRIBUTING HARASSMENT TO THE "EMPLOYER"

A. GENERAL PRINCIPLES: COMMON LAW RULES OF AGENCY

The core federal statutes impose liability on *"employers,"* not on individuals. *Fantini v. Salem State College,* 557 F.3d 22 (1st Cir. 2009). However, recovery against individuals for harassment may be possible under state law and for racial harassment under the Reconstruction Era Civil Rights Acts such as 42 U.S.C. 1981 and 1985(3). Moreover, the federal statutes do not create absolute liability on "employers" for all work place activity of its agents or employees. It is necessary to attribute to the "employer" the harassing actions of its employees. Common law rules of agency are the starting place for determining which acts of an employer's agent can be attributed to the employer. *Burlington Industries, Inc. v. Ellerth,* 524 U.S. 742 (1998).

(1) Managers: Common law rules of agency treat executives and independent managers of an enterprise as the alter ego of the "employer." Accordingly, all actions of high level managers are attributed to the manager's "employer." *Townsend v. Benjamin,* 679 F.3d 41 (2d Cir. 2012).

(2) Co-workers: The common law will attribute actions of a rank-and-file worker to their employer only if the worker was authorized to take the challenged action, the employer ratified the action, or the employer was negligent in assigning or controlling the actions of the harassing co-worker.

Co-worker harassment of which the employer has knowledge can be considered ratification of the harassment when the employer fails to take prompt remedial action. Actionable negligence similarly requires a combination of knowledge by the employer of the co-worker's behavior and the employer's inaction in the face of such knowledge. *Vance v. Ball State University,* ____ U.S. ___, 133 S.Ct. 2434 (2013). Employers will not be liable for harassment by the victim's co-workers until plaintiff demonstrates that responsible management had, or reasonably should have had, notice of the harassment taking place, and with such knowledge failed to take prompt and effective remedial action. *Id.*

(3) Supervisors: Mid-level employees who do not manage the enterprise, but who have been delegated authority to influence decisions affecting the allocation of tangible job benefits, such as dismissal, discipline, promotion, reassignment to significantly different jobs and pay can be broadly designated as "supervisors." Employer liability for a supervisor's actions depends on whether the supervisor exercised the delegated authority to affect tangible job benefits or only harassed the employee, and by this created a hostile working environment.

B. SUPERVISORS AND THE "FARAGHER DEFENSE" GENERALLY

(1) Tangible Job Benefits: "If the supervisor's harassment culminates in a tangible employment action the employer is strictly liable." *Vance v. Ball*

State University, supra. Even if the employer was unaware of the discriminatory motive behind the supervisor's actions or had in place policies expressly forbidding such discrimination and had made reasonable efforts to monitor its policies, the supervisor's discrimination in allocating tangible job benefits is attributed to the employer. It is no defense that the supervisor had engaged in a "lark or frolic" of his own for which the employer received no benefit. *Meritor Savings Bank, FSB v. Vinson,* 477 U.S. 57 (1986) (Denying job benefits because employee rejected the supervisor's sexual relationship attributable to the employer).

(2) Intangibles (Hostile Environment): When a supervisor badgers, bullyrags, threatens, demeans, or harasses an employee without affecting adversely the victim's tangible job benefits the employer will be liable for such harassment, but may avoid liability by establishing an affirmative defense that has two basic prongs. (1) The employer exercised "reasonable care to avoid harassment and to eliminate it when it might occur," and (2) The employee unreasonably failed to "take advantage of the employer's safeguards." *Faragher v. City of Boca Raton,* 524 U.S. 775 (1998); *Burlington Industries v. Ellerth,* 524 U.S. 742 (1998).

C. "FARAGHER DEFENSE"

(1) "Reasonable Care:" To defend against a supervisor's creation of a hostile work environment the employer first must demonstrate that prior to the alleged harassment it had taken affirmative, proactive steps to avoid and eliminate supervisory harassment. This prong probably requires employers to satisfy four elements:

(a) The employer should have a clear policy that unambiguously forbids harassment. A broad, general policy prohibiting "discrimination" ordinarily will not suffice. *Cf., Hall v. Bodine Elec. Co.*, 276 F. 3d 345 (7th Cir. 2002), which held that an expressed anti-harassment policy was not required where the employer had provided clear channels for reporting complaints about objectionable behavior.

(b) The non-harassment policy should be disseminated among employees. An obscure wall posting normally is inadequate. *Cf., Hill v. General Finance, Inc.*, 218 F.3d 1305 (11th Cir. 2001), holding that absence of specific notice to supervisors was not fatal where there were known processes for communicating complaints, harassment issues had been discussed in open meetings, and the specific policy had been posted in a personnel office and placed in files to which all employees had access.

(c) Management must reasonably monitor compliance, which requires pro-active oversight of supervisors. Making no "attempt to keep track of supervisors" can be fatal to the defense. *Faragher, supra.* Required monitoring of supervisors may be satisfied by periodic training or by designating an EEO officer whose job is to regularly monitor employee behavior.

(d) Reasonable procedures for receiving and resolving harassment complaints *must* be established and clearly communicated to all employees. *Faragher* stated that for a policy to be reasonable it needs to "include * * * assurance that the harassing supervisors could be bypassed in registering complaints." Procedures that *require* the employee first to complain to her tormentor cannot be reasonable. *See, Gorzynski v. JetBlue Airways Corp.,* 596 F.3d 93 (2d Cir. 2010), where the policy *permitted* reporting first to the harasser. The fact that the victim followed that alternative by complaining to her harasser was reasonable compliance with the obligation to invoke the employer provided procedures.

(2) Unreasonable Inaction of the Employee: The second prong of the *Faragher/Ellerth* defense requires the *employer* to demonstrate that the employee unreasonably failed to invoke the employer's procedures. If the employee's failure to invoke established and reasonable procedures is shown to be unreasonable, defendant has a defense to the supervisor's harassment. However, if the employer fails to establish that the employee's failure to invoke the employer's procedures was unreasonable, the employer will not be accorded the protection of the defense, and thus will be held liable for any actionable harassment committed by the supervisor.

The issue of reasonableness is one of fact, and a jury could find that failure to invoke procedures was "reasonable" given a close personal relationship and significant age difference between the harasser and the victim. *Monteagudo v. AELLA,* 554 F.3d 164 (1st Cir. 2009). A reasonably based fear of actual retaliation for complaining, or a reasonable belief that her complaint would not be taken seriously, likewise may justify an employee's inaction. *Leopold v. Baccarat, Inc.,* 239 F.3d 243 (2d Cir. 2001). However, a victim doing no more than posting on her office door, without comment, a copy of the employer's anti-harassment policy, followed by a delay of months before she invoked the employer's processes, was not reasonable. *Taylor v. Solis,* 571 F.3d 1313 (D.C. Cir. 2009).

(3) Claiming the *"Faragher* Defense:" "Supervisor" Defined: Unlike discriminatory behavior by co-workers where common law rules of agency determine employer liability for co-worker created hostile environment, a hostile environment created by supervisors is attributable to employers, unless the employer carries the burden of establishing the "*Faragher* defense." As a consequence, a narrow definition of "supervisor" gives employers greater protection against liability. The EEOC, supported by some lower courts, had held that an employee is a "supervisor" if he has been given broad authority to "direct or oversee" the work of the victim. Thus, a "team leader" or "crew chief" that assigns daily tasks, determines the order of breaks, handles paper work, or similar responsibilities would be a supervisor, in which case the employer would be liable for harassment by such a "leader" unless the employer established the exonerating affirmative defense. *Vance v. Ball State University,* ___ U.S. ___, 133 S.Ct. 2434 (2013), rejected this broad definition and held that for the purposes of an employer's vicarious liability, an employee is a supervisor only "if he or she is empowered by the employer to take tangible job actions against the victim." Accordingly, a "leader" whose authority did not extend to affecting tangible benefits, is not a supervisor. The employer will be liable only if the plaintiff can establish that the employer was negligent by failing to take reasonable remedial action.

D. *FARAGHER* DEFENSE TO CONSTRUCTIVE DISCHARGE

An employer is absolutely liable for the direct or indirect action of a supervisor that results in a discharge. *Vance v. Ball State University,* ___ U.S. ___, 133 S.Ct. 2434 (2013); *Staub v. Proctor Hospital,* ___ U.S. ___, 131 S.Ct. 1186 (2011)(employer liable when supervisor with discriminatory motive influenced the final decision-maker). As *Faragher* expressly limited its defense to actions of supervisors inflicting *intangible injuries*, the question arose as to whether the defense would be available when the hostile working conditions created by supervisors were so intolerable that the employee resigned (*i.e.,* was "constructively discharged"). *Supra,* 25.05. On one hand the treatment precipitating the "discharge" involved intangible working conditions. On the other, a discharge is a tangible job action not subject to the *Faragher* defense.

Resolving this issue, *Pennsylvania State Police v. Suders,* 542 U.S. 129 (2004), held that as a constructive discharge claim "stems from, and can be regarded as an aggravated case of sexual harassment, or hostile work environment," the

Faragher defense is available to defendants charged with a constructive discharge.

25.07: "PROMPT, EFFECTIVE REMEDIAL ACTION"

A. NOTICE

Employer liability for harassment committed by supervisors begins with resolving whether the employer may assert the *Faragher* affirmative defense. *Supra,* 25.06. If the defense is not established, the employer will be liable even when the employer had no notice of the supervisor's behavior. However, if the employer had made reasonable attempts to prevent the harassment, provided reasonable procedures for employees to complain about perceived harassment, and the employee has reasonably invoked those procedures, the employer, now on notice, must take prompt and effective remedial action. Failure to take such action will result in liability.

As noted above, the employer will not be liable for harassment committed by co-workers unless the victim establishes first that the employer knew or reasonably should have known of the harassment. Absent proof that the employer had effective "notice" of the harasser's behavior, actions of co-workers will not be attributed to the employer.

Necessary notice need not come from the victim's complaint or by supervisors actually witnessing abuse, but can be based on "inquiry notice." That is, when surrounding circumstances such as general bawdiness, graffiti, or complaints of others concerning the behavior of the harasser would lead reasonable managers to make further inquiry, the employer is held to have notice or knowledge of what a reasonable inquiry would have disclosed. Once effective notice has been received, the employer's obligation is to take "prompt and effective remedial action." *Haugerud v. Amery Sch. Dist.*, 259 F.3d 678 (7th Cir. 2001).

B. INVESTIGATION

Upon having notice of hostile conditions created either by a supervisor or co-workers, the employer's first obligation is to undertake a reasonable inquiry into the accuracy of the allegations. Doing nothing in response to notice of possible harassment cannot be reasonable.

If a reasonable investigation produces a reasonable conclusion that the allegations are unfounded or insufficient to create an abusive or hostile environment, and on this basis the employer takes no action against the alleged harasser, the employer will not be liable even if it is proved later that the initially alleged harassing events took place. An employer need not accept the uncorroborated allegations of the victim, but may require some reasonable confirmation. *Adams v. O'Reilly Automotive, Inc.*, 538 F.3d 926 (8th Cir. 2008). An investigation may be reasonable even if it does not include confronting the alleged perpetrator. *Sutherland v. Wal–Mart Stores, Inc.*, 632 F.3d 990 (7th Cir. 2011).

C. REMEDIAL ACTION

If a reasonable person would conclude from the investigation that illegal harassment was probable, the employer must take remedial action that is both "prompt and effective." What constitutes "prompt effective remedial action" is a question of fact that varies with the circumstances. Generally, the action must protect and reassure the victim and have a prophylactic effect sufficient to deter future harassment. *Mockler v. Multnomah County,* 140 F.3d 809 (9th Cir. 1998).

It is not reasonable to involuntarily transfer the victim. *Cadena v. Pacesetter Corp.,* 224 F.3d 1203 (10th Cir. 2003). That the victim is "insignificant" and the harasser "too valuable" to offend is not a reasonable basis either for inaction or for the transfer of the victim. *Id.* Informal or jocular reprimands or requests for the harasser to "behave himself" are unlikely to be seen as either reassuring to the victim or effective in deterring future harassment. At the other extreme, reasonable remedial action for a first offense rarely demands the discharge of the perpetrator. *Wilson v. Moulison North Corp.,* 639 F.3d 1 (1st Cir. 2011). Progressive discipline usually is appropriate. For a first, relatively minor offense, a written warning that further misbehavior would result in serious discipline such as transfer, demotion, salary decrease, or perhaps eventual dismissal, may be reasonable. *Id.* Mandatory counseling or training can be an important aspect of effective remedial reaction. A remedy usually considered necessary for serious harassment is the transfer of the harasser to different job duties that eliminates or significantly reduces contact with the victim. *Sutherland v. Wal–Mart Stores, Inc.,* 632 F.3d 990 (7th Cir. 2011). For criminal behavior such as sexual assault, very hurtful or humiliating behavior, that would include cursing a worker with racial insults, or for recidivist behavior, the discharge of the harasser may be the only remedy that effectively meets the goals of protection, reassurance, and deterrence. *Intlekofer v. Turnage,* 973 F.2d 773 (9th Cir. 1992).

Graffiti and offensive materials, regardless of their source, must be promptly removed and reasonable steps taken to see that such displays are not repeated. Steps should be taken to identify and discipline offending employees. *Daniels v. Essex Group, Inc.,* 937 F.2d 1264 (7th Cir. 1991).

CHAPTER 26

ADVERTISEMENTS, INTERVIEWS, INQUIRIES AND MEDICAL EXAMINATIONS

26.01: ADVERTISEMENTS, NOTICES, SOLICITATIONS

Covered entities are prohibited from printing, publishing, or causing to be printed or published "any notice or advertisement * * * indicating a preference, limitation, specification, or discrimination" for a protected class. 42 U.S.C. 2000e–3(b). "Boys" or "girls" help-wanted notices indicate proscribed sex discrimination. Facially neutral solicitations for "students" or "recent graduates" is suspect as indicating an age preference. 29 C.F.R. 1625.4(a). This restriction on notices and advertisements does not violate the advertiser's free speech and press guarantees of the First Amendment. *Pittsburgh Press Co. v. Pittsburgh Comm'n on Human Rel.,* 413 U.S. 376 (1973).

While the EEOC has standing to enforce these prohibitions, it is unclear what remedy, if any, an individual reader of the advertisements could claim. An advertisement indicating an age or sex preference is "direct evidence" of proscribed motivation. *Woody v. Covenant Health,* 81 U.S.L.W. 1632 (E.D.Tenn. 5/8/13).

26.02: APPLICATIONS, INTERVIEWS, INQUIRIES

A. TITLE VII AND THE ADEA

Questions asked of applicants, on applications or during interviews, are not covered by the above restraints on "notices and advertisements." However, when questions are directed at women, but not men, minorities but not whites, and the applicant's response is used to make the job decision, this action constitutes illegal discrimination. To illustrate, in *Howard v. Roadway Express, Inc.*, 726 F.2d 1529 (11th Cir. 1984), the employer asked black, but not white applicants about their criminal background. When the background information secured by the inquiry was the basis for the black applicant's rejection, the rejection was discrimination because of race. Similarly, asking women applicants whether they are, or are planning to become, pregnant, will be pregnancy discrimination if the woman applicant is not selected based on her response. Even questions asked of all applicants, such as "family plans," number of children, and child care responsibilities may suggest that in rejecting a woman the employer made stereotyped distinctions between men and women regarding such family responsibilities. *See, Chadwick v. Wellpoint, Inc.*, 561 F.3d 38 (1st Cir. 2008).

Testing women for fertility or for pregnancy can be discrimination because of sex which could be justified only if the employer can establish that non-pregnancy is a bona fide occupational qualification.

Norman–Bloodsaw v. Lawrence Berkeley Lab., 135
F.3d 1260 (9th Cir. 1998). Regular or pervasive
inquiries of women employees as to whether they
are pregnant or about their childbearing and child
care plans may create an actionable hostile work
environment. *Walsh v. National Computer Sys. Inc.,*
332 F.3d 1150 (8th Cir. 2003).

B. GINA

The Genetic Information Non–Discrimination Act,
42 U.S.C. 2000ff (GINA), makes it unlawful "for an
employer to request, require, or purchase genetic
information with respect to an employee or a family
member of the employee." This prohibition applies
to individuals regardless of whether they suffer
from an impairment, disability, or any particular
genetic condition. This prohibition has a number of
qualifications and exceptions that include the
purchase of commercially and publicly available
documents, other than medical data bases or court
records, "inadvertent requests" for a medical history
pursuant to the employer providing health care
services, and securing information authorized or
required under federal or state family and medical
leave statutes, such as FMLA. Thus, requiring an
employee seeking leave to care for her own illness or
that of a child, spouse or parent to provide a
physician's certification of the medical condition is
not a proscribed inquiry. *Lee v. City of Columbus,*
636 F.3d 245 (6th Cir. 2011). Subject to certain
employee protections, an employer also may monitor
employees for the biological effects of their exposure
to toxic substances in the workplace where the

monitoring follows governmental standards and the employer receives outcomes in aggregate terms.

C. THE ADA

The ADA severely limits inquires about potential medical conditions and the administering of medical examinations. Restrictions apply to three categories: (1) Applicants, (2) Post *offer*, and (3) Post *employment*. Drug testing is excluded from the limitation. Employers are free to administer pre- or post-employment drug tests, and thus recovering addicts may be subjected to more frequent drug testing than other employees without subjecting the employer to liability based on discrimination against individuals with an addiction (a protected disability). *Buckley v. Consolidated Edison, Co.,* 127 F.3d 270 (2d Cir. 1997).

(1) Applicants

The Act prohibits: (a) all pre-offer medical examinations, (b) inquiries as to whether the applicant considers himself to have a disability, or (c) questions that might disclose a disability, such as medications being taken, injuries, records of hospitalization, insurance claims, and applications for workers compensation benefits. The prohibition against inquires applies to all individuals whether or not they suffer from any condition and even if the records disclose no evidence of a disability. A nondisabled individual who is asked such questions may recover damages from the employer whether or not the individual is hired. *Griffin v. Steeltek, Inc.,* 261 F.3d 1026 (10th Cir. 2001). If the responses to a forbidden inquiry disclose a potential medical impairment, and the applicant is rejected, it may be inferred that the employer discriminated against the individual because he was "perceived" to be suffering from a disability. An employee who provides false answers to questions the employer may not legally ask may not be terminated because the employee provided "false information." *Downs v. Mass. Bay. Transp. Auth.,* 13 F.Supp.2d 130 (D. Mass. 1998).

Proscribed medical inquiries do not include a description of job requirements and essential job duties, followed by questions as to whether the applicant possesses the credentials and ability to perform those duties. Thus, if the job requires driving a truck, the employer is permitted to ask: "Do you have a driver's license, and are you willing and able to drive this truck?"

(2) Post Offer

After an applicant is tendered a firm offer of employment an employer may require a medical examination as a condition of the offeree commencing employment if all new employees are subjected to the examination, results and information are kept confidential, and the information is not used in a manner inconsistent with the ADA. This means, for example, that all persons who have been offered truck driver jobs now may be given reasonable hearing and eye sight examinations, and that the offer may be revoked for those who fail. Applicants offered pipefitters jobs may be given a *relevant* physical examination. If the examination discloses that an offeree could not lift 100 lb., the offer may be revoked on the basis of the examination if, but only if, the ability to lift 100 lbs was an essential duty of a pipefitter. *Fuzy v. S & B Engineers & Constructors, Ltd.,* 332 F.3d 301 (5th Cir. 2003).

(3) Post Employment

Employers are permitted to require post-employment examinations of employees if the examination narrowly focuses on the specific ability to perform necessary job functions. For example, regular eye and hearing tests may be administered to drivers. Cardiovascular examinations may be given to employees in particularly strenuous jobs or which involve high risks to themselves or others should they suffer a collapse. 42 U.S.C. 12112(d)(4)(B). If the job involves high risks of infection of others, as would be the case for food handlers or health care workers, employers may test these employees for infectious diseases. *Tice v. Centre Area Trans. Auth.,* 247 F.3d 506 (3d Cir. 2001).

Employees seeking medical leave under the Family and Medical Leave Act are required by that Act to provide, upon request by the employer, certification of their medical condition. *Supra,* 24.03. Employers requiring such certification would not violate ADA. *See,* 26.02(b).

An employer may condition a return to work of an injured or previously disabled employee on the employee passing a job related physical examination or performance test given to determine the employee's fitness to perform essential job duties. *Porter v. United States Alumoweld Co.*, 125 F.3d 243 (4th Cir. 1997).

Encouraging, but not requiring, all employees to have physical examinations as part of a general wellness program is permitted, as long as employees are not discriminated against for refusing to take an examination or based on the results of the examination.

D. EMPLOYEE POLYGRAPH PROTECTION ACT, 29 U.S.C. 2001

(1) General Prohibition

This Act prohibits *private* employers not involved in handling controlled substances from: (1) requiring, requesting, or causing employees or applicants to take lie detector tests or similar truth probing techniques; (2) using, accepting, referring to, or inquiring about the results of such tests; and (3) discharging, disciplining, or discriminating against employees or applicants who refuse to take such a test or in relying on the results of such tests.

(2) Exception

The Act permits employers to require and to use polygraphs pursuant to an *ongoing investigation* of an economic loss where: (1) the employee being tested had access to the missing property, (2) the employer had a reasonable suspicion that the employee was involved, and (3) the employee is provided with an explanation of the loss and the basis for the employer's suspicion. If authorized, the test questions may *not* inquire into sexual matters, political beliefs, or labor union activity. The employee being tested must be given an advance copy of the questions. The employee may have counsel present during the test. Test results, papers, and completed test markings must be provided the tested employee.

(3) Enforcement

Individuals enforce the Act through private judicial actions. If plaintiff establishes that his refusal to take an *unauthorized* test or that the results from that *unauthorized* test were used to discriminate against him, defendant may avoid liability by proving that it would have taken the same action notwithstanding the test or its results. *Worden v. SunTrust Banks, Inc.,* 549 F.3d 334 (4th Cir. 2008). 29 C.F.R. Part 800. Successful plaintiffs are entitled to reinstatement with seniority and back pay, compensatory damages, and their attorneys' fees. *Mennen v. Easter Stores,* 951 F.Supp. 838 (N.D. Iowa 1997).

E. CITIZENSHIP AND IMMIGRATION STATUS

The Immigration Reform and Control Act, 8 U.S.C. 1324A, *requires* employers to verify the eligibility of applicants to work in the United States. Failure to conduct such verification can subject the employer to civil and criminal penalties. Thus, inquiries into an applicant's nationality, and eligibility for employment in the United States, not only are permissible, they are required.

While citizenship status inquiries are required, the Act makes it illegal for an employer to discriminate against applicants on the basis of national origin or their "citizenship status." "Citizenship status" protects only U.S. citizens and "intending citizens" against discrimination. "Intending citizens" are defined as lawfully admitted resident non-citizens who have applied for citizenship "on a timely basis" and are "actively pursuing" U.S. citizenship. *Supra,* 7.02. Immigration reform is currently pending in Congress.

CHAPTER 27

RETALIATION ("REPRISAL") FOR "PARTICIPATION" OR "OPPOSITION"

27.01: GENERALLY

The core statutes prohibit discrimination against individuals because they have made a charge, testified, assisted, or *participated* in any manner in an investigation, proceeding, or hearing under the Act, or have "*opposed* any practice made unlawful" by the Act. 42 U.S.C. 2000e–3(a). By protecting "individuals" the statutes implicitly protect former employees from future retaliation. For example, a defined employer may not give bad references to an individual's prospective employers because the individual had participated in EEOC proceedings or had opposed perceived illegal practices of the former employer. *Robinson v. Shell Oil Co.,* 519 U.S. 337 (1997).

While 42 U.S.C. 1981, and the ADEA as applied to federal employees, have no expressed non-retaliation provisions, both statutes implicitly prohibit retaliation using standards similar to the expressed statutory protection. *CBOCS West v. Humphries,* 553 U.S. 442 (2008); *Gomez–Perez v. Potter,* 553 U.S. 474 (2008).

27.02: "DISCRIMINATION"

The protection against retaliation requires only "discrimination" because of protected activity. It is not necessary for the "discrimination" to adversely affect a "term or condition of employment." The standard is whether the employer's retaliatory action "might have dissuaded a reasonable worker from making or supporting a charge of discrimination." *Thompson v. North American Stainless, LP,* ___ U.S. ___ 131 S.Ct. 863 (2011). Personal slights or minor adjustments of job duties would not be "discrimination" as they would not dissuade a worker from engaging in protected activity. However, assignment of an employee to a different, less prestigious, and somewhat more arduous job could be a deterrent, and thus would be actionable "discrimination." *Burlington Northern & Santa Fe Ry. Co. v. White,* 548 U.S. 53 (2006).

In some instances discrimination against an individual for the protected activity of others is proscribed, even though the plaintiff himself did not file or support a charge of discrimination. Shortly after a fellow employee, who was plaintiff's fiancée, filed an EEOC charge, plaintiff was discharged. Although the adverse action was not taken against the fiancée—the person who filed the charge—plaintiff was "aggrieved by the alleged unlawful employment practice" under 42 U.S.C. 2000e–5(b)(f)(1), and thus had standing to sue. Plaintiff stated a claim because his discharge could reasonably dissuade his co-workers, including his fiancée, from filing charges or supporting protected activity. *Thompson v. North American Stainless, LP, supra.* The Court sketched the parameters of the protection: "[F]iring a close family member will almost always meet this standard [of dissuading a reasonable employee from making or supporting a charge], and inflicting a milder reprisal on a mere acquaintance will almost never do so, but beyond that we are reluctant to generalize."

27.03: PROTECTED ACTIVITY

A. GENERALLY

There are two classes of activity protected by the statutes. The first is actual participation in enforcement proceedings ("participation clause"). The second protects unofficial, more informal, opposition to practices made illegal by the Act ("opposition clause"). It is important to distinguish between "participation" and "opposition" because "participation" receives more complete, if not absolute, protection, while protection for "opposition" is qualified.

B. "PARTICIPATION"

(1) What It Is

"Participation" includes filing of charges or lawsuits, giving testimony as part of *state* or federal enforcement proceedings or during discovery, as well as supplying information to state and federal enforcement agencies (not limited to the EEOC). It includes more informal communications, such as letters, to enforcement agencies. *Pettway v. American Cast Iron Pipe Co.,* 411 F.2d 998 (5th Cir.

1969). Protection extends to oral complaints, charges, or communications such as telephone calls and personal visits to an enforcement office. *Kasten v. Saint–Gobain Performance Plastics Corp.,* 563 U.S. ___, 131 S.Ct. 1325 (2011) (FLSA).

Mere threats by the employee to file an EEOC charge may well be protected "opposition," but are not "participation." *EEOC v. Johnson Co.,* 18 FEP 896, 19 EPD 9016 (D.Minn. 1978). *Cf., Croushorn v. Bd. of Trustees,* 518 F.Supp. 9 (M.D. Tenn. 1980) (unconditional statement that employee was preparing an EEOC charge was protected "participation").

Reasonable gathering of evidence by an employee or the employer's EEO officer for *pending* litigation or in response to filed EEOC charges may be "participation" in those proceedings. *Grant v. Hazlett Strip Casting Corp.,* 880 F.2d 1264 (2d Cir. 1989). However, *McKennon v. Nashville Banner Pub. Co.,* 513 U.S. 332 (1995), implied that clandestine gathering and copying of confidential information in *anticipation* of possible litigation was neither "participation" nor protected "opposition."

When an employer's internal investigation of possible discrimination is precipitated by an EEOC charge, statements to the *employer* as part of the employer's investigation may be "participation." *EEOC v. Total Systems, Inc.,* 221 F.3d 1171 (11th Cir. 2000). However, in *Townsend v. Benjamin,* 679 F.3d. 41 (2d Cir. 2012), the employer's human resources director conducted an investigation into an employee's claim of sexual harassment *prior to* the victim filing an EEOC charge. The director was disciplined. His pre-charge investigation was held not to constitute "participation."

Refusal to settle or waive claims pending before the EEOC or the courts is participation, and may not be the basis for discipline. *Goldsmith v. Bagby Elevator Co.*, 513 F.3d 1261 (11th Cir. 2008). However, it is not unlawful retaliation to insist, as a condition of continued employment, that employees agree to submit *future* discrimination claims to private arbitration. *Weeks v. Hardin Mfg. Corp.*, 291 F.3d 1307 (11th Cir. 2002).

(2) Protection Accorded

(a) Absolute

Early, and still leading, authority held that "participation" was absolutely privileged. *Pettway v. American Cast Iron Pipe Co.*, 411 F.2d 998 (5th Cir. 1969). "Protection is not lost if the employee is wrong on the merits of the charge, nor is protection lost if the contents of the charge are malicious as well as wrong." *Booker v. Brown & Williamson Tobacco Co.*, 869 F.2d 1304 (6th Cir. 1989). Such an absolute privilege was seen as the only way to insure that an employee would freely invoke and participate in enforcement proceedings.

(b) Good Faith

Some courts have limited the privilege to good faith participation, refusing to protect charges or statements that are made frivolously or in bad faith. "[I]t cannot be true that a plaintiff can file false charges, lie to an investigator, and possibly defame co-employees, without suffering repercussions." *Gilooly v. Mo. Dept of Health & Senior Serv.*, 421 F.3d 734 (8th Cir. 2005).

(c) Reasonable

Clark County School Dist. v. Breeden, 532 U.S. 268 (2001), indicated that *good faith* allegations in an EEOC charge are protected participation even if the allegations are not *objectively* reasonable. *Accord, Glover v. South Carolina Law Enf.*, 170 F.3d 411 (4th Cir. 1999). Nevertheless, some courts hold that "completely groundless" or unreasonable charges are not protected. *Johnson v. ITT Aerospace*, 272 F.3d 498 (7th Cir. 2001). Participation was held unprotected if the participation violated other legitimate employer rules. Thus, supplying the EEOC with documents that supported plaintiff's charge was unprotected because releasing these particular documents violated "privacy interests." *Vaughn v. Epworth Villa*, 537 F.3d 1147 (10th Cir. 2008) (ignoring the fact that communications to the EEOC are confidential and cannot be disclosed by the EEOC to the public).

C. "OPPOSITION"

(1) To What?

The core statutes make unlawful, discrimination because the individual "*opposed* any practice made unlawful." 42 U.S.C. 2000e–3(a). The language has not been interpreted to require that the practice opposed be found to violate the law. The statutes protect opposition to "practices" that could *reasonably be perceived* as unlawful. "When an employee communicates to her employer a belief that the employer has engaged in * * * a form of employment discrimination, that communication virtually always constitutes opposition to the activity. It is true that one can imagine exceptions, * * * but these will be eccentric cases." *Crawford v. Metro Gov't of Nashville,* 555 U.S. 271 (2009).

Clark County School Dist. v. Breeden, 532 U.S. 268 (2001), involved one of the exceptional, "eccentric cases." The Court concluded that a single off-color comment followed by male co-workers laughing could not reasonably be perceived to create an unlawful hostile working environment, and thus plaintiff's objections thereto were not protected "opposition." Removing a hangman's noose or sexist graffiti and objecting to, as well as rejecting, sexual advances would seem to be protected opposition. *Ogden v. Wax Works,* 214 F.3d 999 (8th Cir. 2008).

Requests or demands to implement policies clearly beyond the scope of the statutes, such as demands for *paid* child care leave or adoption of an affirmative action program probably are not "opposition" to reasonably perceived *illegal* action. *Holden v. Owens–Illinois, Inc.,* 793 F.2d 745 (6th Cir. 1986). Complaints about staff cutbacks and the employer's formula for calculating pension contributions, not tied to any alleged age or sex discrimination, were not protected opposition. *Smith v. Lafayette Bank & Trust Co.,* 674 F.3d 655 (7th Cir. 2012).

Some courts have given an exceptionally narrow interpretation to what a reasonable person would consider unlawful. Based on the fallacious assumption that "all persons are presumed to know the law," one court has held that no reasonable person would believe that a practice violates the law if binding precedent within its jurisdiction had held otherwise. Thus, a black employee could be dismissed for raising objections to racial slurs directed at others because the slurs had not yet reached the level that this particular circuit had considered necessary to constitute a hostile environment. *Butler v. Alabama Dep't of Transp.,* 536 F.3d 1209 (11th Cir. 2008). A female employee complained about favoritism shown to paramours of a supervisor. This was held to be unprotected because paramour preference had been held not be a form of sex discrimination that violates Title VII. *Kelly v. Shapiro & Assoc.,* 716 F.3d 10 (2d Cir. 2013). Presumably, as sexual orientation is not a class protected by current federal law, an employee who objects to homophobic slurs does so at his/her own risk.

The wording of the core statutes, as well as the Court's interpretation of them, suggest that to be protected the opposition must be to a *"practice"* that a reasonable person in the position of plaintiff might consider illegal. *Crawford v. Metro Gov't of Nashville, supra.* One lower court held, however, that plaintiff's objection must be, not just to the "practice," but also to the perceived *illegality* of the practice. The court assumed that the employer's advances toward plaintiff might well constitute actionable sexual harassment. However, as plaintiff's expressed "opposition" was to the sexual advances, not to their perceived illegality, the opposition was unprotected. *Tate v. Executive Mgt. Serv.,* 546 F.3d 528 (7th Cir. 2008). In this court it would seem that if a black employee asks a supervisor to stop using a racist slur because the term was personally insulting, his request is not protected opposition unless the employee had in mind at the time of the objection that the supervisor's slur would violate Title VII.

(2) "Opposition"

Protected "opposition" to employer perceived discrimination includes making internal complaints about perceived discriminatory treatment, filing discrimination grievances with a labor union, enlisting the aid of civil rights organizations, circulating petitions or publishing advertisements, writing letters to legislators, and making critical statements to the media. *Fine v. Ryan Intern. Airlines,* 305 F.3d 746 (7th Cir. 2002). Urging or participating in lawful, peaceful striking, picketing, or consumer boycotts can be protected opposition. *Payne v. McLemore's Wholesale & Retail Products,* 654 F.2d 1130 (5th Cir. 1981).

"Opposition" goes beyond positive, direct action. *Crawford v. Metro. Gov't of Nashville,* 555 U.S. 271 (2009), involved an employee who responded to employer questions asked as part of the employer's investigation of sexual harassment claims made by plaintiff's co-worker. Plaintiff recited facts relating to her treatment by the supervisor charged with the harassment. Plaintiff was disciplined for the answers she gave. The Court held that plaintiff's response to questions was protected opposition even though it did not involve active or consistent opposition to a practice. "Opposition," the Court held, includes inaction, doing nothing or "standing pat," as one might silently "oppose" slavery without actively speaking against it. Clearly, then, the Court concluded, a response to an employer's questions regarding alleged illegal treatment of a co-worker is protected "opposition." Accordingly, accompanying or giving "moral support" to a co-worker who files a complaint with the employer's human resources office is protected "opposition." *Collazo v. Bristol–Meyer Squibb Mfg. Co.,* 617 F.3d 39 (1st Cir. 2010). A supervisor who refused to discipline a worker because the supervisor believed to do so would be illegal, likewise, would be protected. *EEOC v. St. Ann's Hosp.,* 664 F.2d 128 (7th Cir. 1981).

Opposition to the employer's actions outside of the *employment relationship* are not protected. For example, objecting to a teacher's perceived favoritism toward a Caucasian *student* was not protected as it was not an objection to discrimination covered by Title VII. *Artis v. Francis Howell N. Band Booster Ass'n, Inc.,* 161 F.3d. 1178 (8th Cir. 1998). A release of a police department report that was critical of the department's *policing* practices was not protected opposition to the employment practices of the department. *Bonn v. City of Omaha,* 623 F.3d 587 (8th Cir. 2010).

(3) Opposition Limits

Activity that is unlawful, such as trespass, assaults, or other violent behavior is not protected simply because the opposition is directed at the employer's perceived discrimination. *Green v. McDonnell Douglas Corp.,* 463 F.2d 337 (8th Cir 1972). Nor is activity protected if it undermines the policies of other federal statutes, such as the National Labor Relations Act. Thus, demanding that the employer disregard a collective obligation to a labor union, urging an illegal secondary boycott, or making a demand for the employer to engage in improper collective bargaining will not be protected. *Emporium Capwell Co. v. Western Addition Comm. Org.,* 420 U.S. 50 (1975) (picketing and boycotting that undermined policies of the NLRA are not protected by Title VII).

Lawful opposition also must be reasonable under the circumstances. An employer may dismiss an employee if it has a good faith belief that the employee consciously misstated a material fact. In sum, lies about an employer are not protected opposition. *EEOC v. Total System Serv. Inc.,* 221 F.3d 1171 (11th Cir. 2000). Maligning the quality of the employer's *products or services*—to be contrasted with an attack on its employment practices—is fundamental employee disloyalty that is unprotected. *Hochstadt v. Worchester Foundation for Exp. Biology,* 545 F.2d 222 (1st Cir. 1976). Protected opposition does not extend to "dubious self-help tactics or work-place espionage in order to gather evidence of discrimination." *Argyopoulos v. City of Alton,* 539 F.3d 724 (7th Cir. 2008).

Disrupting the work of other employees or copying and distributing confidential documents that seriously undermine a confidential working relationship is not protected. *Jennings v. Tinley Park Comm. Consol. School Dist., No. 146,* 864 F.2d 1368 (7th Cir. 1988). *McKennon v. Nashville Banner Pub. Co.,* 513 U.S. 352 (1995), assumed that unauthorized copying of confidential information, done in fear of, and in defense against, *anticipated* age discrimination by her employer, was not protected opposition.

Managers or supervisors have been held to a higher standard of "loyalty" in opposing their employer's practices than have lower level workers. *EEOC v. Crown Zellerbach Corp.,* 720 F.2d 1008 (9th Cir. 1983), held that lower level employees writing letters to the parent corporation and to local officials, picketing the mayor's office, sending a letter to a major customer which alleged "bigoted racism" was protected opposition. However, *Pendelton v. Rumsfeld,* 628 F.2d 102 (D.C.Cir. 1980), involved the employer's EEO counselors who called a news conference and publicly complained that management had been unresponsive to civil rights complaints. The court held that such public confrontation by employees with special responsibilities to management was not protected. Similarly, an executive's public complaints about the company's failure to hire women were not protected, in that a managerial employee should have worked internally to address the problem and exercised restraint in making critical public pronouncements that would undermine his ability to do his job. *Novotny v. Great American Fed. Sav. & Loan Ass'n.*, 539 F.Supp. 437 (W.D. Pa. 1982).

27.04: PROVING RETALIATORY MOTIVE

A. CIRCUMSTANTIAL EVIDENCE AND "TEMPORAL PROXIMITY"

Plaintiff has the burden of proving that the discrimination was because of her protected participation or opposition. This could be accomplished through "direct" or verbal evidence of a retaliatory motive, such as a supervisor commenting, "she should have never filed that complaint." In the absence of such verbal evidence, improper motivation can be proved by circumstantial evidence, such as a distinct pattern of an employer discriminating against workers who engage in protected activity.

The "temporal proximity" between the employee's protected action and the employer's act of discrimination is sufficient to create an inference that the employer's action was motivated by the employee's protected activity. *Clark County School Dist. v. Breeden,* 532 U.S. 268 (2001). To create this inference the time lapse between the two events must be "very close." *Breeden, supra,* held that a 20 month period between plaintiff's filing of an EEOC charge and the challenged transfer was not sufficiently close to sustain a finding that the defendant was motivated by plaintiff's charge. The Court cited with approval lower court decisions which held that the temporal proximity of 3 and 4 months between the events was insufficient to sustain a judgment for plaintiff. Subsequent decisions have held that even a one month gap between protected activity and the act of discrimination is insufficient, standing alone, to create an inference of retaliation. *Smith v. Fairview Ridges Hosp.*, 625 F.3d 1076 (8th Cir. 2010).

The *Breeden* Court emphasized, too, that to create an inference of improper motivation plaintiff must establish that the decision-maker was aware of the plaintiff's protected activity. No inference of improper motivation could be drawn if the supervisor charged with retaliatory motive was unaware that plaintiff had filed an EEOC charge.

B. MIXED MOTIVES

Clark County School Dist. v. Breeden, supra, observed that employers need not suspend previously planned actions simply because the employee engaged in protected activity. Employers may assert that, notwithstanding the fact that the employee engaged in known protected activity, legitimate reasons, such as economic pressures or plaintiff's poor job performance, motivated the employer's action. Fact finders are then confronted with assertions of legitimate reasons in the face of plaintiff's evidence of retaliatory motive.

Violations of the substantive, or status based, provisions of Title VII found in 703 (42 U.S.C. 2000e–2) are established if plaintiff proves that "a" proscribed factor motivated the decision. The statute specifically provides that a claim by defendant that it would have made the same decision on legitimate grounds is no defense to liability, but only affects plaintiff's ability to secure the remedies of damages, reinstatement, and back pay. 42 U.S.C. 2000e–2(m). *Desert Palace Inc. v. Costa,* 539 U.S. 90 (2003).

Gross v. FBL Financial Serv., Inc., 537 U.S. 167 (2009), held that as the ADEA has no statutory requirement similar to Title VII, ADEA imposes on plaintiff the burden of proving that age was "the" motivating factor for defendant's discrimination. *Supra,* 16.09. The question remained as to whether retaliation claims under 704 of Title VII (42 U.S.C. 2000e–3) would follow *Desert Palace, Inc. v. Costa, supra,* or *Gross* v. *FBL Financial Serv. Inc., supra.* The issue arises because, unlike section 703 of Title VII, the retaliation provisions of section 704 simply prohibit discrimination "because of" protected participation or opposition.

A number of lower courts had held that the causation standard of 704 should be based either on an assumption that 703(m) causation standards implicitly applied to 704 or on *Price Waterhouse v. Hopkins,* 490 U.S. 228 (1989), which held that an employer would be liable if plaintiff proved that a proscribed factor was "a" motive behind the action, but defendant could avoid liability by proving that it would have made the same decision, on legitimate grounds. *See, supra,* 16.08B.

University of Texas, S.W. Medical Ctr. v. Nassar, ___ U.S. ___, 133 S.Ct. 2517 (2013), however, followed the reasoning of *Gross.* In the absence of the statute changing the causation standard (as was done in

703(m)), the "because of" language found in both the ADEA and section 704 of Title VII "requires plaintiff to show that the harm would not have occurred in the absence of—that is but for—plaintiff's protected activity." The Court relied on the premise that common law tort liability depends upon plaintiff proving such "causation in fact," and absent an express statutory alteration, the common law principle should govern. Indeed, Congress' failure to the extend the 703(m) "a motivating factor" standard to 704 indicated its intent to limit 703(m) to class-based, or status, discrimination. Finally, the Court held that 703(m), added in 1991, replaced the *Price Waterhouse* analysis of the Title VII causation standard.

Prior decisions had held that 42 U.S.C. 1981 (proscribing race discrimination) and the federal sector ADEA provision *implicitly* proscribe retaliation for asserting such claims, and that the *Price Waterhouse* shifting burden analysis sets plaintiff's burden to establish the causation necessary for liability. *E.g. Gomez-Perez v. Potter,* 553 U.S. 474 (2008)(federal employee ADEA retaliation). The *Nassar* Court held that these decisions were inapplicable to Title VII retaliation claims because 704 is part of a detailed statutory scheme expressly proscribing retaliation which set the "because of" standard for causation. This distinction suggests that notwithstanding *Gross* and *Nassar,* retaliation claims brought under statutes which lack express non-retaliation provisions may continue to apply the *Price Waterhouse* shifting burdens approach to liability.

Many Title VII charges involve claims of both status-based discrimination and retaliation for the employee's assertion of status discrimination. Claims of race discrimination that violate 42 U.S.C. 1981 may be joined in the Title VII suit. In such cases juries will be required to apply three different standards for liability: (i) Title VII status claim "a" motivating factor (*Desert Palace*); (ii) 1981 race claim: shifting burdens of liability (*Price Waterhouse*); and (iii) the retaliation claim: "the" motivating factor (*Nassar*).

27.05: NATIONAL LABOR RELATIONS LEGISLATION

The National Labor Relations Act, 29 U.S.C. 157 and 158, (NLRA) and the Railway Labor Act, 45 U.S.C. 151, (covering rail and airline employees) provide potentially broader protection against retaliation than do the core statutes. These statutes prohibit discrimination against an employee for engaging in any "concerted activity" for their "mutual aid and protection." 29 U.S.C. 158(a)(3). Activity will be "concerted," if it is joined by more than one employee or by one employee acting on behalf of other persons.

"Mutual aid and protection" broadly includes concerted opposition to perceived discrimination in all forms, including sexual orientation or citizenship, and protects demands for the employer to undertake affirmative action or other programs benefiting workers. *New Negro Alliance v. Sanitary Grocery Co.,* 303 U.S. 552 (1938). For example, an employee who had discussions with other employees about obtaining maternity and child care leave, and requested the employer provide such leave for its employees was engaged in "concerted activities for mutual aid and protection," and could not be discriminated against for this activity. *Boese Hilburn Electric Serv. Co.*, 313 N.L.R.B. 372 (1993).

Enforcement of the NLRA is by the National Labor Relations Board, and is triggered by charges filed by aggrieved persons with the Board. Hearings are held before the Board, which issues findings and conclusions subject to review by an appropriate United States Court of Appeals.

PART 5

COMPLIANCE AND ENFORCEMENT

CHAPTER 28
REMEDIES

28.01: REMEDIES INTRODUCED

Title VII and the ADA provide that when the defendant "[h]as intentionally engaged in * * * an unlawful practice * * * the court may enjoin * * * the practice or order such affirmative action as may be appropriate, but is not limited to reinstatement or hiring, * * * with or without back pay * * * or any other equitable relief as the court deems appropriate." 42 U.S.C. 2000e–(5) (g). Amendments in 1991 to Title VII and the ADA allow juries to assess compensatory and punitive damages, subject to fixed dollar amount limits. 42 U.S.C. 1981A(a)(2). Punitive damages are not recoverable against governmental employers.

The ADEA differs somewhat. It incorporates the remedial provisions of the Fair Labor Standards Act which authorizes back pay, as well as hiring, reinstatement, and equitable relief. Except for unlawful retaliation, the ADEA does not provide for compensatory or punitive damages, but does authorize statutory liquidated damages for willful violations in an amount equal to the assessed back wages. 29 U.S.C. 626(b).

The Equal Pay Act and the Family and Medical Leave Act (FMLA) provide for payment of back wages, plus an amount equal to back wage liability as liquidated damages. The FMLA also allows for reinstatement with full benefits of employees discriminated against for the exercise of the leave rights granted by the Act. 29 U.S.C. 2612–2614.

An employee who resigned, but did so under circumstances that made her continued employment "intolerable," will be considered "constructively discharged," and thus will be entitled to the same remedies as a person actually discharged illegally. *Supra,* 25.05.

Even if plaintiff establishes defendant's illegal motivation, if defendant demonstrates that it would have made the same decision on legitimate grounds, such proof will preclude plaintiff from securing a hiring order and the recovery of back wages and damages. 42 U.S.C. 2000e–4(g)(2)(B).

28.02: GENERALLY: THE "MAKE WHOLE" OBLIGATION

The grant of any remedy appears to be based on a judicial finding that discrimination is "intentional." However, "intentional" has been construed to mean that the activity found to be discriminatory was not accidental. Remedial powers are not dependent upon proof that defendant intentionally violated the law.

Moreover, the statutory terms "may" and "with or without back pay" suggest broad discretion in trial courts to balance various equitable concerns, such as defendant's good faith, as a basis for denying a successful plaintiff monetary or injunctive relief. The Court has narrowly circumscribed this apparent discretion.

Albemarle Paper Co. v. Moody, 422 U.S. 405 (1975), involved the trial court's denial of back pay to victims of a discriminatory discharge based on the employer's good faith and plaintiff's initial disclaimer of a desire to recover back pay. The Court reversed, quoting from the legislative history:

> The person aggrieved, * * * so far as possible, [must] be restored to a position where they would have been were it not for the unlawful discrimination. * * * It follows that, given a finding of unlawful discrimination, back pay should be denied only for reasons which, if applied generally, would not frustrate the central statutory purposes of eradicating discrimination * * * and making persons whole for injuries suffered * * *.

Franks v. Bowman Transp. Co., 424 U.S. 747 (1976), involved a trial court's denial of retroactive, remedial seniority running from the date of the illegal denial of the position until the date of employment. The denial of remedial seniority was based upon the assumption that to do so would undermine legitimate seniority expectations of "innocent" incumbents, which seniority rights are specifically preserved by the seniority proviso of 42 U.S.C. 2000e–2(h). The Court reversed addressing first the seniority proviso, which the Court held applied only to possible liability based upon good faith use of seniority, and did not limit the remedial provisions of the statute requiring "make whole" remedies for found violations. *Supra,* 19.04. The Court then held that undermining the seniority expectations of incumbent workers was an insufficient reason to deny the full seniority necessary to "make whole" victims of illegal treatment.

As immigration law forbids the employment of undocumented workers a court, not only may not, but must not, order the hiring or back pay for individuals not entitled to legal employment. *Hoffman Plastic Compounds, Inc., v. NLRB,* 535 U.S. 137 (2002).

28.03: BACK PAY

Rarely, if ever, can back wages be denied. *Albemarle Paper Co. v. Moody, supra.* The statutory term "wages" is not limited to lost salary, but includes regularly granted pay increases, bonuses, lost fringe benefits, such as vacation pay, retirement plan contributions, stock options, meal or housing subsidies, and profit sharing distributions. *Munoz* v. *Oceanside Resorts, Inc.,* 223 F.3d 1340 (11th Cir. 2000).

For employees who are victims of compensation discrimination, the employer must increase the compensation to that of comparable employees, plus provide back pay for the difference that runs for the length of time of the discriminatory pay difference. Under the core statutes back pay may not be recovered from a date more than two years prior to the filing of a charge. 42 U.S.C. 2000e–5(g). Willful violations of the Equal Pay Act allow recovery of up to three years of back wages. Back pay liability toward a rejected applicant may be tolled at the point the employer unconditionally offers to hire the plaintiff, even if the offer does not include an offer of retroactive seniority. *Ford Motor Co. v. EEOC.,* 458 U.S. 219 (1982).

Any amounts actually earned through alternative employment prior to reinstatement or an unconditional offer of employment will be deducted from the gross amount of back pay liability otherwise due. 42 U.S.C. 2000e–5(g)(1). The nature of plaintiff's alternative employment is immaterial. "Collateral source" benefits such as social security, unemployment, welfare benefits, or income from investments are not "interim earnings" that must be deducted. *Gaworski v. ITT Commercial Finance Corp.,* 17 F.3d 1104 (8th Cir. 1994). Uncertainty or difficulty in calculating the amount of a back pay award does not warrant its denial or reduction. Doubts are resolved in favor of the injured employee. *Salinas v. Roadway Exp., Inc.,* 735 F.2d 1574 (5th Cir. 1984).

In addition, "amounts *earnable with reasonable diligence*" by the successful plaintiff "shall operate to reduce the back pay otherwise available." 42 U.S.C. 2000e–5(g)(1). To secure this reduction *defendant* carries the burden to prove that: (1) positions similar to that wrongfully denied plaintiff were available in the geographical area, and (2) plaintiff failed to exercise reasonable diligence in seeking out such positions. *Ford v. Nicks,* 866 F.2d 865 (6th Cir. 1989). Availability of similar positions can be established thorough help wanted advertisements or testimony of career placement experts.

Plaintiff has no obligation to seek or accept positions that are significantly different from the one wrongfully denied. *EEOC v. Guardian Pools, Inc.,* 838 F.2d 1507 (11th Cir. 1987). That plaintiff has moved from the community, started a business, or has accepted significantly different employment, does not conclusively establish plaintiff's lack of due diligence. *Id.*

Back pay may be tolled during any period that plaintiff is unavailable for work, as where she became disabled (unless the disability was caused by the employer's illegal action) or has been incarcerated. If defendant can demonstrate that plaintiff engaged in misconduct discovered after he was illegally denied employment, back wages may be denied from the point that plaintiff would have been lawfully discharged or was rendered otherwise unqualified for employment. *McKennon v. Nashville Banner Pub. Co.,* 513 U.S. 352 (1995). *See, supra,* 14.03(a).

Pre-judgment interest on unpaid back wages running from the date of the unlawful employment denial will be added to the award. *Barbour v. Merrill,* 48 F.3d 1270 (D.C.Cir. 1995). Post-judgment interest will be added to the final award.

Liability for back pay is both joint and several among defendants. Thus, where a union and employer are found liable, as where there is a discriminatory collective bargaining agreement, plaintiff may collect full back wages from either defendant, and there is no right of contribution between defendants. *Northwest Airlines, Inc. v. Transp. Workers Union,* 451 U.S. 77 (1981).

28.04: HIRING AND REINSTATEMENT WITH SENIORITY

The statutes specifically authorize reinstatement or hiring. Hiring into the position wrongfully denied usually is necessary to "make whole" the victim, and is denied only in unusual circumstances. Rarely, however, will a court order an incumbent employee to be bumped or removed in order to hire the plaintiff. *Cf. Walters v. Atlanta,* 803 F.3d 1135 (11th Cir. 1986). The uniqueness of the job denied caused irreparable harm, warranted a hiring order that effectively resulted in plaintiff replacing the individual who had been given the job. When there is no current vacancy, the court will order defendant to hire the plaintiff into the first comparable vacancy available, with "front pay" compensation until such time as the plaintiff is actually hired or plaintiff secures substantially equivalent employment elsewhere.

An "acrimonious" relationship between the successful plaintiff and a supervisor is not itself a satisfactory reason to deny reinstatement. Courts "must be careful not to allow an employer to use its anger or hostility toward the plaintiff for having filed a lawsuit as an excuse to avoid plaintiff's reinstatement." *Hicks v. Forest Preserve Dist. of Cook County,* 677 F.3d 781 (7th Cir. 2012). Occasionally, when the job involves a close and confidential relationship with the defendant, or where acrimony is so intense that it precludes plaintiff's successful job performance, a hiring remedy may be denied with defendant ordered to grant preferential hiring into similar positions when they arise, plus "front pay" as compensation until such time as an appropriate job is tendered. *Che v. Mass. Bay Transp. Auth.,* 342 F.3d 31 (1st Cir. 2003).

Upon being (re)hired, successful plaintiffs must be awarded the seniority and similar benefits they would have received had they not been discriminatorily denied the position. Good faith of the employer and impact on "innocent" incumbents is no basis for denial of such remedies to the reinstated employee. *Franks v. Bowman Transp. Co., supra.*

28.05: "FRONT PAY:" INTERIM ALTERNATIVE TO HIRING

Compensation is not an open alternative to hiring. Compensation alternatives to (re)hiring are appropriate *only* in unusual situations where reinstatement is not appropriate.

[W]hen an appropriate position for the plaintiff is not immediately available without displacing an incumbent employee * * * [or] is not viable because of continuing hostility between the employer or its workers, or because of the psychological injuries suffered by the plaintiff as a result of the discrimination, courts have ordered front pay as a substitute for reinstatement. * * * [F]ront pay is simply money awarded for lost compensation during the period between the judgment and [the eventual] reinstatement or in lieu of reinstatement. *Pollard v. E.I. duPont de Nemours & Co.*, 532 U.S. 843 (2001).

When front pay is appropriate, it has been ordered in the form of a lump sum that attempts to forecast future lost wages and reduces them to current value. That such an amount is speculative is not grounds for denial. *Suggs v. ServiceMaster Educ. Food Mgt.*, 72 F.3d 1228 (6th Cir. 1996). Or, the trial court may order and monitor regular payments to the successful plaintiff until such time as the plaintiff is employed by defendant or secures equivalent employment elsewhere.

28.06: DAMAGES: COMPENSATORY AND PUNITIVE

A. GENERALLY

Originally, Title VII did not provide for damages or for a trial by jury. Amendments in 1991 authorized awards of both compensatory and punitive damages for illegally motivated discrimination and a trial by jury on factual issues of liability and the extent of damages. However, the amendments placed dollar amount limits on total damage liability that range from a low of $50,000 for smaller employers to a high of $300,000 for employers of 500 or more employees. Back wages and front pay are *not* considered "damages" to be calculated in determining the statutory cap. The ADA contains identical provisions. In addition, no damages may be collected where defendant "demonstrates good faith efforts in consultation with [the plaintiff] to identify and make reasonable accommodation" for plaintiff's disability. 42 U.S.C. 1981A(a)(3).

Neither the ADEA nor the EPA provide for such damages. The statutory provisions for liquidated damages is deemed a substitute. Damages may be recovered under 42 U.S.C. 1981, and are not subject to the Title VII statutory cap. *Bogle v. McClure*, 332 F.3d 1347 (11th Cir. 2003).

Plaintiffs may also join claims under state tort law, which usually allow damage recovery without regard to statutory caps. Federal law does not pre-empt state law that expands upon federally authorized remedies.

B. COMPENSATORY DAMAGES

Monetary awards to compensate plaintiff for miscellaneous non-wage pecuniary losses and for non-pecuniary injuries such as humiliation, emotional distress, inconvenience, loss of enjoyment of life, injury to reputation or professional standing, loss of credit, and aggravation of pre-existing physical or mental conditions, may be recovered. 42 U.S.C. 1981A(b)(3). Such damages are not presumed to flow from discrimination. Plaintiff must prove actual injury with "competent evidence." *Carey v. Piphus,* 435 U.S. 247 (1978). Plaintiff's own testimony as to specific manifestations, preferably supported by documentary evidence, is sufficient. Expert evaluations are not required. *Kucia v. Southeast Ark. Comm. Action Corp.,* 284 F.3d 944 (8th Cir. 2002).

Compensatory damages can be collected against governmental employers. *West v. Gibson,* 527 U.S. 212 (1999). The 1991 Amendments expressly provide that the authorization of compensatory damages does not apply when liability is based on disparate impact. 42 U.S.C. 1981A(a)(1).

C. PUNITIVE DAMAGES

Monetary awards designed to punish wrongdoing and deter future illegal conduct are known as "punitive damages." To be entitled to punitive damages a successful plaintiff must establish more than improperly motivated discrimination but that the employer acted "with malice or with a reckless indifference" to plaintiff's rights. *Kolstad v American Dental Ass'n.,* 527 U.S. 526 (1999). Imputing liability to an employer based on the malicious acts of employees is insufficient, standing alone, to establish employer liability for punitive damages. Thus, an employer liable for harassment by plaintiff's co-workers based on the employer's failure to take effective remedial steps to end the harassment will not be subjected to punitive damages absent a showing that the employer's inaction was made with "malice" or in "reckless disregard" of the plaintiff's rights. *May v. Chrysler Group, LLC,* 716 F.3d 963 (7th Cir.2013). Punitive damages can be awarded, however, upon proof that an investigation into alleged discrimination proved to be a sham designed to protect certain employees. *Bruso v United Airlines Inc.,* 239 F.3d 848 (7th Cir. 2001).Employers are not subject to punitive damages for discriminatory acts of mid-level managers or supervisors that were made contrary to employer policies and where the employer made good faith efforts to comply with the statutes. Reliance on the advice of counsel usually precludes a punitive damage award. *Farias v. Instructional Sys.*, 259 F.3d 91 (2d Cir. 2001). However, even strong anti-discrimination policies alone will not preclude punitive damages for intentional discrimination by high level executives. *McInnis v. Fairfield Communities, Inc.*, 483 F.3d 1129 (7th Cir. 2006).

Punitive damages can be used only to punish behavior that bears some relationship to the plaintiff, and cannot be assessed simply because defendant is an unsavory character or be used as a method of transferring wealth. *State Farm Mut. Auto Ins. Co. v. Campbell,* 538 U.S. 408 (2003). Punitive damages do not require a back wage award, and thus are appropriately awarded to plaintiffs who have been subjected to severe intentional harassment. *May v. Chrysler Group, LLC,* 692 F.3d 734 (7th Cir. 2012). Punitive damage awards do not require significant actual injury to plaintiff. However, the lack of actual damage can be a factor in limiting the *amount* of punitive damages awarded. *BMW of North America v. Gore,* 517 U.S. 559 (1996).

In determining the amount of the award the jury should be instructed to consider the intensity and duration of the conduct itself, defendant's mental attitude, and the size and financial situation of the defendant, and the court may reduce any award that is excessive in light of the these factors.

Title VII specifically exempts all governmental employers—state, local, and federal—from punitive damages awards. 42 U.S.C. 1981A(a)(1).

28.07: LIQUIDATED DAMAGES

The Equal Pay Act, the Family and Medical Leave Act, and the ADEA allow for recovery of "liquidated damages." The EPA and FMLA automatically add an amount equal to the back pay award, thus doubling back pay liability. However, trial courts are granted discretion to reduce or eliminate the liquidated amount if *defendant* carries the burden of proving that it acted on a reasonably based, good faith belief that its actions did not violate the law.

The ADEA also allows an award equal to back pay liability as liquidated damages, but to secure the liquidated damages the *plaintiff* has the burden to establish that defendant acted "willfully." 29 U.S.C. 626(b). In disparate treatment cases involving a discharge or refusal to hire, "willful" means no more than defendant was motivated by plaintiff's age. As defendant was found to have discriminated "willfully" when the fact finder concluded that defendant acted "because of" plaintiff's age, to secure the liquidated amount plaintiff "need not additionally demonstrate that the employer's conduct was outrageous, provide direct evidence of the employer's motivation, or prove that age was the predominant rather than a determinative factor." *Hazen Paper Co. v. Biggins,* 507 U.S. 604 (1993). However, where the discrimination involves the application to plaintiff of a broad, established policy such as the employer relying on age being a bona fide occupational qualification for the particular job, liquidated damages cannot be imposed simply because the employer was generally aware that the ADEA was "in the picture," and that there was a possibility that the policy violated the Act. In this context, "willful" means that the employer either knew that the policy violated the Act, or in adopting and applying it, "showed disregard for the matter." *Trans World Airlines, Inc., v. Thurston,* 469 U.S. 111 (1985).

Liquidated damages authorized by the ADEA may not be collected against federal employers. *Smith v. Office of Personnel Mg't,* 778 F.2d 258 (5th Cir. 1985).

28.08: INJUNCTIVE RELIEF

The statutes give trial courts broad, equitable powers to order prospective actions, to cease discriminatory behavior, such as harassment, to eliminate or modify practices having an adverse effect on the protected class, such as discriminatory tests or policies, and require defendant to take steps to eradicate continuing effects of the discrimination such as expunging files and posting notices of its non-discrimination policies. The trial court may order the defendant to undertake monitoring activity, and to take protective, proactive, and reassuring measures such as requiring supervisors to undergo training. The court may maintain its equitable jurisdiction over the parties after judgment and require the employer to make compliance reports to the court and may appoint monitors to oversee compliance. Failure to comply with court orders will subject defendant to civil contempt liability.

28.09: AFFIRMATIVE ACTION

Remedial authority of trial courts extends to "such affirmative action as may be appropriate." 42 U.S.C. 2000e–5(g). This has been interpreted to allow trial courts to order adoption of reasonable affirmative action plans that set specific race or sex numerical goals and establish timetables for meeting these goals. To warrant such a remedy the plaintiff must prove that plaintiff's class has been victimized by the employer's "persistent or egregious" discrimination, and that race or sex based affirmative action is necessary to "dissipate the lingering effects of pervasive discrimination." *Local 28, Sheet Metal Workers Int'l Ass'n v. EEOC,* 478 U.S. 421 (1986). *United States v. Paradise,* 480 U.S. 149 (1987), sanctioned an order requiring the hiring of equal numbers of black and non-black applicants until 25% of defendant's officer corps was black.

The "reasonableness" parameter of trial court discretion to order race or sex conscious remedies is set by the Constitution. Generally, this means that any work place goal must not be greater than the percentage of victimized class in the available workforce. Moreover, a court may not "unduly trammel" the interests of white incumbent workers by requiring their discharge or establish a "quota" system that excludes consideration of qualified white males. The plan may not override the operation of a bona fide seniority system that would in an economic down turn require retention of recently hired minority employees while more senior white employees were laid off. *Firefighters Local 1748 v. Stotts,* 467 U.S. 561 (1984). Once the goal of a reasonably balanced work force is achieved the court must dissolve the plan's use of race or sex ratios. *Quinn v. City of Boston,* 325 F.3d 18 (1st Cir. 2003).

Non-parties to the discrimination lawsuit that produced the court's order of affirmative action, such as white workers disappointed by the effects of the plan on them, may not later challenge the judicially ordered affirmative action if they had notice or otherwise had an opportunity to object to the provisions or intervene in the litigation but failed to do so. Nor may a non-party challenge the ordered plan in subsequent litigation where a party to the original suit adequately represented the non-party interests and challenged the order on the same legal grounds. 42 U.S.C. 2000e–2(n).

28.10: ATTORNEYS' FEES AND COSTS

A. GENERAL ENTITLEMENT

Many public law statutes that depend on individual enforcement initiatives, including the anti-discrimination statutes, authorize a prevailing plaintiff to recover from defendant reasonable attorneys' fees and related costs of the litigation. The ADEA allows only prevailing *plaintiffs* to recover their attorneys' fees. Title VII and the ADA provide that "the court, *in its discretion*, may allow the *prevailing party* other than [the EEOC or

United States] a reasonable attorney's fees as part of costs." 42 U.S.C. 2000e–5(k).

Notwithstanding the apparent grant of trial court discretion, in fact, trial courts have very little. *Christiansburg Garment Co. v. EEOC,* 434 U.S. 412 (1978), held that "a prevailing *plaintiff* ordinarily is to be awarded attorneys' fees in all but special circumstances." The "make whole" remedial goal of the statutes, as well as the burden of enforcement that the statutes place on private parties make an award of a "reasonable" attorneys' fee necessary. Rarely present are "special circumstances" that would warrant a complete denial. As attorneys' fee allowances are designed to allow plaintiffs to retain competent counsel, they cannot be awarded to a plaintiff who represents himself. *Kay v. Ehrler,* 499 U.S. 432 (1991).

An award of attorneys' fees to a successful *defendant* may be made only upon proof by defendant that "plaintiff's action was frivolous, unreasonable, or without foundation." To hold otherwise would unduly discourage legitimate enforcement efforts. Rarely have defendants been successful in establishing that a plaintiff acted so "frivolously" that a fees award against the plaintiff is warranted. That the EEOC did not find "reasonable cause" or that plaintiff's law suit was dismissed on summary judgment does not establish that plaintiff's claim was unreasonable or frivolous. *Walker v. NationsBank of Fla.,* 53 F.3d 1548 (11th Cir. 1995). In the event that a complaint has a frivolous claim that is combined with non-frivolous claims, defendant may recover its attorneys' fees only for the portion of the fees expended defending the frivolous claim. *Fox v. Vice,* ___ U.S. ___, 131 S.Ct. 2205 (2011).

Fee awards run against the named parties, not against the opposing attorney. However, courts have inherent power to assess fees or allocate litigation costs against attorneys who act vexatiously. *Roadway Exp. Inc., v. Piper,* 447 U.S. 752 (1980).

B. PREVAILING PLAINTIFF

The statutes do not define when a party is "prevailing." The general principle: "[P]laintiffs may be considered 'prevailing parties' for attorneys fees purposes if they succeed on any significant issue in litigation which advances some of the benefit the parties sought in bringing the suit." *Texas State Teachers Ass'n v. Garland Ind. School Dist.,* 489 U.S. 782 (1989). A settlement followed by a consent decree which granted plaintiff some of the relief sought in the complaint can give plaintiff "prevailing" status even if the final decree resulted in dismissing the complaint. *Farrar v. Hobby,* 506 U.S. 103 (1982). However, the fact that the law suit may have stimulated a change in the policy being challenged and resulted in plaintiff withdrawing the complaint does not make plaintiff a "prevailing party." *Buckhannon Bd. & Care Home, Inc. v. West Va. Dept. of Health & Human Res.,* 532 U.S. 598 (2001).

Plaintiff who establishes defendant's illegal motivation is a "prevailing party" entitled to attorneys' fees even if defendant demonstrates that it would have made the same decision on legitimate grounds and thus need not hire the plaintiff or pay plaintiff back wages and damages. 42 U.S.C. 2000e–4(g)(2)(B). *Desert Palace, Inc. v. Costa,* 539 U.S. 90 (2003).

Recovery of nominal damages may make plaintiff a "prevailing party," but failure to secure any other meaningful relief or remedy means that "the only reasonable fee is usually no fee at all." *Farrar v. Hobby, supra.*

Plaintiff's victory must not be fleeting. That is, a plaintiff who prevails on procedural motions or secures preliminary injunctive relief, but ultimately loses on the merits, is not entitled to recover the fees attributable to these preliminary successes. *Sole v. Wyner,* 551 U.S. 74 (2007).

C. CALCULATING A "REASONABLE" FEE

While the statutes allow recovery of fees that are "reasonable" they provide no indicia of "reasonableness." The Court has dictated that a strong presumption of "reasonableness" comes from the calculation of a "lodestar." The "lodestar" first identifies the prevailing hourly rate charged by attorneys practicing in the community who have the experience and background similar to that of the prevailing party's attorney. That reasonable rate is not set by nor limited to the rate charged the plaintiff by her attorneys (who may have been working pro bono or on a contingent fee arrangement that provided for a payment of any eventual monetary recovery). Nor is the reasonable rate influenced by the fact that plaintiff's attorney worked for a legal aid society, civil rights organization, or an academic institution whose salaries from the organization may not reflect "prevailing rates," and who may have charged the plaintiff little if anything for their services. *Blum v. Stenson,* 465 U.S. 886 (1984).

Generally, the prevailing rate is that of lawyers in the community where plaintiff lives or where the litigation takes place, not the rate from the community where the attorney actually practices. Only if the plaintiff cannot find competent local counsel may the prevailing rates for his attorneys outside of the community be used in the calculation. *Mathur v. Bd. of Trustees of Southern Ill. Univ.,* 317 F.3d 788 (7th Cir. 2003) (Chicago attorney conducted southern Illinois trial. Chicago prevailing rate was "reasonable").

The second component of the "lodestar" calculation is the number of hours the attorneys reasonably committed to the successful claims. Plaintiff cannot include time spent on issues where he/she did not prevail unless plaintiff can show that unsuccessful and successful claims shared a "common core of facts" or were "based on related legal theories" making the time expended on each inseparable. *Hensley v. Eckerhart,* 461 U.S. 424 (1983). The time for which fees must be awarded includes pre-trial procedures, such as discovery, pursuing state and federal administrative exhaustion requirements, settlement negotiations, and post-trial proceedings through final appeals and post-appeal hearings on attorneys' fees and compliance. *Pennsylvania v.*

Delaware Valley Citizens' Council for Clean Air, 478 U.S. 546 (1986).

The final "lodestar" is the prevailing hourly rate of the attorneys multiplied by the reasonable number of hours spent on the successful claims. Plaintiff carries the burden of establishing the reasonableness of this lodestar calculation which must be supported by precise documentation. The trial court has discretion to deny hours expended or determine that the number of attorneys involved was excessive in light of the complexity of the issues. The goal is to insure compensation adequate for plaintiff to secure competent representation, not to enrich their attorneys.

The lodestar amount carries a strong presumption of its reasonableness, and may be adjusted only for extraordinary reasons. Upward enhancement may not be based on the fact that the attorney had agreed to a contingent fee arrangement where the attorney would be paid nothing if plaintiff did not prevail. *Burlington v. Dogue,* 505 U.S. 557 (1992). Nor is the lodestar amount to be enhanced based only on the "superior performance" of plaintiff's attorney in that ability is often subsumed in the lodestar calculation. *Perdue v. Kenny A.,* 559 U.S. 542 (2010). An enhancement may be warranted where plaintiff can identify a factor that the lodestar does not adequately take into account, and prove with specificity that an enhanced fee is justified, such as where the performance of the attorney was not only extraordinary, but was well beyond that expected from those of similar experience or background on which a lodestar would be based, and that this extraordinary performance expedited the proceedings. Long delay in securing a final judgment may warrant an upward adjustment that reflects the attorney's loss of use of the funds ultimately found due. *Missouri v. Jenkins,* 419 U.S. 274 (1989).

Downward adjustments are more common and allowed where the performance of the attorney was so unusually poor or so inefficient that it inflicted on the court and the defendant unreasonable delay and unnecessary expenses, such as where plaintiff's attorney made vexatious motions, repeated demands for continuances or made excessive discovery requests. Pursuing a strategy that required a second trial or rejecting settlement offers that far exceeded the amount eventually recovered may result in a deduction from the lodestar amount. *Shott v. Rush–Presbyterian–St. Luke's Med. Ctr.,* 338 F.3d 736 (7th Cir. 2003).

D. "COSTS"

A successful plaintiff also may recover court costs such as filing fees, jury fees, and deposition costs. Plaintiff may recover expenses directly attributable to the litigation: fees of experts, such as statisticians, physicians, accountants, testing psychologists, stenographers, notary fees, etc. Recoverable direct costs and litigation expenses are distinct from indirect, non-recoverable "overhead," for which clients are not normally billed separately, such as ordinary internal photocopying, telephone communication expenses, capital investments in computers, fax machines, salaries of clerical and administrative staff, office rent, utilities, etc. Payments to paralegal assistants for time directly attributable to the litigation are expenses that can be recovered. *Missouri v. Jenkins,* 491 U.S. 274 (1989).

CHAPTER 29

ENFORCEMENT PROCEDURES IN THE PUBLIC FORUM: NON–FEDERAL DEFENDANTS

29.01: INTRODUCTION

Ultimately, rights and remedies under the statutes are enforced through lawsuits filed by the individual or government enforcement agencies (primarily EEOC). The three core statutes require victims to navigate and exhaust complex pre-suit administrative procedures with confusing and relatively short time limitations. Title VII and ADA processes are identical. The ADEA is similar, but with significant differences. Distinct procedures apply to federal government employees. *Infra,* Chapter 30.

Federal district courts, as well as state courts of general jurisdiction, have subject matter jurisdiction to hear and resolve the federal statutory claims. *Yellow Freight System, Inc. v. Donnelly,* 494 U.S. 820 (1990). Federal courts may entertain state law claims pursuant to the "pendant jurisdiction" established by the federal claim. While state courts of general jurisdiction also have subject matter jurisdiction over federal claims, federal administrative requirements must be exhausted before any court may entertain the federal law claims.

The Equal Pay Act and Reconstruction Era Civil Rights Acts (42 U.S.C. 1981 and 1983) impose *no* administrative prerequisites to filing a law suit. The EPA has a simple two year statute of limitation for recovering back wages (3 years if plaintiff can prove the violation to be "willful"). Race discrimination claims under 42 U.S.C. 1981 involving *compensation* and *intangible* job benefits such as harassment have a four year statute of limitation. 28 U.S.C. 1658(a). *Fonteneaux v. Shell Oil,* 289 Fed.Appx. 695 (5th Cir. 2008). Claims involving *hiring or discharge* under the Reconstruction Era Civil Rights Acts are subject to no explicit federal statute of limitations, but federal courts impose state law limitations applicable to civil rights actions.

29.02: BEGINNING THE PROCESS: THE "CHARGE"

Enforcement of the core statutes is begun by the victim filing an administrative charge. This is a mandatory obligation, "impervious to judicial discretion." *National R.R. Passenger Corp. v. Morgan,* 536 U.S. 101 (2002). The statutes require the charge to be in writing, under oath, and contain such information as the EEOC requires. 42 U.S.C. 2000e–5(b). By regulation the EEOC requires that a charge: (1) name the person charging discrimination and the entity allegedly discriminating; (2) outline the nature of the action taken against the charging party (*e.g.,* hiring, firing, compensation, harassment); (3) state the basis of the alleged discrimination (*e.g.,* race, sex, national origin, religion, age, disability), and (4) set the time and place of the alleged discrimination.

For convenience the EEOC provides a simple form. However, no specific format is demanded. Any *written* communication, such as a letter, containing the critical information is sufficient so long as the document can be construed as a request for agency action. *Federal Express v. Holowecki,* 552 U.S. 389 (2008). A completed EEOC "intake questionnaire" can be a "charge." *Clark v. Coats & Clark, Inc.,* 865 F.2d 1236 (11th Cir. 1989). A telephone complaint or a personal appearance at the EEOC office with only an oral allegation does not suffice.

EEOC regulations allow amendments to remedy *technical* defects in the charge. In *Edelman v. Lynchburg College,* 535 U.S. 106 (2002), plaintiff faxed a timely letter to the EEOC that contained the critical information. However, the letter was not "under oath" as required by the statute. The EEOC responded by asking plaintiff to complete a form charge that included the required oath. Plaintiff returned the charge with proper oath but *after* the statutory time limit for filing charges. The Court held that the unverified faxed letter was a "charge," and the formal verified charge was a technical "amendment" that related back in time to the original filing.

Amendments that raise new legal theories, such as adding a count of disability discrimination to a charge alleging only age discrimination, are not "technical amendments," and thus do not relate back to the time of the initial filing. *Manning v.*

Chevron Chemical Co., LLC., 332 F.3d 874 (5th Cir. 2003).

It is important to frame charges with care, not only because major amendments made after the time limits on filing will be untimely, but because any judicial complaint must be based on the allegations in the charge, or those so closely related thereto that they could be expected to grow out of an EEOC investigation of the claims in the charge. *Deravin v. Kerik,* 335 F.3d 195 (2d Cir. 2003). *Infra,* 29.11.

29.03: "FILING" THE CHARGE: EXHAUSTION OF STATE PROCEDURES

Ultimately charges must be filed with the appropriate district office of the EEOC. The statutes prescribe a complex two-step process that requires "exhaustion" of any existing state processes. Title VII and the ADA envision *sequential* filings. A charge must <u>*first*</u> *be filed with any state agency* enforcing the state's fair employment law. A charge first *deposited* with the EEOC will not be considered *"filed"* with the EEOC until *after* a charge has been filed with the state agency and state procedures have been "exhausted." *Mohasco Corp. v. Silver,* 447 U.S. 807 (1980).

Agreements between the EEOC and state enforcement agencies, however, provide that charges originally *deposited* with the EEOC that have not been first filed by the claimant with the state agency, will be referred by the EEOC to the appropriate state agency. This referral by the EEOC will satisfy the statutory requirement that a charge be first filed with a state agency. *Love v. Pullman Co.,* 404 U.S. 522 (1972).

Required exhaustion of state processes occurs when the charge is resolved by the state agency, the state agency waives further jurisdiction, or 60 days have lapsed after the charge was filed in the state agency. A charge originally deposited with the EEOC and referred to a state enforcement agency, will be reactivated by the EEOC automatically upon the lapse of 60 days following the referral or by the state agency dismissing the charge or waiving further jurisdiction over the charge. The charge is deemed "filed" with the EEOC on the date of this reactivation without the necessity of the charging party taking a formal step to re-file the charge with the EEOC. *EEOC v. Commercial Office Products Co.,* 486 U.S. 107 (1988). States are not required to either resolve the dispute or retain jurisdiction for the full 60 days allowed by the federal statute, but at any time may waive further jurisdiction, and by this waiver permit the "filing" of an EEOC charge. *Id.*

The ADEA also requires the filing of both state and federal charges. However, unlike Title VII and the ADA, the ADEA does not require a sequential filing. A charge may be filed with the state agency either before, simultaneously with, or even after the EEOC charge is filed. All that is required is that no judicial law suit may be filed until 60 days after the filing of the state and federal charges. *Oscar Mayer & Co. v. Evans,* 441 U.S. 750 (1979).

29.04: TIME IN WHICH THE CHARGE MUST BE FILED

The three core statutes have the same time limitations on filing charges. In those few jurisdictions that have no state EEO enforcement agencies, a charge must be filed with the EEOC within 180 days of the discriminatory act.

In the vast majority of states—those with EEO enforcement agencies—a charge must be "filed" with the EEOC within 300 days of the discriminatory act, or within 30 days from the date the state agency terminates its proceedings, whichever is *earlier*.

The Title VII and ADA requirement that the charge is "filed" with the EEOC only *after* the exhaustion of state processes (*supra,* **29.03**) produces a *de facto* time limit of 240 days for *depositing* a charge with the EEOC. In *Mohasco Corp. v. Silver,* 447 U.S. 807 (1980), a charge was *deposited* first with the EEOC 291 days after the discriminatory act. The EEOC promptly referred the charge to a state agency. The state agency retained jurisdiction over the charge for the full 60 days allowed by Title VII. Thereupon, the EEOC reactivated the charge originally deposited with it—351 days following the discriminatory act. As the charge was not *"filed"* with the EEOC until the date on which the EEOC reactivated the previously deposited charge, the charge had not been "filed" within the statutory time limit of 300 days. Even though first deposited with the EEOC within 300 days, the charge was "filed" 51 days late.

If a charge is deposited with the EEOC *after* 240 days, but within 300 days, often with urging from the EEOC, the state agency may immediately waive its jurisdiction, allowing the EEOC to reactivate the charge within 300 days. This would produce a timely filing of the charge. *EEOC v. Commercial Office Products Co.,* 486 U.S. 107 (1988). However, there is no assurance that a waiver will be sought or that the state agency will be willing to comply.

Thus, the only way to *insure* a timely filing is to: (1) file a charge with the state agency within 240 days of the discriminatory act, await 60 days for the state to act and thereafter immediately "file" an EEOC charge, or (2) deposit a charge with the EEOC *before* 240 days have lapsed from the discriminatory act and assume that the EEOC will promptly refer the charge to the state agency and will promptly reactivate the charge upon the lapse of 60 days.

Under the ADEA, when the state has an age discrimination enforcement agency the Act simply requires the filing of a charge with the EEOC within 300 days of the discriminatory act and the filing of a state agency charge either before, after, or simultaneously with the EEOC charge. (Filing with the EEOC must come within 180 days of the discrimination in states with no age discrimination enforcement agency.) The ADEA imposes a 60 day waiting period after a timely EEOC charge and 60 days after the filing of a state charge. After those 60 day waiting periods, a suit may be filed. The mandatory 60–day waiting period to allow state and federal agency action can run concurrently.

29.05: THE DISCRIMINATORY ACT

All the statutes measure the time in which the victim must trigger enforcement mechanisms from the date of the discriminatory act. Identifying the discriminatory act is critical but often difficult.

A. HIRING AND PROMOTION

The time to file a charge runs from the point the applicant has unequivocal notice of the job denial coupled with an awareness of surrounding facts that disclose possible illegality, such as knowledge that a person of a different class has been selected to fill the vacancy for which plaintiff applied. *Colgan v. Fischer,* 935 F.2d 1407 (3d Cir. 1991).

B. DISCHARGE AND DISCIPLINARY ACTIONS

The time to file a charge for dismissal and disciplinary action is measured from the date the employee is informed of the employer's decision and is aware of facts that would put a reasonable person on notice of possible illegality. The critical date is *not* necessarily the employee's last day of work or the date that the discipline was actually imposed. The critical date is the one on which the employee learns of the employer's *decision. Delaware State College v. Ricks,* 449 U.S. 250 (1980), illustrates. An untenured college faculty member was notified that his application for tenure would be denied, and according to college policies, he would be terminated at the end of the next following academic year. Upon receiving the notice of denial, the faculty member filed an internal grievance which, if successful, would have resulted in the reversal of the decision and the grant of the requested tenure. The grievance was unsuccessful, and the grievant was so notified. Plaintiff completed the school year and soon thereafter filed a charge. The Court held that the discriminatory act occurred upon plaintiff receiving notice of the initial decision that he would not be retained. Time for filing a charge of discrimination ran from the employer's communication of the *decision* to terminate plaintiff's employment. Moreover, the pending internal grievance appeal of the initial decision did not toll the running of the time until the grievance was resolved against plaintiff.

Knowledge of information that would put a reasonable person on notice of illegal discrimination also is critical. For example, when plaintiff was discharged he was told that his position had been eliminated for economic reasons. Plaintiff later learned that the position had not been eliminated, and defendant was seeking applicants to fill the position previously held by plaintiff. Later still plaintiff learned that the position had been filled by someone substantially younger than himself. *Jones v. Dillard's Inc.,* 331 F.3d 1259 (11th Cir. 2003), held that the time for filing an EEOC charge should be measured, not from the date of discharge, but from the date plaintiff learned that the position he once held had been filled by a younger person. Only at this point did plaintiff have a reasonable basis for believing that he had been a victim of age discrimination.

C. HARASSMENT

Creating a hostile working environment, or harassment, unlike a discharge, often does not involve a single discrete act or decision, but becomes actionable only after two or more instances of abusive behavior which may be separated by weeks or months. In such cases each discrete act of harassment triggers a new time for filing a charge, and courts may evaluate events falling outside the statutory period to determine whether illegal harassment has occurred. *National R.R. Passenger Corp. v. Morgan,* 536 U.S. 101 (2002).

D. COMPENSATION

Under the EPA, each pay period in which an employee is underpaid constitutes a distinct violation for which the underpaid employee is entitled to recover the underpayment as back wages. Suit for recovery of back wages due can be brought within two years after each underpayment, three years if the violation is willful.

Title VII also provides that back pay may be recovered for two years from the filing of a charge. *Bazemore v. Friday,* 478 U.S. 385 (1986), held that even though the lower pay of black employees was based on legal, pre-Act racial classifications, each post-Act pay check reflected discrimination because of race. Each pay check reflecting the lower pay of the black workers triggered anew the charge-filing period. Back pay thus could be recovered for up to two years prior to the filing of a charge. However, *Ledbetter v. Goodyear Tire & Rubber Co.,* 550 U.S.

618 (2007), distinguished *Bazemore* and held that when an employee's salary was set by a performance evaluation, the discriminatory act was the evaluation, not the receipt of the pay check based thereon. Thus, the time to file a charge was measured from the date of the discriminatory *evaluation*.

Congress immediately amended the core statutes to overturn *Ledbetter*. The Ledbetter Fair Pay Act provides that a discriminatory practice occurs "when a discriminatory compensation decision or other practice is adopted, when an individual becomes subject to a discriminatory compensation decision * * * or when an individual is affected by application of a discriminatory decision or other practice including *each time wages, benefits, or other compensation is paid.* * * *" P.L. No. 111–2. The Act applies only to pay claims pending after May 27, 2007.

The Ledbetter Fair Pay Act has been held inapplicable to charges of a discriminatory failure to promote, even though the denial of promotion later resulted in lower future salary. The "discrete discriminatory act" of the promotion denial, not the consequential lower salary, triggers the obligation to file the charge. *Noel v. The Boeing Co.,* 622 F.3d 266 (3d Cir. 2010).

E. DISPARATE IMPACT

Lewis v. City of Chicago, 560 U.S. 205, (2010), held that the reasoning of *Ledbetter v. Goodyear Tire & Rubber Co., supra,* was inapplicable to cases in which alleged liability was based on the impact of a system, such as a test. When the act is discriminatorily motivated "plaintiff must demonstrate deliberate discrimination within the limitations period. But for claims that do not require discriminatory intent, no such demonstration is needed."

Lewis v. City of Chicago, supra, reaffirmed, but distinguished, *United Air Lines, Inc. v. Evans,* 431 U.S. 553 (1977), where a female plaintiff previously had been discharged based on a sexually discriminatory "no marriage rule." At the time of her discharge, she filed no challenge. Plaintiff was reinstated some years later, but with her seniority and salary calculated as though she were newly hired. When economic conditions resulted in her being laid off because of her low seniority, the Court held that plaintiff had no actionable claim notwithstanding that her lack of seniority could be traced to the long past discriminatory discharge. Plaintiff's current furlough was caused by her low seniority status which was not a discriminatory act. Her challenge to the furlough was thus premised upon the *illegal motivation* for the original dismissal for which the time had long passed for filing a charge.

By contrast, *Lewis* involved an objective test taken a year earlier, which test was used to rank the applicants. Based on plaintiffs' performance on the test, plaintiffs were denied promotions in favor of white applicants with higher scores. Plaintiffs might have challenged the results of the test itself before the impact was felt. However, denial of the promotion based on a device having an adverse impact was itself a discrete act that permitted a challenge to the test measured from the date the promotion was denied.

Similar to *United Air Lines v. Evans, supra, AT & T Corp. v. Hulteen,* 556 U.S. 701 (2009), involved a past failure of the employer to give the same pension accrual rights to those on pregnancy leave as it did for other forms of leave, which would be a clear violation of the Pregnancy Discrimination Act of 1978 (PDA). The employer refused to make requested adjustments to its pension plan to give equal credit for pregnancy leave prior to the effective date of the PDA. Using reasoning similar to that in *Ledbetter v. Goodyear Tire & Rubber Co., supra,* the Court held that the lower pensions received by women was a consequence of legal discrimination and thus was not a new and distinct act of discrimination from which to measure the time to file a challenge. To hold otherwise, the Court reasoned, would give the PDA retroactive effect. The Ledbetter Fair Pay Act had no application because plaintiffs were not affected by the application of a system that was *illegally* discriminatory.

F. SENIORITY SYSTEMS

By statute, challenges to the bona fides of seniority systems may be timed from "when the seniority system is adopted, when an individual becomes subject to the seniority system, or when a person aggrieved is injured by the application of the seniority system." 42 U.S.C. 2000e–5(e)(2). However, the fact that the application of an otherwise bona fide seniority system tends to perpetuate past discriminatorily motivated discrimination does not prohibit the use of that system. Nor is a layoff resulting from the application of an otherwise bona fide system a discrete discriminatory act that permits a charge to now be filed that would permit a challenge to long-past discriminatory treatment. *United Air Lines, Inc. v. Evans,* 431 U.S. 553 (1977). *Supra,* Chapter 19.

29.06: TIME EXTENSIONS: WAIVER, ESTOPPEL, AND TOLLING

Time limits are *not* jurisdictional in that for equitable reasons time for filing may be extended by the court on the basis of waiver, estoppel, or tolling. *Zipes v. Trans World Airlines, Inc.* 455 U.S. 385 (1982).

Waiver occurs if the defendant appears to relinquish the right to demand a timely filing, such as where the employer tells the employee that it will not assert the time limits during internal grievance processing or settlement discussions.

Estoppel is similar to waiver in that it involves conduct or representations on which the individual reasonably relies, as where defendant misleads the charging party by providing inaccurate legal advice or is disingenuous as to relevant facts. *Coke v. General Adj. Bureau, Inc.,* 640 F.2d 584 (5th Cir. 1981).

Tolling takes place when particular circumstances make it unfair or inequitable to demand strict compliance with the letter of the law and there is no counterbalancing prejudice on the defendant for allowing the extension. Tolling typically occurs during a period when the aggrieved individual is incapacitated through illness or injury or relies on erroneous advice from the courts or enforcement agencies regarding charge-filing obligations. *Canales v. Sullivan,* 936 F.2d 755 (2d Cir. 1991). Tolling is not allowed for the "garden variety of excusable neglect" such as failure of the victim to make a reasonable inquiry into the facts, ignorance of his legal rights, or failure to secure counsel. *Irwin v. Veterans Admin.,* 498 U.S. 89 (1990).

Pursuing internal or collective bargaining grievances, including arbitration, does not toll the statutory filing period. Even filing a lawsuit alleging illegal discrimination under a different statute, such as 42 U.S.C. 1981 or the Equal Pay Act, does not toll the time required to file a Title VII charge. *IUEW v. Robbins & Meyers, Inc.,* 429 U.S. 229 (1976).

A class action suit filed under Rule 23, Fed.R.Civ.Proc., can proceed if any member of the putative class has filed a timely charge. *Infra,* 29.13. There is no requirement that each class member file a charge. However, if the class action petition is denied or decertified by the court, which would then require each member of the putative class to proceed individually, the time limits for filing the individual charges will be tolled during the period that the class action claim was pending. *Crown Cork & Seal Co. v. Parker,* 462 U.S. 345 (1983).

29.07: CHARGE PROCESSING

Upon the charge being filed, the EEOC has exclusive jurisdiction over charges under Title VII and the ADA for 180 days. Under the ADEA, the EEOC has 60 days of jurisdiction. The statutes direct the EEOC to notify the charged party of the pending charge and thereafter to investigate the allegations to determine if there is "reasonable cause" to believe the statute has been violated. If "reasonable cause" is found, the EEOC is directed to attempt a resolution by "compromise, conciliation, and persuasion." The EEOC has exclusive jurisdiction during this period to file a judicial action against the charged party. Where the charged party is a state or local government, the EEOC refers the charge to the Attorney General.

29.08: PRIVATE ENFORCEMENT: AWAITING THE "RIGHT TO SUE"

If the EEOC does not file suit by the end of its period of exclusive jurisdiction (180 days under Title VII and the ADA; 60 days under the ADEA), the charging party may file a private judicial action against the charged party. Under Title VII and the ADA, the charging party may initiate litigation against the charged party only *after* the charging party receives from the EEOC a "notice of right to sue." On its own initiative the EEOC *may* terminate its jurisdiction and at any time issue a "notice of right to sue." When demanded by the charging party after 180 days from the filing of the charge, the EEOC *must* issue a "notice of right to sue."

Thus, under Title VII and the ADA, the charging party has an option. The charging party may allow the EEOC to retain jurisdiction over the charge until such time as the EEOC terminates its proceedings and issues on its own initiative a "notice of right to sue." Or, the charging party may demand the "notice of right to sue," which, after the lapse of 180 days, the EEOC must promptly issue. Notice of right to sue is not expressly required for suits under the ADEA.

29.09: FILING THE SUIT: TIMES AND LIMITATIONS

A. GENERALLY

The charging party must file a complaint in a court of general jurisdiction (state or federal) within 90 days of the receipt of the "notice of right to sue." The date of the discriminatory act—critical in determining the time in which to file a charge—is not material in setting the time to file a judicial complaint. Receipt of the "notice of right to sue" is presumed to occur within a reasonable time following the EEOC's mailing the notice to the charging party's last known address.

A complaint placed in the mail 90 days from the receipt of the right to sue notice that was not received by the court until five days thereafter has not been *filed* within the required 90 days. *See, Hallgren v. United States Dep't of Energy,* 331 F.3d 588 (8th Cir. 2003).

Absent a demand from the charging party, the EEOC is not required to issue a right to sue notice within any particular period of time. However, excessive delay by the charging party in requesting a right to sue notice that results in prejudice to the defendant may result in the judicial complaint being dismissed based on the doctrine of laches (inequitable delay) or be a basis for the trial court to limit the amount of a back pay award. *National R.R. Passenger Corp. v. Morgan,* 536 U.S. 101 (2002).[1]

Failure of the EEOC in its statutory obligations to notify the charged party or to undertake "compromise, conciliation, and persuasion" does not limit or preclude the *charging party's* right to sue. *Russell v. American Tobacco Co.,* 528 F.2d 357 (4th Cir. 1975).

B. THE JUDICIAL COMPLAINT

A complaint, at a minimum, must meet the "notice pleading" requirement of Rule 8(a)(2), Fed.R.Civ.Proc. ("a short plain statement of the claim showing that the pleader is entitled to relief"). While *Swierkiewicz v. Sorema, N.A.,* 534 U.S. 506 (2002), struck down a local court rule requiring extensive fact pleading in civil rights cases, *Ashcroft*

---

[1] The time to file an age discrimination suit under the ADEA is far from clear. The 1991 Civil Rights Act provided that suits under the ADEA, similar to Title VII and the ADA, must be filed within 90 days from the receipt of the "notice of right to sue." However, there is no statutory demand that a "notice of right to sue" is necessary under the ADEA or that the EEOC has clear authority to issue such notices. Prior to 1991 courts utilized a two year statute of limitation measured from the point of the discriminatory act.

v. Iqbal, 556 U.S. 661 (2009), required more than a "the defendant-unlawfully-harmed me accusation," and more than "labels and conclusions or a formulaic recitation of the elements of a cause of action." A complaint will not suffice if it "tenders naked assertions devoid of further factual enhancement." *See, Holmes v. Gates,* 403 Fed.Appx. 670 (3d Cir. 2010).

While the federal rules direct liberal amendments to defective complaints, a document that does not satisfy Rule 8 is not a "complaint," and an amended complaint that satisfies Rule 8 filed after the lapse of 90 days from the receipt of the right to sue notice may be untimely. *Baldwin County Welcome Ctr. v. Brown,* 466 U.S. 147 (1984).

C. APPOINTMENT OF COUNSEL

Courts are authorized to appoint counsel prior to a suit being filed to assist the charging party and, upon a showing of poverty, waive filing costs and fees. 42 U.S.C. 2000e–5(f)(1). Appointment of counsel and waiver of filing fees requires a formal petition from the charging party. In evaluating the petition the court will consider the financial resources of the petitioner, the potential merits of the claim, and documented but unsuccessful attempts to secure legal representation. A petition for fee waiver or appointment of counsel will not be considered a complaint unless the supporting documents meet the Rule 8 requirements. However, time for filing a complaint will be tolled pending a trial court's resolution of the petition for appointment of counsel or waiver of filing fees. *Baldwin County Welcome Ctr. v. Brown, supra.*

D. EXTENSIONS

The 90–day period in which to file a judicial action is not a jurisdictional command. Courts have the power to toll or extend the filing period for equitable reasons, such as the incapacity of the plaintiff, waiver, or estoppel. *Supra,* 29.06. Time for filing a complaint is not extended by the "garden variety of excusable neglect," including negligence of plaintiff's attorney. Thus, where the charging party's attorney was absent from his office when the notice of right to sue was delivered to the office, or where the charging party or his attorney failed to keep the EEOC informed of correct mailing addresses, resulting in delay in delivery of the notice, are not grounds for a time extension. *Irwin v. Veterans Administration,* 498 U.S. 89 (1990).

29.10: PUBLIC SUITS

A. GENERALLY

Upon a timely charge being filed, the EEOC may sue the charged party in its own name. The EEOC may not sue until it has satisfied the statutory requirements of notifying the charged party and attempting conciliation and settlement of the charge. Conciliation efforts must be more than pro forma demands for full compliance, setting an arbitrary "take it or leave it" deadline that allows for no interactive discussion and possible compromise. *EEOC v. Aspludh Tree Expert Co.,* 340

F.3d 1256 (11th Cir. 2003). Once a private party files suit, the EEOC is limited to intervention in the private action. Once the EEOC sues in its own name, the charging party is precluded from separately suing but may intervene in the EEOC suit.

There are no expressed time limitations on the EEOC filing suit. It is not implicitly limited by the 180–day period during which it has exclusive jurisdiction, the 90–day filing period imposed on private suits, or the combination of these time periods. Moreover, as a federal agency, the EEOC is not constrained by any state statutes of limitations. *Occidental Life Ins. Co. of Cal. v. EEOC,* 432 U.S. 355 (1977). However, when inordinate, inexcusable delay prejudices the defendant, the defense of laches may be imposed to bar the EEOC suit. *EEOC v. Great Atlantic & Pacific Tea Co.,* 735 F.2d 69 (3d Cir. 1984). A seven year delay between receipt of the EEOC charge and the EEOC filing suit allowed defendant to assert the defense. *EEOC v. Propak Logistics, Inc.,* (W.D. N.C. 2012), 96 EDP 44,501.

B. "PATTERN OR PRACTICE"

The EEOC (or Attorney General where defendant is a state or local government) may challenge a "pattern or practice" of Title VII violations. 42 U.S.C. 2000e–6. While a charge needs to be filed before the agency may sue alleging a "pattern or practice," it is not necessary for all persons within the scope of the suit to have filed individual charges. The agency may proceed to represent this group without securing class certification pursuant to Rule

23, Fed.R.Civ.Proc. The outcome of the litigation will bind all individuals within the general class for which the action was filed. *General Tel. Co. of the Northwest v. EEOC,* 446 U.S. 318 (1980).

29.11: SCOPE OF THE COMPLAINT: RELATIONSHIP TO THE CHARGE

The parameters of the complaint, public or private, and thus the litigation, are set by the original charge. *Supra,* 29.02. Only parties named in the charge may be named defendants, and only the precise form of discrimination alleged in the charge may be litigated, unless the claims raised in the litigation are so closely related to those in the charge that the new or expanded claims would reasonably flow from an EEOC investigation. For example, a charge asserting age discrimination would not allow a complaint that the plaintiff was also a victim of sex discrimination. *Ajayi v. Aramark Business Services Inc.,* 336 F.3d 520 (7th Cir. 2003). The discrimination involved two distinct statutes, and an EEOC investigation would be unlikely to explore possible sex discrimination. A charge that asserts only "age" discrimination may not allow pleading that a neutral factor had an unlawful adverse *impact* on plaintiff's age group. The nature of the discrimination—impact—would not necessarily flow from an investigation into a general allegation of "discrimination." *Allen v. Highlands Hospital Corp.,* 545 F.3d 387 (6th Cir. 2008). By contrast, a non-white charging "national origin" discrimination and asserting favoritism shown "Irish–Americans" would allow a complaint of "race" discrimination because an EEOC investigation into this charge could be expected to explore the possibility that race was the basis of favoring Irish–Americans. *Deravin v. Kerik*, 335 F.3d 195 (2d Cir. 2003).

29.12: JUDICIAL PROCEEDING: *DE NOVO* JURY TRIAL

Whether litigated in state or federal courts, all claims are tried *de novo*. Findings by administrative agencies, such as an EEOC "reasonable cause" determination, in no way restrict complete re-adjudication of plaintiff's claims. *McDonnell Douglas Corp. v. Green*, 411 U.S. 792 (1973). Even if the state administrative proceedings provided a full, fair, and complete adversarial hearing, conclusions of state agencies made pursuant to charges required by the federal statutes are not preclusive in subsequent federal litigation. *Astoria Fed. Sav. & Loan Ass'n v. Solimino*, 501 U.S. 104 (1991). However, if a state administrative determination was reviewed and confirmed by the state *courts*, and the judicially confirmed findings preclude further litigation in the state courts, federal courts must give similar preclusive effect to the findings. *Kremer v. Chemical Const. Corp.*, 456 U.S. 461 (1982).

Whether administrative findings, not confirmed by a court, will even be admitted into evidence, depends on the nature of the finding and the degree of party participation. If the trial court determines that an agency finding or EEOC determination would unduly prejudice the jury in light of the finding's probative value, the administrative findings may be excluded. *Young v. James Green Mgt., Inc.,* 327 F.3d 616 (7th Cir. 2003).

There is a right to trial by jury on all factual claims for which compensatory or punitive damages may be collected. Plaintiff must make a timely demand for trial by jury, or the right will be waived.

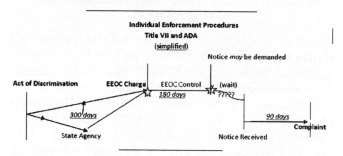

29.13: FUTURE LITIGATION: JUDICIAL PRECLUSION

Prior *judicial* determinations under different federal statutes may or may not have preclusive effect depending upon the application of complex rules of res adjudicata and collateral estoppel. Generally, prior adjudication will preclude subsequent litigation if the earlier *judicial* findings resolved or could have resolved the same factual or legal issues. For example, a plaintiff who files a claim of race motivated discrimination under 42 U.S.C. 1981, may not thereafter file a second race motivated discrimination claim under Title VII as the factual and legal issues are virtually identical under the two statutes. However, the assertion or finding of "disability" under the Social Security statute did not preclude disability claims under the ADA as the factual and legal basis for claims under the two statutes were different. *Cleveland v. Policy Mgt. Sys. Corp.,* 526 U.S. 795 (1999).

29.14: PRIVATE CLASS ACTIONS

A. GENERALLY

A class action is a procedural device that permits representatives to sue on behalf of numerous individuals similarly situated, where claims present a common core of legal and factual issues. All individuals that are within the "certified" class will be bound by any outcome unless they affirmatively elect to be excluded from the class. Rule 23, Fed.R.Civ.Proc. Title VII and the ADA allow true class actions. The ADEA and EPA do not, in that individuals must affirmatively consent to "opt into" the designated class.

Agreements that permit only individual claims, precluding persons from joining class-wide litigation, are not *per se* unconscionable. *AT & T Mobility, LLC v. Concepcion,* 563 U.S. ___, 131 S.Ct. 1740 (2011). Thus, an employer may be immunized from class action suits by securing agreements from its employees clearly stating that they will not join a class action suit.

A person or persons petitioning to create a class must demonstrate four prerequisites set by Rule 23(a). If the four prerequisites of Rule 23(a) are established, the petitioner must establish *one* of the three alternative routes to certification set forth in Rule 23(b).

B. THE FOUR PREREQUISITES OF RULE 23(A)

Rule 23(A) imposes four prerequisites: (1) "numerosity"—that the putative class is so large that joinder of individual claims is not practicable; (2) "commonality"—the questions of law or fact must be "common" to all members of the class; (3) "typicality"—the claims of the named parties seeking the class certification are typical of the claims of the unnamed class members; and (4) "adequacy of representation"—the named parties must demonstrate that they can fairly and adequately protect the interests of the class in that they are represented by competent counsel and that there are no significant conflicts of interests. *General Tel. Co. of Southwest v. Falcon,* 457 U.S. 147 (1982).

C. THE THREE ALTERNATIVES OF RULE 23(b)

If the prerequisites of Rule 23(a) are satisfied, Rule 23(b) provides alternative routes to class certification, *one* of which must be satisfied: (1) there is the possibility of inconsistent adjudications if individual suits were pursued, creating incompatible standards for defendant, and that class certification would not substantially impair the ability of non-class members to protect their individual interests, (2) defendant allegedly acted on grounds generally applicable to the class, making final injunctive relief appropriate, *or* (3) the questions of law or fact in common to class members predominate over questions affecting individual members.

D. WAL–MART STORES, INC. V. DUKES

Wal–Mart Stores, Inc. v. Dukes, 564 U.S. ___, 131 S.Ct. 2541 (2011), involved allegations of sex discrimination in pay and promotions in all Wal–Mart stores nationwide, a class that would exceed 1.5 million women. The lower court found that plaintiffs met all four threshold requirements of Rule 23(a) and the specific alternative of 23(b)(2) in that defendant had acted on grounds generally applicable to the women employees making final injunctive relief appropriate. The Court reversed, unanimously agreeing that 23(b)(2) was the inappropriate option, suggesting that 23(b)(3) may have been satisfied in that common questions appeared to predominate over individual claims. The majority, however, also held, perhaps gratuitously, that plaintiff had failed to satisfy the threshold requirement of 23(a)(2). Since salary and promotions were made individually by each store manager applying their own, largely subjective standards, there were no common questions of fact or law applicable to this multi-store class.

The decision may not directly limit class actions to impact challenges of specific selection procedures or expressed company-wide discriminatory policy such as the assertion of a BFOQ for a particular job. Even when "final" decisions are made by local managers, plaintiffs may be able to satisfy the 23(a)(2) "commonality" requirement if there is a specific, centrally directed policy that permits or encourages discriminatory outcomes or there is a level of company control, review, or direction over individual units that was not present at Wal–Mart. *McReynolds v. Merrill Lynch, Pierce, Fenner & Smith, Inc.,* 672 F.3d 482 (7th Cir. 2012).

The *Wal–Mart* ruling not only undermines many nation-wide class actions, it may significantly limit the use of class action suits in the same store or a small number of small enterprises under a common manager. While the treatment of same-store employees should satisfy the "commonality" requirement of 23(a)(2), the relatively few affected employees in a single store may fail to meet the "numerosity" requirement of 23(a)(1).

Once a class is properly certified the trial court has wide discretion to manage the process such as notice, participation of individuals claimants, severance of liability and remedy trials, etc. *Hoffman–LaRoche, Inc. v. Sperling,* 493 U.S. 165 (1989). All members of the certified class will be bound by the outcome and may not proceed individually.

CHAPTER 30

FEDERAL EMPLOYEE ENFORCEMENT

30.01: INTRODUCTION

Enforcement procedures available to federal executive department employees are dramatically different from those used in claims against non-federal employers. 29 C.F.R. Part 1614, and www.eeoc.gov. The essential difference is that the *employing agency* takes and investigates the initial complaint and ultimately may render a final decision that is subject to judicial challenge. The involvement of the EEOC is through its administrative judges who serve as neutral fact finders where the complainant requests a hearing prior to the employing agency's final decision on the complaint. Time limitations, too, are different from those applicable to non-federal complainants.

Disability discrimination claims are brought under the Rehabilitation Act of 1973, not the ADA, but use the procedures prescribed by Title VII. The ADEA makes administrative exhaustion optional. While the EPA sets forth no administrative prerequisites to exhaust, an EPA complainant may invoke Title VII procedures.

30.02: CONTACT, INVESTIGATION, AND COMPLAINT

The federal employee or applicant must first contact an Equal Employment Opportunity (EEO) Counselor *at the agency where the alleged discrimination occurred.* This contact must be made within 45 days of the discriminatory act. The EEO Counselor is directed to conduct an investigation and attempt informal resolution. If the allegation is not resolved, the complainant is notified of his/her right to file a formal complaint with the employing agency. The formal complaint must be filed within 15 days from the receipt of the notice. The employing agency may reject the complaint and issue a final order of dismissal. Alternatively, the agency may accept the complaint and conduct its own investigation.

30.03: EEOC HEARING AND AGENCY DETERMINATION

At the conclusion of the employing agency's investigation, the complainant may request either a hearing before an EEOC administrative judge or an immediate final decision by the employing agency. Upon a request for a hearing, an EEOC judge in the geographical location where the complaint arose processes the complaint, rules on motions, oversees discovery, and if material issues of fact exist conducts a formal adversarial hearing. The EEOC judge renders a decision and, if warranted, orders hiring or reinstatement, and awards back wages, compensatory damages, and attorneys' fees. The agency head (or designee) must implement or decline to implement the judge's decision.

30.04: APPEAL TO THE OFO

A complainant who receives an unfavorable decision from the employing agency may appeal to the EEOC's Office of Federal Operations (OFO). This appeal must be filed within 30 days of the receipt of the employing agency's final decision. If the agency rejects the judge's decision, the agency must, upon rejection, simultaneously file an appeal with the OFO.

The OFO will examine the administrative judge's legal conclusions *de novo* and the judge's factual findings under a "substantial evidence" standard. The OFO can affirm, modify, or overturn the employing agency's final decision. An OFO finding against the agency will include ordering the agency to provide appropriate remedies. *West v. Gibson,* 527 U.S. 212 (1999).

30.05: JUDICIAL COMPLAINT: ALTERNATIVE ROUTES

A. IMMEDIATE SUIT

Complainants who receive unfavorable final decisions from the employing agency may file a lawsuit in federal district court without seeking a review with the EEOC. The complaint against the agency head must be filed within 90 days from the receipt of the employing agency's final decision.

B. SUIT AFTER EEOC DECISION

If the complainant elected to appeal the employing agency's decision to the EEOC, and the OFO renders an unfavorable decision, the complainant must file suit within 90 days from the receipt of the EEOC's final decision on appeal.

As in the private sector, time limitations are not jurisdictional, and thus are subject to equitable tolling. Tolling, however, is not appropriate for a "garden variety of excusable neglect." *Irwin v. Veterans Admin.*, 498 U.S. 89 (1990). *See, supra,* 29.06.

C. SUIT AFTER 180 DAYS

While Title VII and the Rehabilitation Act require complainants to exhaust administrative procedures, "exhaustion" requires only that the complainant contact the employing agency's EEO Counselor (45 days from the discriminatory act), file a formal complaint with the employing agency (15 days from receipt of notice of right to file), and wait 180 days for the employing agency to complete its investigation. If the employing agency has not completed its investigation within 180 days, the complainant *may* file suit at any time thereafter. The law suit terminates the administrative process.

30.06: THE LITIGATION

The agency head, not the employing agency, is the proper defendant, and must be named in the complaint. The complaint must meet the "notice pleading" requirements of Rule 8, Fed.R.Civ.Proc.

Notwithstanding the often extensive record and findings compiled during the administrative process, the federal district judge adjudicates plaintiff's claim *de novo. Chandler v. Roudebush,* 425 U.S. 840 (1976). Suits under Title VII and the Rehabilitation allow trial by jury.

30.07: AGE DISCRIMINATION: SPECIAL PROCEDURES

Under the ADEA, all the complainant is *required* to do is notify the EEOC of an intent to sue the employing agency within 180 days of the discriminatory act, and wait 30 days. After 30 days have passed and the allegation has not been resolved, the complainant may file the suit. There is no expressed time limit within which suit must be filed. *Stevens v. Secretary, Dep't of Treasury,* 500 U.S. 1 (1991)(1 year, six days is timely). However, an ADEA claimant *may* elect to invoke the administrative complaint resolution process established by Title VII. If so, the processes and time limitations for filing appeals and law suits are applicable. *Supra,* 30.01–30.05. There is no right to a jury trial against federal agencies under the ADEA.

30.08: REMEDIES

Successful plaintiffs under Title VII and the Rehabilitation Act are entitled to hiring with seniority, back wages, compensatory (but not punitive) damages, and attorneys' fees under standards similar to those applicable to non-federal plaintiffs. The ADEA allows neither compensatory nor liquidated damages against federal employers. *Villescas v. Secretary of Energy,* 311 F.3d 1253 (10th Cir. 2002). Attorneys' fees under the ADEA are available under the Equal Access to Justice Act. Because administrative processes under the ADEA are optional, attorneys' fees attributable to exhaustion of those processes may not be recovered. *Nowd v. Rubin,* 76 F.3d 25 (1st Cir. 1996).

CHAPTER 31

PRIVATE, NON–JUDICIAL RESOLUTION

31.01: WAIVERS, SETTLEMENTS, RELEASES

Prospective waivers of *future claims of substantive statutory rights* are unenforceable. 29 U.S.C. 626(f)(1)(C). Releases or settlements of *possible or pending claims* based on defendant's *past* conduct will be enforced if the party establishes that the settlement and release were made knowingly and voluntarily. Where plaintiff's attorney made a verbal offer to settle a pending suit that was accepted in writing by the employer, plaintiff is bound even though plaintiff did not personally agree to the terms or sign the documentation. *Quesada v. Napolitano*, (5th Cir. 2012) (unpublished), 96 EPD 44790. Attempts to *force* a waiver, release, settlement or arbitration of pending claims on threat of discharge is unlawful retaliation. *Goldsmith v. Bagby Elevator Co.,* 513 F.3d 1261 (11th Cir. 2008).

The ADEA specifies seven elements that are required for an effective waiver of existing age discrimination claims: (1) *"Plain English:"* the waiver must be in language reasonably understood; no "legalese" or "fine print." (2) *"Unambiguous:"* the waiver must refer specifically to the rights being waived; no general release of "any and all claims." (3) *"New Consideration:"* value must be provided other than that which the employee had previously received or was entitled to receive. (4) *"Advised:"* employees must be told that they may consult legal counsel prior to signing the waiver. (5) *"Waiting period"* of 21 days between the presentation of the waiver document and its execution by the employee. (6) *"Cooling off:"* the executed waiver must be revocable for 7 days following its execution, and (7) *"Disclosure:"* where the waiver is undertaken as part of group incentive the employer must identify the classes affected, eligibility factors, time limitations, and those selected and excluded from the incentive program. 29 U.S.C. 626(f).

A waiver not meeting these statutory standards cannot be enforced against the employee, even if the employee retains the consideration paid by the employer in return for the release. *Oubre v. Entergy Operations, Inc.*, 552 U.S. 422 (1998). Failure of the employer to establish these elements of a "voluntary" waiver only prohibits reliance on the waiver as a defense to liability. Securing a waiver that fails to meet the statutory standards is not itself a violation of the law, nor does it establish that the employer engaged in illegal age discrimination.

These specific waiver provisions are directly applicable only to age discrimination claims. However, they specify some of the general elements required by common law contract principles to establish the voluntary nature required of liability waivers such as the requirement for consideration, reasonably clear language, and avoidance of unconscionability. Employers wanting to be assured that waivers of possible violations of Title VII and the ADA were executed voluntarily and with knowledge would be well advised to follow ADEA safe harbor provisions.

31.02: ARBITRATION

A. GENERALLY

Arbitration is a private method of binding dispute resolution that is created by a contract between the parties. The arbitration agreement (or contract) will require that defined disputes between the parties be resolved following a prescribed, usually informal, but adversarial proceeding conducted by an impartial third person, the arbitrator. The arbitration is conducted by a pre-agreed protocol that is often referenced in the agreement to arbitrate.

Agreements to arbitrate are routinely enforced by the courts, and judicial review of arbitration awards is extremely limited. Typically, the arbitration contract provides that the arbitrator's award will be "final," and thus the parties ostensibly waive the right to file lawsuits on issues covered by the arbitration contract. Requiring employees, as a condition of their employment, to agree to arbitrate *future* discrimination claims is neither *per se* unconscionable nor does it violate the statutes. *Weeks v. Harden Mfg. Corp.*, 291 F.3d 1307 (11th Cir. 2002).

B. ENFORCEABILITY

A series of early cases strongly indicated that any prospective waiver of the statutory right to seek judicial remedies for violation of substantive civil rights could not be enforced by employers. *Alexander v. Gardner–Denver Co.,* 415 U.S. 36 (1974) (union agreement to arbitrate all disputes could not be enforced against employee asserting Title VII claims); *Barrentine v. Arkansas–Best Freight Sys. Inc.,* 450 U.S. 728 (1981) (waiver of right to judicial remedies for violation of Fair Labor Standards Act unenforceable); *McDonald v. City of West Branch,* 466 U.S. 284 (1981) (arbitration agreement could not waive judicial access to resolve claims under 42 U.S.C. 1983).

This trend was reversed in *Gilmer v. Interstate/Johnson Lane Corp.,* 500 U.S. 20 (1991), which relied upon the Federal Arbitration Act, 9 U.S.C. 1, (FAA) to hold that a stock broker's registration agreement that required all disputes between the broker and his employer to be resolved by arbitration was enforceable, and that agreement effectively waived the broker's right to seek judicial resolution of his ADEA claim.

Although the FAA exempts from its coverage "contracts of employment," *Circuit City Stores, Inc. v. Adams,* 532 U.S. 105 (2001), held that the exemption was applicable only to seamen, railroad employees, and employees engaged in interstate transportation. Moreover, *Circuit City Stores, id,* held that the FAA pre-empted state law to the extent that state law broadly declared agreements in employment contracts to waive access to courts a violation of state public policy.

14 Penn Plaza, LLC v. Pyett, 556 U.S. 247 (2009), expanded *Gilmer* and *Circuit City Stores,* by further narrowing to near extinction pre-*Gilmer* decisions. The Court held that if the language of a collective bargaining agreement *between union and employer* to arbitrate disputes *clearly and unmistakably* included claims under the employment discrimination statutes, *individual employees* covered by the collective agreement would be precluded from seeking judicial remedies for statutory violations. That is, the union could waive the individual's access to the courts to protect individual rights that are granted by federal statutes. The employee could protect his federal statutory rights only through the agreed arbitration forum (which would be controlled by the union, subject only to the union's general "duty of fair representation" of employee interests imposed by the labor relations statutes).

EEOC v. Waffle House, Inc., 534 U.S. 279 (2002), held, however, that arbitration agreements to which the EEOC was not a party did not preclude the EEOC from seeking relief for individuals even if the individuals had agreed to arbitrate, rather than litigate, their claims.

C. UNENFORCEABLE AGREEMENTS

While *Circuit City Stores, Inc. v. Adams, supra,* held that the FAA preempted a blanket declaration that *all* agreements to arbitrate statutory claims were unenforceable, the Court allowed that state contract law would determine whether *a particular* arbitration contract was valid and enforceable. *Wright v. Universal Maritime Corp.*, 535 U.S. 70 (1998), held that, even under federal law principles, to be effective the waiver of statutory rights must be "clear and unmistakable." Some lower courts have used this leeway to find that an arbitration clause using broad "fine print," legalese would not be binding if no reasonable person would understand such language to be a waiver of this significant right to seek judicial remedies. *Ingle v. Circuit City Stores*, 328 F.3d 1165 (9th Cir. 2003). Even clear arbitration clauses have been held to be unconscionable, and thus unenforceable. *Ingle v. Circuit City Stores, supra*. The contract doctrine of unconscionability evaluates both the substantive one-sided "unfairness" of the terms and the procedural unfairness by which such terms were secured, such as vast differences in bargaining power, undue pressure, etc. That the agreement was an "adhesion agreement" imposed as part of a "take it or leave it" condition of employment could establish the one-sided nature of the process. When coupled with such procedural overreaching, the agreement may be substantively one-sided, and thus unconscionable, if the process fails to provide for: (1) neutral arbitrators or effective employee participation in the selection of arbitrators, (2) an employer obligation to disclose relevant materials and allow employee access to witnesses, (3) written arbitration awards, (4) remedies comparable to those available in federal courts, and (5) no more than "reasonable" costs or arbitrator fees. *Cole v.*

Burns Int'l Security Serv., 105 F.3d 1465 (D.C.Cir. 1997); *Hooters of America v. Phillips,* 173 F.3d 933 (4th Cir. 1999).

The extent to which fairness requires that fees of the arbitrator and related costs be borne by the employee has been elusive. American Arbitration Association (AAA) protocols require that in arbitrations conducted under their auspices, the employer must pay 100% of the arbitrator's fee. (www.naarb.org/due_process). However, *Green Tree Financial Corp. v. Randolph,* 531 U.S. 79 (2000), affirmed a lower court confirmation of an arbitration agreement that required the claimant to pay 50% of the arbitrator's fees. The Court stated that an agreement to arbitrate would become unenforceable only if the financial burden on the claimant effectively precluded the claimant from being able to access this forum. The parties' agreement requiring equitable cost sharing thus may override the AAA protocol directing otherwise. *Brady v. Williams Capital Group, L.P.,* 14 N.Y.3d 459, 928 N.E.2d 383 (2010).

D. AWARD ENFORCEMENT: JUDICIAL REVIEW

Arbitration awards are subject to extremely limited judicial review, and, in most cases, are routinely enforced. The FAA allows awards to be vacated by courts only if procured by corruption, fraud, or undue means; where the arbitrator is guilty of misconduct; or the arbitrator's award is in excess of the authority granted by the contract. 9 U.S.C. 10(a).

Courts set aside awards only if the arbitrator ignores the evidence and dispenses his/her own brand of work-place justice. They reject the arbitrator's legal conclusions only if the award is in "manifest disregard of the law that results in significant injustice." *First Options of Chicago, Inc. v. Kaplan,* 514 U.S. 938 (1995). Thus, mere mistakes in interpreting the statute or interpreting the statutes differently than have the courts, does not warrant denying enforcement of the award. It is the arbitrator's interpretation of the law, not that of the courts, that the parties agreed to accept. *Williams v. Cigna Financial Advisors, Inc.,* 197 F.3d 752 (5th Cir. 1999) (ADEA claim).

The agreement to arbitrate or the resulting award has been set aside in rare cases where the award clearly violates a fundamental public policy, such as requiring an employer to hire an undocumented alien. However, the "public policy" exception is narrowly construed. *Eastern Associated Coal Corp v. UMW,* 531 U.S. 57 (2000), held that an arbitration award directing reinstatement of a truck driver who had previously failed two random drug tests did not violate public policy.

INDEX

References are to Pages

Compensation systems, 293
Grooming, impact of on race, 222
Lay-offs, impact of, 217
Model of proof, 51, 215
Nepotism, 223
Physical requirements,
    Height and weight, on women, 218, 221, 250
    Pregnancy, 219
Proving with statistics, 217, 222
Reconstruction Era Civil Rights Act, 53, 215
Recruiting systems, impact of, 217
Seniority, 259
Subjective systems, 255
Veterans preferences, 252

DISPARATE TREATMENT
See also, "Motive"
"Because of" 45, 148
Compensation, 290
Disparate impact as justification for, 142, 242
Individual, model of proof, 147 167
"Pattern or Practice," proof of, 197

DRESS CODES
See "Grooming"

DRUGS
Addiction to, as disability, 104
Impact, 220
Rules regarding, 104
Testing for, 105, 247, 374

DUTY OF FAIR REPRESENTATION
Union obligation, 49

EDUCATION
Adverse impact
    Business necessity of, 248, 249
    Proving impact of, 215, 217
Equal Pay Act, "factor other than sex," 286
"Factor other than age," 231
Qualification under the Americans with Disabilities Act, 106

"ENGLISH ONLY"

ENVIRONMENT, HOSTILE

EQUAL EMPLOYMENT OPPORTUNITY COMMISSION (EEOC)

Record keeping requirements, 22
Suits by, 21, 425, 444

EQUAL PAY ACT
Generally, 4, 271
"Bennett Amendment," effect on, 289
Comparison between male and female, 281
Coverage of, 271
Defenses,
Generally, 282
Merit systems, 283
Quality or quantity of work, 283
Seniority, 282
"Equal work," elements of,
Effort, 276
Responsibility, 276
Skill, 275
Working conditions, 277
Enforcement, 272, 426
"Establishment," 278
"Factor other than sex" defense,
"Factor" defined, 286
Neutrality, 284
Rates of pay, calculation of, 280
Remedies, 272, 413
Statute of limitations, 426

EVIDENCE
See also, "Disparate treatment" and "Motive"
Admissibility of, 157
Circumstantial, generally defined, 167, 291
Compensation discrimination, 290
Context of, 159
Direct, 160
Discharge and discipline, 174
Impact, 215
Indirect, 162
Legitimate non-discriminatory reasons, 177
Lesser discriminatory alternatives, 189
McDonnell Douglas model of presentation, 167
"Me too," 186

REHABILITATION ACT
Americans with Disabilities Act, relationship to, 18
Disabilities discrimination, 18
Federal employment protection, 19

REINSTATEMENT
See, "Remedies"

RELEASES
See, "Waivers"

RELIGION
Generally, Title VII protection of, 83, 88
Accommodation required, 87, 316
Bona fide occupational qualification, 118, 120, 124, 125
Grooming as, 88, 343
Leaves to observe, 316, 318,
Observances and practices of, 83, 316, 343
Secular distinguished, 84
Seniority conflicts, 319

RELIGIOUS ORGANIZATIONS
Coverage of, 33
Discrimination by, 33, 87
Ministerial exemption, 35
Secular activities of, 84, 86

REMEDIES
Generally, 401
Affirmative action, 415
Attorneys fees,
Entitlement to, 416
Calculation of, 419
Back pay,
Caps not applicable to, 409
Constructive discharge, 358
Deductions from,
amounts earnable, 405
interim earnings, 405
misconduct, 406
unavailability, 406
Entitlement to, 403, 404